THE BLITZ

THE BLITZ

CONSTANTINE FITZGIBBON

With drawings by
HENRY MOORE

MACDONALD · LONDON

For Irina
With Affection and Gratitude

CONTENTS

PLATES

INTRODUCTION:
FOR THOSE WHO WERE NOT THERE

Is THIRTY years a long time or a short? It is the generally accepted life-span of a generation. More important, it is the period from birth to maturity, from that maturity to the full awareness of age and death, and soon enough—even for those who die in bed—to death itself. It is half of most men's adult lives that has passed since the winter of 1940 to 1941, the winter of the bombs. For those who are now young, that weird, horrible, brave season must seem at least as remote as the Boer War then did to me, in my own youth. Even London's scars have at long last vanished almost completely. The dome of St. Paul's which presided over it all, over London burning and over the desolate ruins of the next decade, is once again hidden by new buildings, filled with money and pieces of paper which have replaced the old buildings that served the same purpose before the bombers came. Indeed one might almost think that it is the same people who hurry from suburban train to office block, now as then. Often this is doubtless true: the aging clerk was then the young office boy. But many died in that cruel season, the winter of the bombs.

What was it like, the young of today may ask, what was it *really* like? And for the middle-aged, who think they can remember it all so clearly, that is a hard question to answer; for when we examine that most vivid memory it is as though we were revisiting a weird and yet familiar townscape, seen briefly in darkness long ago, when the only light was summer lightning and the sounds were thunder.

And, besides, even as the lightning struck, each man and woman saw only the fragment of the townscape on which his eyes happened then to be fixed.

xi

'It was about twenty past one in the morning, and I was reading *The Taming of the Shrew* in bed, when suddenly all the windows blew in and the room was filled with a greenish dust. When I looked round, all the furniture had moved, not far, it had all just moved round about a foot.'

'He was an extraordinary *looking* dog, a sort of impossible cross between a Pekingese and a bull terrier, bombed out I suppose. Anyhow he just attached himself to our fire station. Quite useless he was—never caught a rat or anything like that —but we got very fond of him. Scared to death of the raids he was, used to hide under things, poor fellow, and when the warning went he howled, just like the sirens, same sort of up and down noise, horrible. When the Blitz finished in the summer he just disappeared, went back to his home maybe. We called him UXB, funny name, but then he was a funny sort of dog himself.'

'When they hit this huge pub they must have smashed every bottle because the booze just poured out into the street and I distinctly remember seeing an old man with a cup, scooping it up out of the gutter.'

'She was buried for hours, and we could hear her swearing away down there. Can't think where she learned the words, a nice little old lady like that.'

'He was a fighter pilot. His mother and father had been killed early in the Blitz, and he was dining with his wife when the place was hit, and she was killed beside him. He went absolutely berserk, ferocious, quite uninterested in his own survival, I'm told. He shot down half a dozen of them before he was killed. That meant the whole family was wiped out.'

'We were sitting on either side of the fire, drinking whisky, when there was the most unholy crash and we found ourselves covered in plaster. Desmond looked at me and said: "You're plastered!" It seemed extraordinarily witty at the time.'

'I had no idea corpses were so small, and at the same time so heavy.'

'It's the stench that I remember, all those tired bodies packed in together. Later, of course, they installed bunks.'

'This damn fool fireman holding the branch thought this was a good opportunity to clean his false teeth. So he held them under the jet, and of course he'd no idea of the power of it. They were simply snatched from his hand and I saw them go hurtling away upwards, snapping, into the flames.'

'How many hundreds of gallons of tea we must have drunk! I can never taste a cup of tea now without seeing again that warden's post down at the baths.'

'The utter exhaustion. . . .'

'The dust and filth. . . .'

'The extraordinary kindness and unselfishness. . . .'

Fragmentary memories, a mosaic of experience, a vast, overwhelming, glorious, tragic, terrifying experience, shared by millions in Silvertown, Wandsworth, Streatham, Westminster, Clapton, the City, Croydon, in all the ninety-five boroughs and districts that then constituted greater London. It is chiefly on this experience that I have drawn, these minute coloured chips that I have collected and put together in an attempt to create a picture of that winter.

My own are as fragmentary as those of the many other voices that will be heard in the pages which follow. I remember, just before the Blitz began, the London streets of the hot August nights when I was on leave before going to Sandhurst. By day the great air battle went on, and I had almost a ringside seat for this, for as a guardsman I had been on duty at Kenley. That was a soldier's battle, and the pilots were gods, and the pretty Waafs did not cry when their lover of last night was not there next evening. But London was something else again.

Every night the bombers could be heard, droning over on their way to Liverpool or the Midlands, and every night London held its breath. Would it be tonight, tomorrow, maybe never? We talked and drank and loved and pretended not to notice when one of us was suddenly, obviously afraid.

I remember a November week-end leave, when the bombing

was heavy, and a friend with whom I was staying, a warden, asked me to help dig out a burst pub. In it, at the back, sat a man with an unspilled pint, but he was spilt, stone dead. I remember another friend coming back from leave in March, sick and white-faced: he had been at the Café de Paris the night before, when it was bombed. And that is almost all that I do remember. This is therefore much, much less my book than the book of all those who have let me record their voices and whose memories I have put together in the pages that follow. And before making the formal acknowledgments, which will be found at the end of this book, I should like to thank them for allowing a stranger to glimpse, through their eyes and voices, emotions of that strange, magnificent winter, which must soon be as lost in the past as are the feelings of the sailors who fought at Lepanto against another merciless enemy.

'*There was Mother, she was an invalid in bed*', says a Bermondsey woman who was a cleaner at a mission down there, in the Surrey Docks, '*and Father was an invalid in bed, and we had this time bomb, you see, at the back of the garden, and the wardens came round and said we'd have to evacuate the house and take shelter elsewhere. So they put us underneath the railway arch, and we all slept there, and of course it was rather cold and damp. Then a gentleman came along, after about three nights, and he said: "There's a billiard hall round the corner", and the gentleman said, "if you care to go in there, since there's only a few of you, you can go in the hall." And naturally we all went, and we got quite one really good happy family.*
'*So we made little beds on the floor for the children, and made them quite comfortable and didn't hear a sound of a night time of anything coming over. Until one night, when there was one great crash, and of course one or two of them got scared. Then a couple of 'em said: "Well, let's have a little sing-song." So we had a nice little sing-song, quietened the children down again, and some of the men played billiards, and then the women said: "Well", they said, "shall we try and get a nap ourselves?" So we tried to have a little*

xiv

nap ourselves, and then another little kiddie woke up. "Is there really anything coming?" "Oh no, no, now go to sleep", she says, "it's quite all right." Off to sleep they went again, and of course nothing happened that night, and nothing the next night, and it was quite all right.

'And of course then when the big night came it was really awful, one great crash and a big flash, and there was a stampede of one or two of them, trying to get out, and they couldn't get out, and then there was a big fire in the shelter, and then I had the misfortune—I lost my mother in there, and I lost my little girl in there.

'And we had to wait, oh, three or four days, before we could find her. We went to the hospitals and couldn't find her, no, nothing there. Then I went round to the baths, and they says: "Well, why don't you go to the mortuary?" Naturally I went round there, and when I got there they just had one there. They asked me to describe my mother, and I did, and it wasn't my mother at all. And then I spoke about my daughter. He says: "How old is she?" I said: "She was eight years old." So he said: "Well, we have one little girl here", he says, "not identified." And when I looked, I'd never seen such a shock in all my life. All her little hair was burned, and her face where she'd put her fingers right across, all the fire was there, and I thought: "Oh dear now, can it be true?" Then I thought to myself: "Well, I suppose the Lord's taken her, you know, to be right out of pain altogether", and I thought to myself, "Well, I'd sooner her go that way than be maimed for life, you know, a little cripple."

'And then I thought to myself: "Well, what about my mother?" And we never did find anything of Mother at all. And I don't think a day goes by without we don't talk of my mother and my little daughter. It was the Lord's way to take her, and not be injured, you know, and I still think that we've got her with us, you see.'

CHAPTER ONE

SEPTEMBER THE 7TH, 1940, was a Saturday. On that Saturday, a warm and sunny day, there occurred an event which had been dreaded for years, expected for over twelve months, and which now had been awaited with mounting certainty throughout that hot summer of battle, and defeat, and death. On September the 7th, 1940, the German Air Force set out to destroy London.

Before describing the events of that day, and of the ensuing fifty-seven nights, when London was bombed each night and often by day as well, and of the six months that followed these, when London continued to be bombed frequently and heavily, it is as well to examine, quite briefly, the emotional, political and military background to the terrible winter that London was about to endure.

The story of aerial bombardment is almost as long as the story of man's ability to fly, though flight was first exploited, from a military point of view, as an aid to vision. In June of 1794, the field of Fleurus was reconnoitred from the air, before the battle, by an early aeronaut, Colonel Coutelle, in a Montgolfier balloon. He was accompanied by General Jourdan's adjutant and perhaps by the general himself, and the resultant victory has been ascribed, at least in part, to this bold and unorthodox exploit. But it is the Austrians who apparently first used lighter-than-air craft for bombing purposes. During the siege of Venice in 1849 small balloons, loaded with bombs equipped with primitive time-fuses, were sent up to drift into the beleaguered city.

The aeroplane was similarly first envisaged as an aid to reconnaissance. In August of 1914 the pilots of such planes,

I

when they met, would shoot at one another with revolvers; such was the genesis of the fighter plane. Later they also carried grenades, which they dropped on the enemy's trenches, and the bomber was born. The first bomb to be dropped by a German aeroplane on British soil—or indeed by any war-plane on a target that was not directly connected with a battlefield —fell near Dover Castle, on December 24th, 1914, and broke a number of panes of glass. The bombing of London, however, which began in 1915, was for the first two years by Zeppelin only. It was expensive and inaccurate, though considerable damage was done and some casualties inflicted on the civilian population. An attempt was made by the Germans to pretend that they were bombing military targets, but in fact it was the civilian population's morale that was their primary objective. The Zeppelin was defeated by the end of 1916, and between May 1917 and May of the following year aeroplanes took over. There were many raids on the capital and other cities which caused quite heavy damage, and proportionately very heavy casualties; in all 1,414 persons were killed and 3,416 wounded. The effect on morale was also quite serious. Scenes approaching panic sometimes occurred. There were stampedes into the tubes and other shelters and on one occasion an A.A. gun crew was almost lynched by an angry mob in Hyde Park because they refused to fire on a plane overhead that was, in fact, British: night raids held up the production of munitions: and over two hundred fighter planes, urgently needed on the Western Front in March of 1918, were kept in Britain to protect and encourage the civilian population. Very few German planes were shot down before the late spring of 1918.

When it is realised that all this was achieved by a numerically very insignificant German bomber force, the 3rd Bombing Squadron, that in only one raid, the last, were more than thirty bombers sent over, and that these carried only a small load of light bombs, it is not surprising that both sides foresaw a tremendous, and perhaps an overwhelming, future for this type of warfare.

Had the war lasted into 1919 the R.A.F., which had already carried out a number of raids on German industrial towns, was planning to launch very heavy attacks of this sort on a very large scale. It seems probable, to judge by the effects of the comparatively light raids already made by the Independent Force, R.A.F., that the results would have been impressive both on German production and on morale.

Such, in very brief summary, was the story of bombing in 1914-18, and its effects were to be studied with great attention by the experts during the next two decades. It had also produced a very deep impression on the popular mind, an impression of horror amounting, in the jargon of the psychologists, almost to a *trauma*. This *trauma*, in its turn, was to have profound effects on the policies of the democracies, and was in due course to be ruthlessly exploited by the dictators, and by the anti-social and suicidal forces within the democracies, for their own admitted or unconscious purposes. But before examining the *trauma*, which helped to condition the frame of mind that prevailed when preparations were being made for Civil Defence and which lasted until the bombing actually began—when the horrible reality replaced the infinitely more horrible dream—let us see what conclusions the policy-makers and the soldiers had drawn from the lessons of 1914-18.

Some, of course, had drawn no conclusions at all, but others, and particularly the more perspicacious airmen, had decided that the key to victory in the next war lay with the air fleets. An exponent of these views in their most extreme form was the Italian, General Douhet, who published his thesis, *The Command of the Air*, as early as 1921. His argument, briefly, was that a bomber force, if properly handled, could knock out an enemy power in a matter of weeks or even days. He did not believe that anti-aircraft guns or fighters could prevent the bombers from attacking and destroying the 'nerve centres' of the opponent's homeland—his railway junctions, ports, key factories and so on—and he stated that the only defence against bombing was counter-bombing.

3

'Air power is a weapon superlatively adapted to offensive operations, because it strikes suddenly and gives the enemy no time to parry the blow. . . . The aeroplane is not adaptable to defence, being pre-eminently an offensive weapon. . . . There is no practical way to prevent the enemy from attacking us with his air force except to destroy his air power before he has a chance to strike at us. . . . *We must . . . resign ourselves to the offensives the enemy inflicts upon us, while striving to put all our resources to work to inflict even heavier ones upon him. . . .*' (General Douhet's italics.)

Such was one essential theory of the use of air power: a tremendous blow given at the earliest possible stage to destroy the enemy's air potential, followed by a succession of hammer blows, also of great violence, delivered against his cities, with objective his industries, his communications and above all his civilian morale. It was calculated that ten planes, each carrying two tons of incendiaries, high-explosives and poison gas, could destroy everything within a circle of 500 metres diameter: to annihilate a city centre measuring three kilometers each way, or roughly the size of the City of London with the Whitehall district, only one attack by a force of 360 bombers would be needed. Thus the next war might be decided by tremendous aerial bombing during the first few days. This theory of the 'knock-out blow' remained, and still remains, an essential element of air force planning against future war.

In Britain the Air Staff, in the words of Mr Basil Collier, foresaw the coming war as 'a slogging match between rival bomber forces', and by the early 'thirties were fully converted to the view that only large-scale offensive bomber action from well-guarded bases could provide Great Britain with the necessary air superiority that would bring victory. It was not, of course, possible for any British Government in the 'twenties or 'thirties to plan, or build, a bomber force capable of delivering a 'knock-out blow' to a potential enemy. The Air Staff therefore worked to build an air force which could parry the enemy's knock-out blow and could then be expanded

4

to defeat that enemy by what came later to be called 'strategic' bombing. But the emphasis, at least until the autumn of 1938, was still very much upon bombers rather than fighters, and twice as much effort was put into the British bomber programme as went into the fighters.

Since no country could afford to keep 'standing patrols' of fighters in the air along its frontiers and coasts, the only hope of defeating bombers by fighters lay in identifying the enemy's course and probable objective at a considerable distance from his target and then converging the airborne defence against the attacking force. This would vastly multiply the efficacy of the individual fighter. But in 1932 no such identification appeared possible. It was obvious, as Mr Baldwin then stated in the House of Commons, that 'the bomber would always get through'.

The picture began to change in the mid-1930's, with the introduction of the radar chain. By 1938 it was becoming plain that the early information supplied by the radar stations on the coast did offer a chance of parrying the enemy's bomber attack by fighter intervention. It was therefore once again considered worthwhile to re-orientate British defensive strategy about the radar chain and the new eight-gun fighter, which combination, indeed, won the Battle of Britain. But that, of course, still lay hidden in the future. Furthermore, though it was no longer believed that the bomber would always get through, it was taken for granted that quite a number of bombers would, particularly by night, and that London would be bombed. So the various British governments still had to plan against this contingency. If there were to be a second world war, and their military advisers were to have judged correctly—as they must assume they had—what then would be the effects of the 'knock-out blow' on London and other primary targets? The answer, also supplied by experts, was an excessively depressing one.

The total weight of bombs dropped by the Germans on Britain during the war of 1914-18 had amounted to some 300 tons, which had caused almost 5,000 casualties, of which one third were fatal, giving a figure of 16 per ton of bombs. But the two big daylight raids on London had caused 832 casualties, or 121 per ton, while the 16 night raids of 1917-18 had caused 52 per ton dropped. As early as 1924, therefore, the Air Staff reckoned that casualties in a future war would be in the nature of 50 per ton of bombs, one third of which would be fatal. In 1934 the Air Staff, using the still illegal German Air Force as their basis of calculation, reckoned that in the foreseeable future the Luftwaffe, were it to operate from bases in the Low Countries, could drop 150 tons of bombs on Britain daily for an unspecified period. In 1938 the Committee of Imperial Defence anticipated 3,500 tons of bombs on London, delivered by 'planes based on Germany, within the first twenty-four hours of attack, followed by 600 tons per day. The figure of 50 casualties per ton was still accepted and, indeed, seemed to be confirmed by reports received from Spain. In April, 1939, the Air Staff, while adhering to the figure of 3,500 tons for the 'knock-out blow', now believed that the Germans could increase their daily bombing to 700 tons and that by April 1940 the figure would be 950 tons per day dropped by some 800 aircraft based in Germany. The Ministry of Health, using these figures which forecast 600,000 killed and 1,200,000 wounded in the first six months, estimated that between 1,000,000 and 2,800,000 hospital beds would be needed for the injured, depending on the length of their stay in hospital. And here it may be of interest, for purposes of comparison, to point out that during the entire blitz of September '40–May '41, London had some 90,000 casualties, of whom just under 20,000 were killed and 25,000 seriously injured: during this period 18,000 tons of bombs were dropped, which, by the 1937 estimate, should have killed over 280,000 civilians. But gas, of course, was not used. The estimate was thus an over-estimate by fourteen-fold.

And the expectation of horror did not end with casualties, though these are perhaps the easiest yard-stick. In late 1938 it was estimated that 500,000 houses would be totally destroyed or rendered uninhabitable by bombing, and that between one and two millions would be seriously damaged. It was believed that the public services would almost certainly break down. A high proportion of the population was expected to flee from the cities, and particularly from London. Winston Churchill, speaking in the House of Commons in 1934, had said: 'This vast mass of human beings, without shelter and without food, without sanitation and without special provision for the maintenance of order, would confront the Government of the day with an administrative problem of the first magnitude.' In fact panic on a nation-wide scale was feared. In London conditions would be horrible beyond belief. During the winter of 1917-18 more than 10,000 people used to crowd into a single tube station for shelter, and on one occasion in February of 1918 almost a third of a million Londoners sought refuge in the tubes. In the incomparably worse bombings now expected, these figures would be much greater. It was feared that the populace would crowd into the tubes, where there were no provisions for food or sanitation, and would refuse to come out. The medical authorities had no doubt that severe epidemics would break out as a result. Apart from disease, madness on a huge scale was expected. In 1939 the Mental Health Emergency Committee reported that psychiatric casualties might exceed the physical by three to one: that is to say, between three and four millions of people would suffer from hysteria or other acute neurotic conditions. It would not even be possible to bury the dead properly, since it would be beyond the resources of the country to provide the necessary timber for coffins. Mass burial in lime pits was envisaged, or even the dumping of bodies from hoppers into the Channel. However, with the city on fire above-ground, the few roads still open crowded with hysterical refugees, and the tubes crammed with starving, panic-stricken masses prey to virulent epidemics, it is hard to see how the corpses could even have been conveyed to the pits.

Such then, at its blackest, was the picture that confronted the Government when it considered the next war. It must be emphasised once again that this picture was not the work of novelists who had read too much Poe and Sade, but was produced by trusted soldiers and civil servants. It must also be remembered that at least until 1938 there seemed almost no defence against the bombing that was expected to produce such conditions in London and the other cities. Those critics who still speak so glibly of Chamberlain's moral cowardice in the autumn of 1938 should remember what, to him, seemed the alternative to the betrayal of the Czechs. What the Government did do in the way both of passive and active defence will be discussed later in this chapter.

This hideous forecast was, of course, very much a secret, but the picture as painted by the writers and publicists was at least as horrifying. H. G. Wells made a film in the middle 'thirties, called *The Shape of Things to Come*, which foresaw another war and the relapse of the Western World into total barbarism; this was quaintly symbolised, if this writer's memory is correct, by a sequence depicting a savage British chieftain of the future pommelling a scantily-clad member of his harem while seated in a broken-down Rolls-Royce pulled by oxen. More serious writers naturally adopted a more serious tone, but it is scarcely an exaggeration to say that—at least until the middle of the Spanish Civil War—the bombing *trauma* had this result: the majority of the French and English intellectuals who were not Communists were pacifists, and some ingenious or ingenuous spirits even managed to be both at once.

We simplify the past. It is obviously as foolish to imagine England in the 'thirties as consisting of a lot of intellectuals reading the productions of Mr Victor Gollancz's Left Book Club and permanently terrified by the prospect of another war, as it is to envisage Edwardian England as one long tea-party on the lawns beneath the elms. But to a certain extent the intellectuals did, as in a distorting mirror, reflect the temper of the country as a whole. The working class, massacred in 1914-18, cheated, as it thought, out of the promised fruits of victory, lied to by its popular press, and later plunged into the hopeless quagmire of mass unemployment, not unnaturally regarded the governing class with deep suspicion and dislike. Why should *we* fight for *them*? was the simple basis of working-class pacificism, which was given an idealistic *raison d'être* by such popular figures as Lansbury and Dr Salter. The Labour Party was not solidly pacifist by any means, and after Hitler had come to power in Germany several of its leaders, some of whom had even gone to prison as conscientious objectors during the First World War, realised that it might be necessary to defend Britain's political liberties by force of arms. But it had a very strong pacifist wing, and most Socialists were, in general, far less interested in international affairs than in the class struggle at home.

The middle classes were as usual curiously silent and it is hard to generalise about their attitude, since for the last two generations fatalism seems to have been a major ingredient of their point of view, save during brief periods of national or social crisis. They were prepared to follow the Government, even into war, but the fact that some two million members of this class evacuated themselves, at their own expense, from their homes in the cities when war was imminent shows that they shared the general terrified foreboding of what that war would bring. A proportion, probably small, of the middle and upper-middle classes believed that in view of Germany's military preponderance—which in practice meant Germany's ability to bomb Britain—we should accept her political preponderance as well, but the dislike of 'the Hun' instilled during the First World War was still very strong, and the out-and-out appeasers-at-any-price were few, as were the Fascists who admired Hitler on so-called ideological grounds.

The Government, then, when it set about to do what it could to lessen the degree of catastrophe which it anticipated in the event of bombing, was dealing with a nation which, if it contemplated a future war at all, did so with emotions ranging from horror and terror to apathy and resignation. A nation, moreover, which was profoundly divided socially and in which the two halves tended to distrust and fear one another. And the genesis of the A.R.P. services was, by a curious coincidence, closely connected with that distrust and fear.

When the first, very tentative, plans for Civil Defence were being discussed in the autumn of 1926, the organisational structure taken as a rough model was that which had been called into existence when the General Strike had threatened the country with chaos. That is to say, it was to be largely a voluntary organisation, whose members would therefore be men, and women, willing to accept responsibility, as had the Special Constables of 1926. Just as the 80,000 specials enrolled before the strike had increased to 200,000 in ten days, so it was hoped that a nucleus of A.R.P. personnel would be able to draw on a similar type of volunteer, and expand rapidly should a crisis develop. This gave its whole tone to the British A.R.P. services, and particularly to the Wardens' Service, in the years to come. Unlike the equivalent German service, it was never a para-military force: its discipline, as will be seen, was primarily that of moral pressure: and its members came largely from the middle classes. In Germany, where for example every concierge had certain duties and thus considerable authority within his building, the A.R.P. service cut across all social distinctions. In England, relying as it did on volunteers, it remained, like all other voluntary work, primarily a middle-class activity, for most workers seldom volunteer and only reluctantly accept even the limited authority of an armband and a whistle. This, in months to come, was to have curious—and at times unfortunate—results in some purely working-class boroughs where there were few volunteers and where the people therefore sometimes felt pathetically neglected and forgotten.

It is not the purpose of this book to give a detailed history of the A.R.P. services, for which the reader is referred to Major

T. H. O'Brien's *Civil Defence*. The Government's policy, however, is of interest. Their plans to avoid, or if it were unavoidable to mitigate, the disaster so gruesomely foreseen, involved action on several different levels. Assuming that they would not succeed in avoiding war, they could hope—and they certainly tried—to prevent the bombing of cities, first, by international agreement, and secondly by disarmament. When the Disarmament Conference finally broke down, after Hitler's accession to power, they could still try to prevent bombing by the policy that has since come to be known as that of the deterrent: they could and did build up the R.A.F. bomber force in the hope that the fear of reprisal would deter the Germans from bombing London. But, with the possible exception of the Ruhr, there was no target in Germany comparable in vital importance to London and the ports in this country. By 1938 it was becoming plain that Hitler was unlikely to be 'deterred' by the threat of counter-bombing. Though the fighters and the radar chain now offered a good prospect of defence, at least by day, it was plain that in the event of war London would be heavily, and probably accurately, bombed at least by night. The Government had therefore to make two further plans. What could be done, apart from strengthening the active defences, before the bombing began: and what must be done during and after the raids?

An individual target could be hidden from the enemy bombers by smoke and camouflage during the day, and by a total blackout after dark. So far as London went, no daytime device could hide the great city, though a lot of time, and paint, was spent in colouring factory chimneys and large buildings a mottled green and buff. This did no harm, paint was plentiful and the broken outlines probably even gave the workers a certain feeling of confidence. Smoke-screens could be, and later were, used to conceal certain small vital targets, and the factories were to be encouraged to burn fuel which produced more smoke than was permitted in peacetime. It was, of course, not possible to blanket London in a permanent pea-souper:

even had it been, this would scarcely have been desirable, and in any case the enemy could simply have dropped his bombs into it. The blackout was another matter. This was a legacy of the First World War, when lights had been dimmed to prevent the enemy from pinpointing his targets. It was decided at an early stage that in the coming war the blackout would be total, all over Britain and Northern Ireland. This again was no direct defence of London, but the blackout, together with the guns and balloons, did provide a certain protection in that it made it very difficult for night bombers to bomb accurately. Had they been able to do so, had the entire weight of each raid been concentrated against one or two boroughs, the casualties would undoubtedly have been heavier—comparable perhaps to the Coventry casualties, but repeated night after night —and above all the effect on civilian morale would have been far graver. More protection than this the blackout could not provide. But nevertheless, as will be seen, Londoners were to attach an almost mystical significance to its strict observation. Finally, the Government could and did ensure that the broadcasting and other wireless stations did not act as beacons to guide the enemy bombers to their targets. Still, London could not be hidden.

If it could not be hidden, and was hardly defensible, would it not be wiser to evacuate the entire population? In 1933, when this problem was first considered, it was thought that some 3,500,000 persons living in inner London, or roughly three-quarters of the population, would have to be moved out. The word 'evacuation' when applied to the plans made at this early date is a euphemism. Great crowds of people were expected to pour out into the countryside and the problem was how to control this mass exodus. This was seen as a police operation. It had earlier been suggested that the police force be enlarged for this purpose, and a cordon thrown around London to prevent 'a disorderly general flight'. Since there were not likely even so to be enough police, and since the military regarded their task as being to fight the enemy, not to control hysterical refugees, the Government found itself forced to consider a planned evacuation. As late as September 1938 the plan was still a very rudimentary one. Had war come at the time of the Czech crisis, the arrangement was that anyone, man, woman or child, who turned up at a main line station would be transported and dumped somewhere in the country. It is not hard to imagine the scenes that would have taken place at Paddington and Euston. After the Munich crisis the question was examined seriously, and the plan that was applied during the following year was agreed.

Government-sponsored evacuation should be limited, broadly speaking, to children, infants with their mothers, expectant mothers, and certain classes of invalids such as the blind: workers and others needed for the war effort were to be encouraged to stay at their places of work: the remainder of the population, many of whom were unflatteringly described as *bouches inutiles*, could go or stay as they pleased, at their own expense: plans were made to evacuate the Government from London, if the need should arise. The results of the evacuation scheme will be described in the next chapter.

Millions of Londoners would thus still have to face the bombs. The first provision that the Government made for their safety, and one which corresponded to the degree of fear this menace inspired, was to give the population the maximum protection against gas. In 1934 defence against gas, namely the production of respirators and anti-gas clothing and the purchase of bleach powder and medical supplies, was financially the largest single item of civil defence. In 1936 plans for the distribution of respirators to all civilians were accepted.

In this same year the Italians used gas against the Abyssinians and this produced a reaction of horror in Britain which is only explicable in its violence in terms of self-identification with the victims. There is no doubt that the people were more terrified of being gassed than of being bombed or deluged with incendiaries. In that year, of the eight Government publications concerned with civil defence, six dealt with chemical warfare.

13

In the first-aid training given to wardens, during the next two years, priority was given to the treatment of gas injuries, and indeed by early 1938 no other first-aid instruction had so far been given. In May of that year the only equipment, apart from some steel helmets, issued to the men and women of the A.R.P. services, and also to policemen and firemen, was anti-gas equipment: respirators, heavy and light anti-gas suits, anti-gas hoods, curtains and gloves, gumboots and eye-shields. During the Munich crisis, gas-masks were issued to almost the entire population. Apart from the digging of trenches, this was almost all that the Government could do for the people during that autumn. It was psychologically a very wise move. To possess at least something, some object, for their own protection even if it were only a respirator, made a great difference, as was shown by the outcry when it was discovered that there were not enough anti-gas helmets for all the babies.

Militarily it was also probably a sound decision. By early 1939 a member of the Government could state in the House of Commons that the anti-gas precautions already in force had rendered the risk of gas attack less likely. Although there is no evidence to show that the Germans ever seriously considered using gas on a large scale against London, it seems probable that they might have done so had it not been well known that London was the best equipped city in Europe to deal with this sort of attack. One aspect, then, of the A.R.P. services was tackled, and at great expense dealt with, once and for all as it turned out, before ever the war began.

In popular estimation the next greatest menace after gas was high-explosive. Fire, which in fact did far more damage than high-explosive, came a poor third. This was a natural reaction, since the people thought that they knew about fires and in any event expected to be able to get away from burning buildings, whereas the bomb that falls from the sky had the fascinating horror of the unknown. And in providing shelter from high-explosive bombs the Government's policy, though it was to prove in general wise, did not, as with the anti-gas precautions, quite correspond with what the people demanded.

As already stated, raids were expected to take the form of short, violent onslaughts, the most violent being the first, delivered at the rate of one or more a day, either by day or by night. It was considered for planning purposes that the average warning period, between the bombers crossing the coast and the bombs actually dropping, would be some seven minutes. It was feared, indeed expected, that the people would panic. The Government's policy was, therefore, to disperse the shelters. There were two principal reasons for this. If huge communal shelters were built, the so-called 'deep shelters' which were the only ones giving full protection even against direct hits, they would have to be fairly widely spaced. It would then take most of the shelterers more than seven minutes to reach them; they would be caught in the streets: and the casualties would be heavy. Also after one or two experiences of this sort, it was feared that a 'deep-shelter mentality' would develop, that is, that many people would go down into the shelters and refuse to come out. This would not only produce feeding, medical, and sanitary problems that were almost insoluble, but would also paralyse the industrial life of London. Crowded shelters, besides being a perfect breeding place for various physical infections, would encourage every form of mass hysteria from defeatism to panic. A subsidiary consideration which influenced the Government against the building of deep shelters was the vast expense.

It is not intended here to go into the deep-shelter controversy to any extent. It was a squalid political campaign, led by the Communists and with parts of the Labour and Liberal Parties lending it their support. A number of left-wing intellectuals and dons were extremely noisy in their attacks on the Government, and the Communists did not hesitate to say that the authorities were deliberately leaving the poor without shelter while the rich were making ready to flee to their mansions in the country. This campaign, begun in 1938, continued up to, and into, the Blitz. From at least August 1939 on, when Russia became Germany's ally, there can be little doubt that the deep-shelter campaign was inspired by motives quite unconnected with any desire to protect the citizens of Great Britain. It was a deliberate attempt to undermine the morale of the people, to spread distrust of the Civil Defence arrangements, and, in fact, to help the Germans in their task of defeating Britain. The forbearance of the Government in dealing with such subversive demagogues and pamphleteers is remarkable.

But the campaign could not have received the support it did had it not corresponded to a basic desire that existed among a large portion of the population of London. The Government policy was dispersal. For this purpose Anderson shelters—those curved-roof, kennel-like constructions of corrugated steel which could protect four or six people from the effects of a near miss—were issued free on a very large scale to the poor, and at a nominal charge of £7 to those who could afford to pay. These were to be half-sunk into backyards, and, as it turned out, provided adequate protection against almost anything save a direct hit. But in the East End many streets consisted of back-to-back cottages and there was thus nowhere to put the Anderson. In those old and often rickety houses attempts to reinforce a ground-floor room with steel supports were not likely to provide much protection. Brick street shelters, originally intended for passers-by caught in a sudden raid, were built in such streets, but these did not look, and indeed, as will be seen, were not always very safe. Besides, many people wanted to go underground. That is what they had done in 1918, and that is what they were determined to do again. They felt happier, and therefore safer, in crowded cellars or tubes. And even when the bombing began, and it was proved over and over again that many of the tubes were not safe and that the shelters beneath the railway arches were often death-traps, a fairly large proportion of East Enders still preferred the quite illusory sense of security engendered by being in a crowded place.

The Government was determined that this time the tubes

16

MORNING, AFTER THE RAID

would not be used for shelter. Not only were many of them very unsafe against the new and powerful bombs, but there was also the danger of flooding. And, finally, if the city above ground were a holocaust, the tubes would provide the quickest and easiest means of transportation and communication. As will be shown, public pressure proved too great and the authorities had to give way on this point when the time came.

Meanwhile through the winter of 1938 and the spring and summer of 1939 the Government continued its policy of issuing Anderson shelters, building brick shelters and reinforcing shelter trenches. Arrangements were made for shelters at factories and other places of work. By the time war broke out shelters, on the dispersal system, were ready for a large proportion of the population, and more were on the way. But there can be little doubt that the inhabitants of the more densely populated boroughs were not satisfied with the arrangements being made on their behalf, and this provided a fertile field for the activities of Communist agitators and other such traitors, as well as for their dupes.

Before ending this introductory chapter, it might be as well to summarise roughly what was the organisation of the A.R.P. services in London when war started, since this remained more or less unaltered throughout the Blitz of the following year.

England was divided into Regions, of which there were nine, and of those the London Region was geographically the smallest. It coincided in area with that of the Metropolitan Police District and thus included parts of the five neighbouring counties as well as Greater London proper. It contained a pre-war population of almost nine millions and stretched from Tilbury in the East to Windsor in the West, from Biggin Hill in the South to a point near St Albans in the North. The Regional Headquarters were in the Geological Museum, Exhibition Road, South Kensington. This sub-division of the country into Regions, based, as stated, on the plans drawn up to deal with internal strife at the time of the General Strike, was intended to ensure governmental control even if communications should break down. Each Region was, in fact, capable of acting as a sort of Home Office in miniature. London Region was unique in that it contained the seat of Government, but the evacuation of the Government departments was envisaged in the event of very heavy air attack, and in such circumstances London Region might well have had a very important administrative function to fulfil.

Beneath the Region was the Group Headquarters. Each group contained a number of boroughs, and its primary task was to move needed reinforcements when a borough was unable to deal with air attack from its own resources. The borough was the tactical unit of Civil Defence, and each had its own Report and Control Centre, usually in the Town Hall. The borough was divided into districts, which might contain as many as 10,000 persons each.

The basic unit was the Wardens' Post. Each Post was manned by from 3 to 6 wardens. In theory there were to be approximately ten Posts to the square mile, and each Post looked after an area containing some 500 persons: in practice some Posts were much larger, some smaller. The Wardens were the backbone of the A.R.P. services. Before the raids began it was their task to issue gas-masks, see that the blackout was enforced, and generally instruct the public. When the raids began, their duty, in theory at least, was principally to pass on information. Each Post was equipped with a telephone, supplemented by runners. The Warden patrolling the two or three blocks of his 'sector' would see a bomb drop, and would assess the nature of the damage and the assistance needed from the specialised services. He would then make his report to the Control Centre, who would send out the specialised services at their disposal—a Stretcher Party, or a Decontamination Squad in the event of gas, or a Rescue Unit to dig out men or women trapped in the rubble. If there was fire they would pass the information to the Fire Service, which had its own hierarchy under the London County Council. If ambulances

were needed—they were only administered by the L.C.C.—
these would be sent. Finally there were the Heavy Rescue, or Demolition Squads, another L.C.C. organisation
consisting mostly of men drawn from the building trade and
equipped with the necessary gear for dealing with major
demolitions. In practice, of course, the Wardens often had to act
as firemen, rescue men and male nurses. And after the raid
was over it was they who guided the homeless to the Rest
Centres, who helped people find their property among the
ruins, who arranged the evacuation of buildings threatened by
unexploded bombs, and who performed a thousand other
tasks of every variety. A Government publication of 1938, *The
Duties of Air Raid Wardens*, had said: 'In time of war, an air-
raid warden should regard himself, first and foremost, as a
member of the public chosen and trained to be a leader of his
fellow-citizens and, with them and for them, to do the right
thing in an emergency.' The great majority of Wardens were
unpaid volunteers, who did a full day's work before reporting
at their Posts. Only some 16,000 London Wardens—out of
some 200,000—were full-time and paid, at the not very
handsome rate of £3 per week. A number were women. The
Wardens, and the firemen, were to be the true heroes of the
Blitz.

CHAPTER TWO

IN FACT the Germans not only did not launch the massive air attack on London, on September 3rd, 1939, but do not even seem to have made any plans for such an attack at this time. In his General Directive No. 1 for the prosecution of the war, dated August 31st, 1939, Hitler laid down: 'The decision regarding attack on London rests with me', and more than a year was to pass before the decision was taken. True, the air raid warning went at once that morning. Sir Winston Churchill has written:

'The Prime Minister's broadcast informed us that we were already at war, and he had scarcely ceased speaking when a strange, prolonged, wailing noise, afterwards to become familiar, broke upon the ear. My wife came into the room braced by the crisis and commented favourably upon German promptitude and precision, and we went to the flat top of the house to see what was going on. Around us on every side, in the clear, cool September light, rose the roofs and spires of London. Above them were already slowly rising thirty or forty cylindrical balloons. We gave the Government a good mark for this evident sign of preparation, and as the quarter of an hour's notice, which we had been led to expect we should receive, was now running out, we made our way to the shelter assigned to us, armed with a bottle of brandy and other appropriate medical comforts.

'Our shelter was a hundred yards down the street and consisted merely of an open basement, not even sandbagged, in which the tenants of half a dozen flats were already assembled. Everyone was cheerful and jocular, as is the English manner when about to encounter the unknown. As I gazed from the doorway along the empty street and at the crowded room below, my imagination drew pictures of ruin and carnage and vast explosions shaking the ground; of buildings clattering down in dust and rubble, of fire brigades and ambulances scurrying through the smoke, beneath the drone of hostile aeroplanes. For had we not all been taught how terrible air raids would be? The Air Ministry had, in natural self-importance, greatly exaggerated their power. The pacifists had sought to play on public fears, and those of us who had so long pressed for preparation and a superior air force, while not accepting the most lurid forecasts, had been content they should act as a spur. I knew that the Government were prepared, in the first few days of the war, with over two hundred and fifty thousand beds for air-raid casualties. Here at least there had been no underestimation. Now we should see what were the facts.'

The fact, on this particular day, was that a single French civilian plane had arrived, unheralded, from France, and the warnings had been sounded as a result. This was not, however, immediately realised even by Londoners, who had been told so repeatedly of the horrors they must expect that the silence on that sunny Sunday morning seemed incredible. Indeed, many people refused to believe the evidence of their senses. The writer of this book, who was in the country at the time, telephoned a young woman in London shortly after mid-day. She had, she said, just left the air raid shelter. There had been a tremendous raid, though luckily not on Chelsea where she was. The destruction in the East End and other parts, however, was appalling. Let it be added that she was neither an hysterical nor a stupid girl. But it had been dinned into her head for years that the moment war broke out the Luftwaffe would 'raze' London to the ground. She could hardly be expected to know that the Luftwaffe staff had never intended to do any such thing.

Indeed, by its very nature the Luftwaffe was ill-suited for operations of this sort. Goering, we are told, admired and accepted General Douhet's theories about the preponderance of air power, and in the early days of the Third Reich would have liked to build a Luftwaffe capable of delivering a 'knock-out blow' against civilian and industrial targets. But he had been over-ruled by the army generals. The Luftwaffe consisted almost entirely of twin-engined bombers and of fighters, excellent planes designed primarily to co-operate with the ground forces in very large-scale land operations. In fact the Luftwaffe was built expressly to fight with the army, in Eastern Europe, against the Russians.

However, even though his Luftwaffe was built for quite other purposes, Goering still cherished an apocalyptic vision, not unlike that of H. G. Wells, of his great air force raining down death and destruction on huge cities filled with hysterical civilians who would immediately surrender. But he never built the four-engined plane needed for strategic bombing, though a former Chief of the Air Staff, General Wever, had pressed for one, which he had called, significantly enough, the 'Ural-bomber'. General Kreipe, who was himself for a short time Chief of Staff of the Luftwaffe, has said of Goering: 'He was entranced by the ideas of General Douhet. I myself doubt whether he ever grasped the full implications of the Italian's doctrine.'

During the first year of the war, the staff plan that did exist at Luftwaffe headquarters for operations against this country was far less ambitious. General Felmy was responsible for this and he had much more modest aims than the massive bombardments favoured by Goering. In view of the immensity of Britain's war potential he did not believe that blanket attacks on cities would be very effective, particularly with the light bombers at his disposal. He preferred a plan of attack against certain types of vital targets, such as the aircraft industry. He was also influenced by a fear, to be only too fully justified, that the bombing of British cities must even-tually lead to reprisals on a truly enormous scale against the German towns.

Felmy, however, disappeared at an early stage of the war and for a most peculiar reason. An officer of his Air Fleet Two, a major, was taking secret documents from one headquarters to another in January of 1940. These were no less than the plans for *Fall Gelb*, the operation against France and the Low Countries. Against orders, this officer went by plane. The plane landed, by mistake, in Belgium, and most of these highly secret papers were captured before the major could destroy them. When Hitler heard of this, he had one of his tantrums and ordered the instant dismissal of the Air Fleet's Commanding General, even though no possible connection existed between the mishap and that most talented airman. Kesselring, a former artillery officer who had only transferred to the Luftwaffe in 1933, took over command of Air Fleet Two. This was clearly a net gain to Goering, who henceforth met little opposition to his grandiose and impractical views.

During the first ten months on the war, then, there was no German plan for the bombing of London. Such an operation was, of course, discussed, but dismissed. General Keitel's instructions for *Fall Gelb*, for instance, issued on the last day of 1939, stated quite clearly: 'attacks [on Britain] which imperil to any great extent the civilian population are to be reserved for cases that demand reprisals'. As late as July of 1940, when Admiral Raeder urged on Hitler that London be bombed, since 'the great mass of people cannot be evacuated', his suggestion was turned down. This, needless to say, was not due to any humanitarian considerations on the part of the German dictator. He hoped that the fear of bombing alone would cause the British to surrender. Should they eventually fail to do so, terror would then bring them to their knees. But this was the final trump, which must not be played prematurely.

That the fear was very great, in September of 1939, cannot be denied. Lord Baldwin, speaking in Parliament in October 1938, had stated that had war come at the time of the Munich crisis, 'there would have been tens of thousands of mangled people—citizens, women and children—before a single soldier or sailor gave his life for his country. That is an awful thought.' It is indeed, despite its phrasing. A woman, questioned by Mass Observation on September 2nd, 1939, that is to say the day before war broke out, said: 'Felt sick at news. Feeling that we'd be for it at once. Woke at three and lay waiting for bombs till time to get up.' Yet on September 4th and 5th, though the citizens of London might still glance apprehensively at the skies, they were, apart from the large number run over in the blackout, quite unmangled. For almost half the Luftwaffe was busy at the other end of Europe, and as already stated the German High Command had, so far as is known, not even sanctioned provisional plans to use the other half against this country.

The first few days of the Polish campaign were a text-book operation so far as the use of air power went. Within twenty-four hours the German fighters had established complete air supremacy over the somewhat antiquated, but by no means insignificant, Polish air arm. Within two days the Polish air force had been destroyed, largely on the ground and by bombing. For the next two days the Luftwaffe concentrated on the Polish centres of communication, and so successfully were these 'nerve centres' attacked that the Poles not only failed to complete mobilisation, but often lost the power to control their own forces in the field. It was not necessary now to carry out 'strategic' bombing of Poland's industrial centres, since the German armour was advancing so rapidly that these were being captured almost as quickly as they could be bombed. This was the method of waging war known as the 'blitzkrieg' or 'lightning war'. Only one more task remained to the Luftwaffe in Poland. In the last stage of the campaign consider-able Polish forces were still resisting in Warsaw, which was under artillery fire. The German bomber force was switched to reinforce the artillery, and Warsaw was heavily and, in part at least, indiscriminately bombed. This must not be regarded, however, as strategic bombing. It was an operation that perfectly, and it turned out uniquely, combined Goering's two conceptions of the use of air power. It was a close-support operation for the army and it was a terror attack on civilians. In so far as its first purpose went, this addition of 'vertical' to 'horizontal' artillery probably hastened the capture of Warsaw. As for terrorisation, the Poles are a brave people. There is no evidence that the bombing of their capital produced any panic or longing to surrender: indeed, what evidence there is points the other way. But it was all over so quickly that it is hard to draw any conclusions. With the help of their Russian allies, the Nazis conquered Poland in just eighteen days. And for all intents and purposes there was to be no more fighting for a further seven months.

Meanwhile, far away in Britain, London was preparing for the attack that did not yet come. A million and a half mothers and children were evacuated from the cities with, in general, remarkable smoothness and, also in general, very small success. Readers interested in that brief-lived experiment are advised to read Professor Titmuss's *Problems of Social Policy*. Had London in fact been heavily bombed, evacuation might have worked. As it was, the refugees from the cities, who were naturally most upset at being thus uprooted from their homes, were very frequently treated with contempt and loathing by their country hosts. Middle-class families in Cheshire or Wiltshire seem to have been quite astonished that children from Bethnal Green and Bermondsey did not have exactly the same *mores*, and even clothes, as their own offspring. Rapidly the mothers returned to their unbombed homes, to look after their husbands, usually taking their children with them. Already as the last evacuation trains arrived at distant country stations, cross little groups of mothers and children could be seen on the opposite platform, waiting for the next train that would take them home. A large proportion of the unaccompanied children followed. By the end of the year, of the million and a half who had left the cities, one million—including almost all the mothers —had returned. By May of 1940 only an estimated quarter of a million children were still living in their wartime foster homes. The long-planned evacuation, on which the Government had set so much store, had been a failure.

Another sort of evacuation was more successful. Something over two million people hurried out of London, under their own steam or in their own motor-cars, as soon as war broke out. Many of them stayed away, and *The Times* was to write, in early 1941, of country hotels 'filled with well-to-do refugees, who too often have fled from nothing. They sit and read and knit and eat and drink. . . .' A high proportion had already reserved accommodation for themselves in safe areas; others just locked up their London flats and drove off. This author remembers a constant stream of private cars and London taxis driving up to his mother's front door in the Thames Valley in September of '39, filled with men and women of all ages and in various stages of hunger, exhaustion and fear, offering absurd sums for accommodation in her already overcrowded house, and even for food. This horde of satin-clad, pin-striped refugees poured through for two or three days, eating everything that was for sale, downing all the spirits in the pubs, and then vanished. This was to happen again, though on a smaller scale, when the bombing actually started a year later. It was undoubtedly an excellent thing that London was rid of these people when it faced the bombs. They would only have been in the way, and they presumably spent a pleasant, if boring, war in their country hotels.

In London, during these months of phoney war, the chief discomfort was undoubtedly the blackout, which to begin with was total, not even torches being allowed in the streets. As the days grew shorter, travelling to and from work in the dark became a protracted and exhausting nightmare. It was danger-ous, too, and the number of road casualties rose sharply, until in December these amounted to no less than forty fatal casual-ties to pedestrians per day. In January the Government was compelled slightly to relax their more stringent rules, which had been frequently enforced with an absurd rigidity. For example, a garage owner was fined five shillings for switching on a neon sign at midday: a woman's baby was having a fit in the night, and she momentarily switched on a light in an uncurtained room, for which whe was fined £3: the Chief Constable of a small country town in Herefordshire announced that it might be an offence to smoke a cigarette in the street if it showed too much light: and a saucy girl who flashed a torch in a policeman's face was immediately arrested by the outraged officer and sent to prison for one month. It may be that she was not saucy at all, but merely frightened of the dark and of the male figure that had loomed up before her. There can be no question that many women in the cities, and particularly those living in the crowded and garishly lit East End, were extremely frightened by a darkness they had never before seen. Apart from the very real danger of falling under an invisible bus, it evoked atavistic fears inherited from our remote ancestors who had lit their fires at the front of their caves to keep the wild beasts at bay. To this must be added horrid folk-memories connected with highwaymen, Jack the Ripper and other such popular figures of Freudian fantasy. Among ignorant and timid women the blackout caused real distress.

On the other hand the belief current at the time that it was a godsend to the criminal classes, and that footpads were roaming the West End, knocking old gentlemen over the head as they emerged onto the steps of their clubs while cat-burglars slithered, invisible, up and down the fronts of luxury blocks of flats, was fortunately quite untrue. As a retired policeman has remarked darkly, the blackout worked both ways. If the copper couldn't see the crook, the crook also had no idea where his enemy might be waiting, and a very large number of war reserve policemen were now on duty. There was, at least during the early months of the war, no marked increase in crime, and large-scale planned robbery actually decreased. Presumably the master criminals were busy installing their families in those country retreats to which we have referred.

27

Later this was to change, but, as will be seen, for reasons not connected with the blackout.

In London the preparations to deal with air raids went on, at a much accelerated pace. Throughout the country one and a half million Anderson shelters had been distributed free, more were on the way, and if in early 1940 there was any London household which did not possess such a shelter, that was not the fault of the Government. The trenches that had been dug in the parks a year before were roofed, revetted and enlarged. The borough councils declared a number of basements and other apparently sturdy edifices public shelters, and proceeded to reinforce those that had need of such support. The public had not been informed that they were to be prevented from using the tubes as shelters, but a number of tube stations in central London were closed so that bulkheads could be installed which, when shut, would prevent flooding. Brick and concrete surface shelters, each to hold fifty people, were rapidly constructed. In fact by the end of the year the Government's arrangements for shelter on the dispersal system were largely completed in the London Region. Apart from the Andersons, public shelters of one sort or another to hold over 800,000 people was ready or nearing completion. As stated in the previous chapter, the defences against gas had reached a high state of readiness even before war began.

A great many men and women volunteered for the A.R.P. services, over one and a half million throughout Britain, and the London services were up to strength. The boroughs had over 9,000 paid Wardens and over 10,000 whole-time members of Stretcher Parties. The Rescue Services, which, it will be recalled, came under the L.C.C., were well organised and contained 12,000 paid members. Recruiting for the Auxiliary Fire Service was going on satisfactorily, and sixty per cent of the war establishment of pumps and other equipment had been issued. The rest was produced by the summer. Report and control centres had been set up in schools and other commandeered buildings. It all went remarkably smoothly, and in view of the enormity of the task, the Government, the London Region, the L.C.C. and most of the boroughs were remarkably efficient.

The main task now was to instruct the public as to what they should do in the event of raids, and this proved difficult for two reasons: the invincible stupidity and frivolity of a large portion of the public, and the growing unpopularity of the A.R.P. services, and particularly of the Wardens, whose jobs it was to give the public that instruction.

Not that the lessons the public had to learn were in any way difficult or complicated. But, as has already been pointed out, the A.R.P. services were largely manned by volunteers, that section of the community which accepted responsibility and was capable of foresight. In London, whose population had shrunk to some five or six millions, almost a million of the best men and women who had not gone off to the forces were directly or indirectly concerned with the A.R.P. Services. A high proportion of the remaining eighty per cent were what Marx called the *lumpen-proletariat*, while a very small proportion were actively disaffected. To instruct such people even in the basic rudiments of self-protection was not easy. Thus a Public Information Leaflet, issued to every household at the beginning of the war, stated in heavy type: IF YOU THROW A BUCKET OF WATER ON A BURNING INCENDIARY BOMB, IT WILL EXPLODE AND THROW BURNING FRAGMENTS IN ALL DIRECTIONS. The leaflet went on to say how these bombs should be smothered in sand or with a sandbag. It all seems simple enough. Yet in late 1939 Mass Observation reported that only one-third of the persons interviewed in London could give a correct answer when asked how incendiaries should be dealt with. The commonest incorrect answer was, 'to throw the bomb into water', or 'to throw water over the bomb'. Other recorded answers included:

'Stand up by a brick wall.'
'Lay on it.'
'Leave it to a Warden.'

'Flop a coat over it, or throw it into a sewer, or anywhere there is water.'

'Pick it up and run it in water.'

'Sit back and hold tight.'

'Leave it where it was and run.'

'Keep the thin places of your house patched up.'

'Put on your gas-mask.'

Most people did not bother to read this or any other of the Public Information Leaflets. Some even regarded them as an obscure insult. One person described his reaction to them as one of 'contemptuous and cynical amusement'.

The bombs had not fallen, and after a brief period which can only be described as one of disappointment a portion of this ignorant mass of persons quite naturally blamed the 'authorities' for the fear they had felt and the inconveniences, such as evacuation or the blackout, that they had suffered. By October, again according to Mass Observation, approximately half the population believed that there would not be any raids. A high proportion of working-class women ascribed this immunity from bombing to the existence of the balloon barrage. In this, since it was visible, they placed an immense trust. Indeed, many of the women who had returned from evacuation gave as their reason for doing so the fact that they had not felt safe in the country. There were no silver balloons floating reassuringly over their heads.

Gas-masks and Andersons, like balloons, were visible, and had the further advantage of being personal possessions. The former was often treated as a sort of charm, even though sometimes known as 'a 'Itler'; and many families expressed their personalities by painting their Anderson, laying lino on the floor and planting flowers around its entrance. On the other hand, when an Anderson became filled with water, this was the fault of the 'authorities' for providing such impractical constructions.

The most obvious target for this deeply rooted, and doubtless healthy, dislike of the authorities was the Wardens. There they were, sitting about all day, being apparently paid for doing nothing, and, what is more, trying to tell *us* what to do in the event of raids that will never happen. Since one of their tasks at this time was the ungrateful one of walking the streets at night and informing householders that their blackout was imperfect, they were regarded as nosey-parkers, too. Since, in the event of repeated and deliberate infractions of the blackout regulations, they had no choice but to inform the police, they were coppers' narks and informers. It is hardly surprising that a Warden, while dutifully making his patrols in the neighbourhood of the World's End, Chelsea, should suddenly have been struck by an accurately thrown boot, while a Bethnal Green Warden has said that he and his fellows were jeered at in the streets for carrying out exercises that would teach them how to help the people.

There was, in fact, a dull resentment against the war as a whole that steadily increased throughout that boring and mildly uncomfortable winter. This was exploited by the Communists and a certain section of the Labour Party. For example, Dr Salter, who represented Bermondsey in the House of Commons, produced a masterly analysis of the war situation in the November, 1939, issue of the Bermondsey Labour Magazine. 'Hitler', he wrote, 'is already defeated. Russia has defeated him, not the British Army or Navy. [This, of course, was after the Russian occupation of Eastern Poland in accordance with the secret clauses of the Molotov-Ribbentrop pact.] His aggression against his smaller and weaker neighbours has been effectively checked. . . . Clearly the best thing to do is to stop the war by a truce. . . .' And in that same month twenty Labour M.P.s, including Lansbury, Salter, Sydney Silverman and R. R. Stokes, published a manifesto headed: PEACE BY NEGOTIATION—NOW! ! ! (Their exclamation marks.) H. G. Wells at this time published his reasons for refusing Government service. He had, it seems, been on the public pay-roll in the First World War, and with sublime modesty and a very curious choice of metaphor he now wrote: 'Once bit, twice

31

shy. I am not going to be a stalking horse for the British Foreign Office again.' Dr Salter, in his little magazine, took this as his text when advising his constitutents not to believe what they read in the papers or heard on the B.B.C.

It is hardly surprising that the Wardens, enforcing unpopular regulations designed to protect the people against air raids that would never take place, in a war that ought to be immediately called off, should have boots thrown at them. They were even attacked, as early as October, as 'slackers and parasites' in the House of Commons, and in January the establishment was cut down, and a number of the paid Wardens dismissed as a result. What is surprising is that so very high a proportion should have remained at their posts, continued their remarkably uninspiring training, and thus have been able to carry out their function so efficiently and bravely when the time came.

The Auxiliary Fire Service had never been up to strength and in June of 1940, to increase recruiting for this rather unpopular form of service, the Government announced that men between the ages of 30 and 50 might volunteer for the Auxiliary Fire Service instead of doing the normal military service for which they would otherwise be conscripted. When the Blitz started, the Fire Service therefore consisted of three distinct types of men: the regulars of the London Fire Brigade, most of whom were ex-service men with a tight discipline, a profound belief in the virtues of metal-polish and drill, and a deep conviction of their own superiority to the Auxiliaries: men of the Auxiliary Fire Service who for reasons of patriotism, a fondness for bonfires or some other motive, had joined the Fire Service before, or in the early stages of, the war: and men who, after June of 1940, regarded life in the Fire Service as preferable to the Army, Navy or Air Force. Quite a number of those intellectuals who had inclined to pacifism before the war, but who now did not feel that they could object to military service on conscientious grounds, joined the A.F.S. A friend of the author, a writer, has described the men of his station in the following words:

'The thing about my role as a fireman, which I think was in some ways typical, was that I joined the A.F.S. to dodge the army, because I've always had a horror of the army, having had too many relations in it, and being at school a congenital member of the awkward squad. . . . I suppose my sub-station was fairly typical. It was on the fringes of the City and the East End. There was a solid core of taxi-drivers and a sprinkling of waiters—the intellectuals were generally further West—and a few men with little businesses, such as tobacconists and so on, who joined the fire service because they wanted to be able to keep an eye on their businesses and their wives and the rest of it. We had two burglars, one an old professional burglar from Bethnal Green, who came from a very good family and could trace his descent right back for almost three generations of burglars. He was very highly thought of. The other was a much less highly thought of petty crook, and after a time it became the custom in the sub-station to shake him when we came back from a fire. . . .'

On one point all the former members of the A.F.S. with whom this writer has talked, no matter what their motives in joining the service, were agreed: this is that they were extremely shabbily treated by the regulars. This may be pure coincidence, but it seems that in many parts of London the regulars refused to allow the A.F.S. to use their shower-baths, even when returning filthy from a fire: that no attempts were made in the early days to provide them with canteens: and that they were in general treated with the rough contempt that boys of eight receive from their seniors aged eleven. Presumably the junior officers of the London Fire Brigade, who were usually former N.C.O.s in the Army or Navy, were responsible for this. Mr Henry Greene's novel, *Caught*, gives an excellent picture of the relationship between the auxiliaries and the regulars. The resentment engendered must have been very strong indeed, for it has survived dangers shared and innumerable conflagrations extinguished.

The Ambulance Service, it will be recalled, also came under

the London County Council, and though recruiting for this vital duty—and its importance was if anything over-estimated before the Blitz started, on account of the number of casualties expected—was considered unsatisfactory before the war, it soon received many recruits, for it had a very definite appeal to a certain type of man and even more so to the wholly admirable type of young women whose mothers in their tens of thousands had nursed the wounded of the First World War. Many of the girls who are loosely described by the popular press as débutantes knew how to drive a car and now drove ambulances instead. Though the first-aid, ambulance, nursing and medical services would probably have been overwhelmed had casualties been on the anticipated scale, as it turned out they were fully able to deal with the situation that actually arose. Nor did this service, with its obviously humanitarian functions, suffer from the unpopularity of the Wardens or the internal friction of the Fire Service. Even such veteran critics and self-appointed arbiters of social usefulness as Dr Salter and the editor of *The New Statesman and Nation* realised that small popularity was to be gained by decrying ambulance men and sneering at voluntary nurses.

And so the winter of the phoney war went on. The theatres and cinemas, that had all been closed by order, gradually reopened. Rationing, always a thoroughly popular measure with the British since it appeals to the egalitarianism of some and the notorious 'sense of fair play' of others, was introduced and adjudged an immediate success. The popularity of the Minister for Food, Lord Woolton, reached heights only equalled by the unpopularity of his equally hard-worked colleague, the Home Secretary and Minister for Home Security, Sir John Anderson. The men and women of the Civil Defence services continued to train for an eventuality which the majority now believed would never come. The war became known as the Bore War. And the Air Ministry staff increased their estimate of the danger hanging over London's head. The Germans, they now calculated, could drop 2,000 tons of

34

bombs per day for several days, and 700 tons for an unlimited period. They still estimated the probable casualty rate at fifty per ton dropped.

The bombing of Rotterdam was the awakening. When the Germans invaded the Low Countries, on May 10th, they again employed the blitzkrieg tactics which had served them so well in Poland, but now the lightning struck even further from the frontier, for airborne troops were used on what was, for that period, a large scale. Those airborne troops, once they had landed by parachute or glider, became infantry. In place of artillery, they were supported by bombers, particularly dive-bombers, in their attacks on objectives far behind the frontiers. The principal objective, and the one against which the largest force of airborne troops was committed, was Rotterdam and its several airfields.

This operation, unlike the others, was not immediately and entirely successful. General Student, commanding the airborne troops, was held up in Rotterdam. He asked for air support on a large scale. This was given him on May 13th, large areas of Rotterdam were flattened, and many civilians killed. Churchill was to refer to this operation as 'a massacre', and to the Western World as a whole it seemed at that time, and later, a terror attack of the sort that had long been awaited. It also appeared to have achieved the purpose of such attacks, for on the next day the Dutch army laid down its arms.

The Germans maintained, and Kesselring, who commanded the Air Fleet, has continued to maintain, that the bombing of Rotterdam was a purely tactical operation in support of ground troops. The answer seems to be that, as was the case with Warsaw, the bombing of Rotterdam accorded simultaneously with both of Goering's views on the use of air power.

There was no other example of the massive bombing of a civilian target during the Western Campaign, though small forces of German bombers did raid towns in central and southern France with the obvious purpose of inspiring terror in their inhabitants. In this objective they were to a large degree successful. Dread of what the Luftwaffe might do contributed powerfully to the demoralisation of the French. This dread was at least partially responsible for the speed with which the French Government surrendered as soon as the French armies were defeated. In such an atmosphere there could be no question of repeating Gambetta's heroic resistance of 1871, even had this been possible against modern weapons.

Britain was clearly the next on the list, and in June of 1940 the Luftwaffe, now busy installing itself on a great semi-circle of airfields all within easy striking distance of Britain, looked a truly formidable force. It was.

And yet somehow the almost panic terror of 1938 and the less hysterical but perhaps more deep-rooted fears of 1939 hardly re-appeared. The reason for this was twofold. Most important was the new mood of the country, a mood most skilfully tempered and welded by the new Prime Minister. Like his predecessors, he was well aware of the horrors of bombing and he had to rely on the same gloomy estimates that the experts provided, but unlike them he preserved a certain scepticism, and he was not at all frightened. No doubt he remembered the words that he himself had written, nearly twenty-three years before, when, as Minister of Munitions in October of 1917, he prepared a memorandum on the subject of air attacks upon civilians:

'It is not reasonable to speak of an air offensive as if it were going to finish the war by itself. It is improbable that any terrorisation of the civil population which could be achieved by air attack would compel the government of a great nation to surrender. Familiarity with bombardment, a good system of dug-outs or shelters, a strong control by police and military authorities, would be sufficient to preserve the national fighting power unimpaired. In our own case we have seen the combative spirit of the people roused, and not quelled, by the German air raids.'

Now, in 1940, though the forecasts by the experts might be far more terrible than in that earlier war, Winston Churchill knew too much about war to confuse forecast with fact. He made no bones about the grimness of the immediate future, but he did not believe that Britain would be conquered. Nor did the British people. They had no first-hand knowledge of defeat and, being a remarkably unimaginative people, have never been able to conceive of it as more than a theoretical possibility. His determination and their stubbornness during that summer were admirably suited. Sir Winston Churchill has drawn a very clear picture of his own attitude in his *History of the Second World War*. That of the people whom he led is well depicted in Peter Fleming's *Invasion 1940*.

And the word 'invasion' is the key to the second reason for the change of attitude of the country. Hitherto massive bombing had had, as it were, all the publicity. That was the threat, that was the danger. But now it was equalled if not surpassed in the popular mind by the menace of invasion. And against this there was something that every man and woman could do. In October of 1938 and September of 1939 the British, and particularly the Londoners, had envisaged their role in the expected catastrophe as almost entirely a passive one. Huddling in shelters, groping their way through clouds of poisonous gases, dying in the streets, victims. Now, in July of 1940, though they once again expected heavy raids, they saw themselves in another role as well: hurling home-made grenades at German tanks, garrotting Nazi paratroopers in the night; in a word, fighting. Churchill's blood-curdling phrase, 'You can always take one with you', struck a responsive chord. And so the bombing was seen only as a part of the forthcoming battle, not as the final cataclysm.

The grumbling and the whining stopped, almost overnight, and few people paid much attention to those voices which, like gramophone records stuck in one groove, were unable to stop uttering words no longer suited to the country's mood. The Socialists had entered the Churchill Government: the country was united as it has seldom been: this was the period of the 'Dunkirk spirit'. People ceased throwing boots at

Wardens, and were now only too anxious to see that their neighbours, and they themselves, blacked out their houses. Many of those who had withdrawn from the Civil Defence Services volunteered again. Millions joined the Home Guard. And the country's eyes were fixed on the air battle which began in August, and which has gone down to history as the Battle of Britain.

As is known, the German objective during the Battle of Britain was the destruction of the Royal Air Force as a preliminary to the invasion. Goering may have believed that it was possible to defeat Britain by air attack alone, but in this he was not supported by the Army and the Navy nor even by the majority of his own staff officers and commanders. However, the possibility that Goering's theory might be practicable was not ruled out at Hitler's own headquarters.

On June 30th, 1940, Colonel General Jodl, Chief of the Armed Forces Command Staff, prepared a memorandum entitled *The Continuation of the War against England*. (This was produced during his trial at Nuremberg as Document 1776-PS.) It runs as follows:

The continuation of the war against England.

If political methods should fail to achieve their object, England's will to resist must be broken by force.

(a) by attacks upon the English homeland.

(b) by an extension of the war peripherally.

So far as (a) is concerned, there are three possibilities:

(1) Siege.

This includes attack by land and sea against all incoming and outgoing traffic.

Attack on the English air arm and on the country's war economy and its sources as a whole.

(2) Terror attacks against the English centres of population.

(3) Invasion with the purpose of occupying England.

The final victory of Germany over England is now only a question of time. Offensive enemy operations on a large scale are no longer a possibility.

Course (a) was the one selected, and it was followed in three phases, the three phases outlined by Jodl, though in reversed order. This, incidentally, is, so far as the writer knows, the first time that the word 'terror' was quite nakedly used by a responsible German headquarters in describing their own plans. But for the time being Hitler had decreed that London was not to be bombed.

A great deal has been written about the Battle of Britain, and it is not intended here to do more than recapitulate very briefly its connection with the bombing of London. But since the nature of the Battle of Britain, and the objectives of both sides, are intimately connected with the events of the following winter, the course of events must be outlined briefly.

The Luftwaffe had begun by attacking coastal convoys, had then switched to forward airfields, and finally to the sector-stations, the control-centres of Fighter Command. The losses during the first two phases had been heavy on both sides, but because of the radar chain, the excellent system of tactical control based on the Observer Corps and the sector-stations, and the quality of the R.A.F.'s eight-gun fighters and their pilots, the balance was tipping in favour of the Royal Air Force. But the loss of planes in Fighter Command was severe, and reserves were sinking. Though German bomber losses had been considerable, their fighter strength was still large, and their strategy still was to compel, if they could, the British fighters to meet their own. In such a battle of attrition, though the German fighter casualties might be as heavy as, or even heavier than, the British, their aim would be achieved if Fighter Command were destroyed, no matter what the cost in German fighters. For once that was done, the German bombers would have an empty sky from which to destroy the R.A.F.'s bomber bases, attack the Royal Navy, and thus clear the way for their invasion fleet.

From August 19th until the 30th an inconclusive battle raged during the course of which the R.A.F. Fighter Squadrons managed to conserve their strength, while the German bombers carried out a number of sharp raids which caused considerable damage to industrial and other targets. But on August 31st the Luftwaffe switched the main weight of their attack to the sector-stations covering the defence of London, those nerve-centres of Fighter Command, a first-class target. This was the first time during the Battle of Britain that the Germans had concentrated on a vital target, and it paid them handsome dividends. During the first few days of September they caused extensive damage to six of the seven sector-stations in question. To protect them the R.A.F. fighters had to be committed against heavily escorted German bomber groups, and once again Fighter Command's reserves sank dangerously. Had the Germans succeeded in knocking out the sector-stations, and keeping them out, this might have proved no less fatal to Fighter Command, at least in that part of England, than the physical destruction of the R.A.F.'s fighter planes. A few days later Air-Marshal Park wrote: 'Had the enemy continued his heavy attacks against Biggin Hill and the adjacent sectors and knocked out their operation rooms and telephone communications, the fighter defences would have been in a perilous state during the last critical phase when heavy attacks have been directed against the capital.'

But on September 7th the Germans prematurely switched their attack from the sector-stations to London, and, as it turned out, Fighter Command was saved to win its great victory a week later, on September 15th.

It must not be assumed that the Battle of Britain was one distinct engagement, the Blitz, as it came to be called, another. They faded into one another and overlapped. When the Luftwaffe launched its first large daylight attack on London, its objective was still, by attacking vital targets, to get Fighter Command into the air and destroy it. For whatever Hitler may have thought, and however strong the doubts about the feasibility of the invasion cherished by the Army and the Navy, Operation 'Sealion' was still 'on' and the Luftwaffe was still fighting the preliminary phase of that battle. But

Hitler had intended to keep the bombing of London as the *pièce de résistance* of those preliminaries, to be carried out a matter of hours before his invasion flotilla sailed. A directive for the invasion signed by Keitel, and therefore coming directly from Hitler, and dated August 16th, had said: '. . . on D-1 the Luftwaffe is to make a strong attack on London, which will cause the population to flee from the city and block the roads.' On September 6th D-day was fixed for no earlier than September 21st. That is to say, Hitler had changed his mind. Why?

The real answer almost certainly is that he had at last been persuaded by Admiral Raeder and others that 'Sealion' would never in fact take place, or at least not that year. He was already seriously thinking of the attack on Russia, and for this campaign he must, of course, have a Luftwaffe in being. Meanwhile it was worth trying the second of Jodl's three suggested means for knocking Britain out of the war. He, too, had been influenced by all that had been written about terror bombing, and he knew the effect of the attack on Rotterdam. It was on the cards that Britain might cave in if London were reduced to rubble. His bomber force was in the West and had nothing else to do. Furthermore, apart from the long-term policy of blockade by U-boats and other devices, there was no other way that he saw whereby he could hit directly at Britain. He therefore rescinded his decree that London should not be bombed.

The reason he gave, and he gave it in a speech on September 4th, for this sudden change of attitude is a curious one.

One of the sillier manifestations, and incidentally a highly un-Christian one, of the human mentality is the alacrity, when doing something nasty or foolish, to advance as justification that he, or she, did it first. With this in mind, no government, or almost no government, will ever admit that it has launched a war of aggression, but invariably insists that it was only acting to defend its own interests. In almost every country War Ministries are called Defence Ministries and, as we have seen, even Douhet's bombing theories are allegedly devised to 'defend' the homeland. In the Second World War, to judge by the public utterances of those who carried them out, the bombing of civilians was always by nature of reprisals.

Behind closed doors, of course, such pretences are often dropped. Thus on May 14th, 1940, Air-Marshal Dowding, in his protracted struggle to prevent his Fighter Command from being wasted away in France, had urged a bombing raid on the Ruhr in order to draw reprisals upon this country. This was highly logical, since the R.A.F. could, and later did, fight much more effectively from its own bases. Dowding's operation was carried out, 96 bombers bombed the Ruhr on the following night, but the Germans firmly kept their eyes on the main battle and did not take the bait.

When, on August 24th, a few German planes accidentally, and against Hitler's orders, dropped bombs on London, Churchill was quick to order reprisals. On the very next night 81 aircraft of Bomber Command were sent to bomb Berlin. They did little damage. But for the next week the British bombers were over Berlin whenever the weather permitted. This gave Hitler the perfect excuse for reprisals. On September 4th he announced that he intended to wipe out the British cities. On September 5th the appropriate orders were issued for the attack on London. This time the bait, if it was still bait, had been taken. And on September 6th Goering arrived on the Channel Coast to take direct command of the battle of London, a battle in which that inflated personage hoped to win everlasting glory in Valhalla and, incidentally, to end the war.

CHAPTER THREE

ON THAT Saturday afternoon Goering and Kesselring are said to have stood on the cliffs of Cap Gris Nez and watched the bombers of Air Fleet Two form up and set off for London, while the escorting fighters took up their positions above and below the Heinkels and Dorniers. That was at approximately four o'clock. Further to the south bomber after bomber of Sperrle's Third Air Fleet, forming the second wave of the attack, roared along the runways of Normandy and Brittany and was airborne. That afternoon well over three hundred bombers, escorted by about six hundred fighters, flew against London. Compared with the bomber fleets that were to set out, in the other direction, three and four years later this may seem a small force. At the time it was regarded as a huge one. This was the massive attack which, for a decade and more, had been the threat, the nightmare and the fear. There is always a first time, and this was it.

The attack achieved surprise. This may seem curious, since the German bombers had been edging closer and closer to London: the oil installations at Thameshaven, Shell Haven and Purfleet had been bombed and set ablaze two days before, and as already stated an occasional bomber had been unloading over the suburbs and even the centre of the capital for the past fortnight. But nevertheless, Fighter Command Headquarters at Stanmore and Air-Marshal Park's No. 11 Group at Uxbridge covering the approaches to the metropolis did not expect a concentrated attack on London yet. They had every reason to assume that the Luftwaffe would continue its successful raids on the sector-stations, and the fighter squadrons were therefore sent up to intercept such attacks. Indeed, had the Luftwaffe been assigned its targets by the German air-marshals, that is almost certainly what the Luftwaffe would have done. But this operation had been ordered by Hitler and was under Goering's control. Military logic was thus at a discount and surprise was achieved. If it was a strategic blunder—and it is just conceivable that this switching of the bomber fleets to London lost Germany the war—it was a tactical triumph.

The illogicality confused and misled the British Chiefs of Staff. They had assumed, quite correctly as we know, that the German plan for invasion would involve a heavy attack on London immediately before the troop-carrying barges put to sea. Air reconnaissance had revealed that the German preparations in the Channel ports were nearly completed. When, therefore, the Chiefs of Staff, who were actually meeting that afternoon, heard the crashing of the bombs on London and learned that the great attack so long awaited was in fact being delivered on the capital, they reckoned that the invasion was likely to take place within a matter of hours. They therefore issued the code word 'Cromwell' to commands on that same evening. 'Cromwell' meant 'invasion imminent'. They could not be expected to guess at this early hour that the real meaning of the attack was to be exactly the reverse. Hitler, dissatisfied with the results achieved by his airmen and increasingly irritated by the technical advice he was receiving from his sailors and soldiers, was switching to those methods of terror and brutality which had hitherto won him such spectacular victories both in his own country and abroad. The London docks were, of course, a first-class military target, and in this respect the attack on them was fully justified from a military point of view, at least on a long-term basis; for had they been put out of operation, together with Southampton, Bristol and Liverpool, it would certainly have been very difficult, and might have proved impossible, for Britain to continue the war. But all this was far removed from the tactical requirements of the German sailors and soldiers waiting to carry out Operation 'Sealion'. Furthermore, it is hard not to believe that Hitler, in making the long-delayed decision to bomb a target in the middle of London, was not also indulging in that taste for sadism and destruction which was such a marked aspect of his character. But that is speculative and not of great importance. What is important is that the attack on the docks meant a basic switch of German strategy, away from 'Sealion' which then seemed imminent, to a longer-range attack on Britain's communications as a whole and on the morale of the civilian inhabitants of Britain's capital city. Strategically it was a political act of violence. That is why it took the British soldiers and airmen by surprise for half an hour or so.

The first wave came in from the east, with targets the docks below Tower Bridge, Woolwich Arsenal and again the oil installations farther down river. The Thames and Medway guns opened up on the leading formations, flying westwards, at about five o'clock. A quarter of an hour later the first bombs fell on Woolwich Arsenal—a prime military target—and damaged two important factories as well. Other squadrons went on to bomb West Ham, Poplar, Stepney and Bermondsey, the riverside boroughs on either side of the Thames' great double meander where are concentrated the Victoria and Albert Docks, the West India Docks and the vast Surrey Commercial Docks. Having reached their objectives, they turned away to the north, and now they were in their turn attacked by some seven fighter squadrons of Nos. 11 and 12 group. They were roughly handled, but their bombs had exploded where they meant them to, and already fires were starting. Meanwhile the second wave was driving for the capital from the south and southeast. Some of these were intercepted by the R.A.F. fighters before reaching the capital, and one squadron fought a running fight over London. In general, however, the Messerschmitts managed to blast a way through for their bombers and the target area was again heavily hit. The bombs, over three hundred tons of high explosive and many thousands of incendiaries, rained down not only on the docks, but also on the mean, closely packed and highly inflammable rows of little streets that housed the workers and their families. In an hour and a half London received its heaviest daylight raid of the war, and its most concentrated. Though bombs were dropped as far away as Tottenham and Croydon, it was the East End that bore the brunt of it. By half past six that evening whole streets of little two-storey cottages, built as cheaply and quickly as the speculative builders of the nineteenth century could put them up, had collapsed in dust and rubble. To the countryman or the town planner, those grimy, aged, jerry-built dwellings might be nothing but slums, and in retrospect it is often said that the action of the Luftwaffe was comparable to that of the surgeon's knife, removing once and for all a cancerous growth. But for those who lived in those dreary, dirty streets, these cottages and shops and pubs were home. At half past six many of those homes no longer existed. And the fires were only just beginning to catch hold.

Nor was there any chance of extinguishing them before darkness fell, when they would provide a tremendous beacon to draw new bomber formations, with fresh loads of high explosives and incendiaries. During this biggest daylight raid the Germans lost over forty aircraft, but the R.A.F., already stretched almost to snapping point, had lost twenty-eight fighters and seventeen pilots it could ill afford. And the East End was ablaze. Goering might well congratulate himself on a victory. He did so, with his customary ostentation, that same evening, over the German wireless.

The blaze, as the sun sank towards the west, was enormous and visible for miles. From every part of London eyes were turned towards the Isle of Dogs. Mr Maxwell-Hyslop, who worked at what was then the Board of Education, has said:

'We'd been down to Richmond to tea with some friends. We came back on bicycles at about five o'clock and we saw this enormous great mushroom of smoke. It was so big, and towered up in the sky so high, that one couldn't believe it was

46

smoke at all, and for a long time we didn't know what it could be. We'd heard the guns going and we'd heard the sirens going but we never dreamt of anything like this. And then we got up to the top of this rise in Richmond Park and we could see this smoke, this column of smoke, and we said—My goodness, that must be somewhere near Hammersmith. And then we bicycled on, and we said—Well, it must be Chelsea. And finally when we got home, it was only then that we realised it was ten or twelve miles away from us still. And then we went up on the roof of our flat and saw this great horizon plainly, this red column of smoke towering up into the sky, a terrifying sight.'

Far away to the northeast in Woodford, on the edge of Epping Forest, a man remembers: 'A monstrous, monotonous droning proclaimed the coming of the bombers. They swept on south of the Borough. By six o'clock the skies were empty, and all Thameside blazed. As the sun began to sink, the vast expanse of the red glow, to west and southwest, sent a chill to the heart. It seemed that all London was burning.'

William Sansom, in his book *Westminster in War*, has written: 'Towards six o'clock the fiction of unease became fact, the man on the street learned that something had been happening in the East End, something more significant than the ordinary tidings brought by the siren—and Report Centres and other official quarters knew that at last the Luftwaffe had struck hard, there and then, that afternoon, at London proper. The docks were ablaze. And as the sun set, those in the West End streets grew conscious of the unbelievable, for the sunset occurred not only in the accustomed west near Putney and Willesden, but also incredibly in the East over St Paul's and where the City of London was held to lie. That was curious enough— but when the western skies had already grown dark the fierce red glow in the East struck harshly fast and there was seen for the first time that black London roof-scape silhouetted against what was to become a monotonously copper-orange sky.'

47

And, nearer to the fires still, the Dean of St Paul's, Dr Matthews, was on duty that evening with the other guardians of London's own cathedral. 'Inside the Cathedral', he has written, 'the light was such that I have never seen the stained-glass windows glow as they did then.'

Mr Jack Rothmans had joined the A.F.S. before the war, and on the afternoon of September 7th had been having a cold bath in the 500-gallon canvas tank at his sub-station near the Surrey Docks.

'I was drying myself and partly dressed when we heard the sound of planes overhead. We saw them coming in rather fast and low, far lower than I'd ever seen any plane during the war. We saw the bomb bays open quite clearly, but we still thought it was some fun and games exercise over the docks, which we knew nothing about. I don't think it struck any of us that the emblems on the planes weren't British. Then we saw the bombs leave the planes, and everyone ran for cover, buildings tossed about, the ground shook, and the next thing we knew the bells were down and away we went.'

At about eight o'clock that evening the German night bombers took off from their bases again, and a little less than an hour later, as darkness fell and the fires blazed more fiercely, the first bombs were dropped into the holocaust. All London wondered what was happening beneath that pall of twisting, crimson, oily smoke.

The historian of the London Fire Brigade has written, in *Front Line*:

'Four-fifths of the firemen involved had had no prior experience of actual fire-fighting. In normal times a 30-pump fire is a very big fire. Shortly after midnight there were nine fires in London rating over 100 pumps. In the Surrey docks there were two, of 300 and 130 pumps; at Woolwich Arsenal, 200 pumps; at Bishopsgate Goods Yard and at five points on the docks, 100-pump fires. All these were technically "out of hand", that is to say unsurrounded, uncontrolled and spreading. In Quebec Yard, Surrey Docks, was the night's biggest fire

TUBE SHELTER PERSPECTIVE
The Liverpool Street extension

—immense in its area, moving with disconcerting speed, generating terrific heat. It was 30 or 40 times bigger than the great Barbican fire of 1938, the biggest in London's recent history. It set alight the wooden blocks in the roadways, a thing without precedent. A blaze covering such an area is not only worse than a smaller one in direct proportion to its area, but is far harder to fight than its mere extent would suggest. The greater the cumulative heat, the fiercer the draught of cold air dragged in to feed it, and thus the quicker the movement of the fire and the greater the length of its flames. They were so long and their heat so great as to blister the paint on fireboats that tried to slip past under the lee of the opposite river bank 300 yards away. Solid embers a foot long were tossed into streets afar off to start fresh fires. Stocks of timber which the firemen had drenched began at once to steam, then to dry, then themselves to burst into flame in the intense heat radiated from nearby blazes.

'While the men fought this monstrous fire, the enemy continued to drop bombs into it, throughout the night. Time and again these would rekindle an area that had just been laboriously conquered. Only with daybreak could real progress begin. The exhausted men could not be relieved after a normal interval because the brigades were fully extended. Many firemen were at work here for 40 hours, some officers for longer. Such was the baptism of fire of most of London's wartime firemen.

'At Woolwich Arsenal men fought the flames among boxes of live ammunition and crates of nitro-glycerine, under a hail of bombs directed at London's No. 1 military target. But in the docks themselves strange things were going on. There were pepper fires, loading the surrounding air heavily with stinging particles, so that when the firemen took a deep breath it felt like burning fire itself. There were rum fires, with torrents of blazing liquid pouring from the warehouse doors and barrels exploding like bombs themselves. There was a paint fire, another cascade of white-hot flame, coating the

49

pumps with varnish that could not be cleaned for weeks. A rubber fire gave forth black clouds of smoke so asphyxiating that it could only be fought from a distance, and was always threatening to choke the attackers. Sugar, it seems, burns well in liquid form as it floats on the water in dockland basins. Tea makes a blaze that is "sweet, sickly and very intense". One man found it odd to be pouring cold water on hot tea leaves. A grain warehouse when burning produced great clouds of black flies that settled in banks upon the walls, whence the firemen washed them off with their jets. There were rats in their hundreds. And the residue of burned wheat was "a sticky mess that pulls your boots off".'

And an auxiliary fireman has said:

'Most of us had the wind up to start with, especially with no barrage. It was all new, but we were all unwilling to show fear, however much we might feel it. You looked around and saw the rest doing their job. You couldn't let them down, you just had to get on with it. You began to make feeble jokes to each other and gradually you got accustomed to it. . . . The fires had a stunning effect. Wherever the eye could see, vast sheets of flame and a terrific roar. It was so bright that there was no need for headlights.

'On 7th September we took our pumps to East India Dock, to Rum Wharf. The first line of warehouses was ablaze from end to end. I walked down between the two warehouses by myself. Half-way down was a staff car in the middle of the causeway. Standing nonchalantly by it was a young W.A.F.S., outwardly not taking a blind bit of notice of the stuff that was falling pretty thick all round. Seeing her I strolled past as if I was used to walking out in the middle of the falling bombs every Saturday afternoon. We gave each other a sickly smile and I passed on. . . .

'The fire was so huge that we could do little more than make a feeble attempt to put it out. The whole of that warehouse was a raging inferno, against which were silhouetted groups of pigmy firemen directing their futile jets at the wall of flame.

. . . While we were working on our branch—we had to keep in the same position for hours on end, unable to let go of the branch to take cover when bombs fell—a large cargo ship took fire for'ard. . . . We put this fire out in half-an-hour and then returned to our warehouse.

'In spite of the numbness you have time to think a little while you crouch over the branch and I remembered the crowd of women and children whom we had met as we rode in, streaming away from the danger area, carrying bundles over their shoulders. Some would run out into the roadway and call to us to come and attend to their fires. . . .

'Occasionally we would glance up and then we would see a strange sight. For a flock of pigeons kept circling around over-head almost all night. They seemed lost, as if they couldn't understand the unnatural dawn. It looked like sunrise all round us. The pigeons seemed white in the glare, birds of peace making a strange contrast with the scene below.

'When the real dawn came about five, the Germans eased off their blitz. The All Clear raised a weary cheer. At seven o'clock I was hunched half-asleep across the branch holder. At last the relief crews arrived. Knowing that we were returning home gave us that extra ounce of strength without which we could hardly have hoisted the rolled-up lengths on our shoulders.'

There was a quite fantastic quantity of timber stored in the docks, much of it cut from extremely inflammable conifers and some loaded on to barges. These blazing barges were, when possible, cut loose from their moorings and went swinging down the river, only to return, still blazing, on the next tide.

The chaos was enormous. Many of the local fire brigades—that of Poplar, for instance—had been sent away forty-eight hours before to help deal with the fires at Thameshaven and other places lower down the river, and had not yet returned. Fire brigades from other boroughs were sent in to help: one from Wanstead, for instance, fought the blaze in East Ham, and these fire brigades were of course in territory which many of the men and their officers had never set foot in before. All attempts to exercise detailed control of the fire-fighting were soon abandoned. By eight in the evening West Ham alone had called for more than five hundred pumps to deal with its fires. There was great congestion in the narrow streets, many of which were impassable, as pumps and towing vehicles formed traffic jams among the miles of snaking hose. But of water, at least, there was no shortage.

It must not be imagined that the docks were simply great areas of warehouses and wharf and water guarded by night watchmen and fought for by firemen. Many people lived in and among them. Between the Surrey Docks and the river, and again on the north bank, in Silvertown, between the Victoria Docks and the Thames, there were narrow settlements of houses, missions and pubs. The people who lived in these now found themselves surrounded by fire, while the bombs poured down on them from the roaring sky.

In Bermondsey the inhabited strip between the Surrey Commercial Docks and the river is known locally as 'down town'. One main street, Rotherhithe Street, circles the blunt peninsula, with a number of short, narrow lanes running off it, and one road, Redriff Road, cuts through the acres of dock from the 'mainland' to join Rotherhithe Street. There are thus three bridges connecting 'down town' with the great sprawling mass of factories, back-to-back cottages and grimy goods yards that was Bermondsey. When the docks blazed, the people were evacuated from down town and many of them were taken to Keeton's Road School. This building was not an air raid shelter and was in no way prepared as a reception centre. But after all, they had to be taken somewhere. A few hours later this school itself was bombed, and many people were killed.

Here are some descriptions of the afternoon and night of September 7th-8th, 1940.

Mr Mills was a Warden at Roper Street, just south of the bridge that carries Redriff Road into the dock area. He is a small, wiry man, in his forties at the time, with a modest manner and a very strong cockney accent. He had been a soldier in the First World War and is not an educated man. His easily forgotten face is the face beneath the steel helmet in the shell-hole at Loos, the face of the soldier plodding in single file, laden down with anti-tank rifle or mortar, through the jungles of Burma; he is also the man streaming with his mates through the gates of the factory or, in bad times, queuing at the Labour Exchange for his unemployment benefit. This, in his own words, is what he remembers of that night:

'We came away from Roper Street, we was stationed down there at the time and we was directed to the Surrey Docks, the Redriff Estate, to evacuate the people from there.' This must have been about six o'clock. 'Well, when we got there we went up as far as the Canada Yard and we couldn't get no further. Also the teams went away from Rotherhithe Baths.' This is a reference to men from another Wardens' Post, coming into 'down town' from the other end. 'They got down there and picked the people up from down there, took 'em to the Keeton's Road School and as soon as they got 'em there they was bombed again and we had to go there, after we got back. Well, coming back from Redriff Road, they was bombing 'em all the time and the dock was all alight, ships blazing and there was a grain warehouse there, just like a furnace.' Some of the bombed-out people from 'down town' believed that the German airmen had seen them trekking to the Keeton's Road School and had therefore bombed it deliberately. Human nature is such that it requires a certain dispassionate objectivity not to assume that one is oneself the deliberate target aimed at by a bomber flying at 250 m.p.h., two, three or four miles up in the sky. 'All the walls was red-hot and then we came back from there, we came under the arch in South-wark Park Road, we got as far as Ambrose Street and he dropped one on the cinema.' This was one of the great railway arches under the main lines running southeast from London Bridge Station. There will be more about these arches later in this book. 'Well, we stopped the lorry outside the London Tea Stores, I think it was, we got underneath the lorry and laying on the ground I could hear somebody crying out— Hurry up and get me out of here. I didn't know where it was, so what I done, I said to the boy, I said—Well, there's someone in trouble here somewhere, so we'd better go and find out where it is.' Boys in their 'teens were attached to the Wardens' Posts as runners, in case the telephone lines should go. Many of the telephone lines in the Surrey Docks area were out that evening. 'So the sound sounded to me as if it was coming from Anchor Street, so we run back to Anchor Street, went along and there was a woman standing at the door and a man. They said—Here y'are, mate, come through here, there's a fire over there. So when we got through the yard we had to scale about four or five walls and then we see the house alight, the shelter, and then the shed, all ablaze. Well, we done no more, we got over the wall and into the shelter.' This must have been an Anderson shelter, reinforced, as they were supposed to be, with sandbags about the entrance and half-buried in a bit of yard between the backs of Anchor Street and the backs of Ambrose Street. 'Everybody was all mixed up there, the sandbags had all blown in on 'em, so I got my number one and he helped me out, he was at the door, and I threw the sandbags out at him to clear the way, then I got five people out. They came out, and I went out altogether. I came out in Ambrose Street and then I went back from there down to the depot again. Now where did we go from there? I think I went to the Old Kent Road, the top of Page's Walk, they'd dropped one there.' This is only just in Bermondsey, for the Old Kent Road is here in Southwark. However, as has been seen, there could be no question on a night such as this of wardens confining their activities to their own post area, or even to their borough. 'And coming back from the Old Kent Road we come down the Tower Bridge Road. The cork factory in Abbey Street, top end. . . . Next, the public house, the Black Man's House they used to call it, and that was all ablaze, but there was no one in there, and then we came out of there and went back again and I know we went out three or four times. I went in Westcott Street, there was another one we went—we was all out—all the teams was out one after the other on that particular night, I can't think where we went to.'

Mr O'Connell was also a Post Warden, of L Post, actually out on Rotherhithe Street. He had been told, before the bombing started, that his was No. 1 Danger Zone, and this was certainly no exaggeration. He, too, was a full-time warden and was on duty that night. 'Our first big fire was at Bellamy's Wharf and following that was one near the Surrey Lock Bridge, which we did our best to try and out, and we did out to a certain extent, and then we followed on with the break of a spell, and then we had the Dixon Street flare up, and that was a terrific fire, and all the personnel in that street did a magnificent job trying to get the incendiaries and everything out. Two firemen who were badly hurt in the fire were brought into my post, which I had to change all their clothes and give them two suits of overalls, and let themself warm themself because they were soaking with oil. And then Capsull's, the paint factory, that went up in the air. We all had an order to watch out for parachutists coming down in the area.' This must have been almost exactly the hour when the Chiefs of Staffs were issuing code-word 'Cromwell'. 'And this certain thing was coming down which we thought all the time was a parachutist, but it happened to be a mine, which fell partly in the dock and set fire to the paint wells, and then we had Bellamy's Wharf, the egg warehouse. Well, Bellamy's Wharf, as we know, we had a vast lot of people under a shelter there, and also in Globe Wharf. I had a tidy few people in there, and in this shelter this night the top of it was well alight. And I called one of my individuals out on the quiet, and I says to him, I said—Bill, we shall have to evacuate the people out of this place. And with that I brought all the people out, even in our own dust carts.' Some of these were the people who were taken to the Keeton's Road School. Meanwhile the raid went on. To add to the problems of the night there were now delayed action bombs lying about, and at least one of these went off in Mr O'Connell's area. 'Thing quietened down a bit after that, and then we had another big fire. And we had a bargeload of very burnable stuff, which was alcohol, and we had to cut that barge a-loose in the river. And then the dock itself was one mass of flame, and the barges of timber which my people cut loose from the sides of the wharves, to save the other timber, but I think it was labour in vain as far as that went.'

Rothmans has said:

'I was struck by the lack of organisation of the dock authorities. I remember when we wanted petrol for our pumps we had to break the locks on the petrol pumps in the dock area because the man in charge was nowhere to be found. I remember too that there were three ammunition ships in the docks and nobody seemed to make any efforts to move them. I know that one exploded. What happened to the other two I never did find out. There was so much noise and so many explosions, and so many thousands of firemen all about you that you were really just concerned with the fire you were working on.

'The night seemed endless, wave after wave, or what seemed like wave after wave of planes, the roar and crackle of the flames, falling buildings, men shouting. It's hard to remember exactly. I suppose when you're engaged on doing one specific thing you're somewhat oblivious to what is going on around you. Though you know there's terrible things going on. I don't think that any of the men with me were any less scared that I was. I know I was scared, and I'm not ashamed to admit it.'

And so the night went on. A warden remembers:

'A bomb dropped down the back of the A.R.P. Post, my Post, it blew the back windows in, because we had no blast wall then—afterwards they put a blast wall up—and it blew the personnel what was left inside the post all over the place. And of course they were just enjoying a cup of tea and they didn't expect it, but still we got it all the same, and after that I had tea for the people, sent down for the people that was in the shelters all the way round and we done the best we could for them.'

Mr Julius was the leader of a stretcher party stationed that night in the Redriff School. He has described the exodus from 'down town' in these words:

'It looked one flaming mass and the flames were terrifically high. To us it seemed a remarkable thing that people could get out of that area, and when we saw—when we saw the people come streaming down from dockland we were absolutely amazed. They seemed to come like an army marching and running from the area. The people coming from down town looked in a very, very bad condition, they were dirty, dishevelled and hurrying to get away.' He remembers being worried lest the three bridges be hit, for if those had gone the people inside the docks would have been trapped. This actually happened across the river in Silvertown, where people were trapped and had to be taken out of their burning streets by boat.

Mrs Finnis was one of those, approximately one thousand, brought out of 'down town': 'It was a Saturday afternoon, and we was indoors in the top floor of Surrey House, Rotherhithe Street, and I'd been doing some shopping and was going out again in the afternoon to do some more shopping when the guns went off, and the planes come over, incendiary bombs were dropped all round us, on to the boats, in the dock, on to the other side by the river, and the place was just like a ball of flame. We couldn't get out. And then they come and fetched us, the wardens come and fetched us, and took us in the shelter, and there we stayed, my husband and me, the two young boys was away evacuated, Ronnie was at the First Aid Post and me other son was in the Home Guard, and we stayed there till the ambulance come along, taking the people to Keeton's Road School. But we just walked along Rotherhithe Street to my mother's, and there we stayed till the rest of the raid was over.'

She was lucky. Miss Greenwood did go to the school.

'The afternoon the docks were on fire, people were going past our house, which was nearby, like refugees more or less, with just bundles, turned out of their places, nowhere to go really. Then it subsided. Then they returned again, and dropped more bombs and eventually the police come along to our houses and demanded that we should come out—we couldn't stay there any longer, so we were made to get out of the homes and were transferred to Keeton's Road School which is quite a distance away. When we got there we found that nearly all the people from down town had been placed there and there wasn't much room. Then our own people came and we took an elderly couple from next door along with us, and we were standing most of the time there, which was a very short time. Then all of a sudden the most horrible roar came along and the place got hit. There was miles of us got buried there, and the A.R.P. fellows were very, very good, trying to dig us out and transfer us on to stretchers in the roadways. There was no conveyance, everything was going on all around us, they couldn't get by the holes in the road to get you through to hospital. We laid there for quite a time. Eventually they got vans and things to put you in, and there we stayed for a time till they were able to get past, to different hospitals. I'm afraid I don't remember very much more about that because I was unconscious.'

Up at the far end of the Spa Road, Bermondsey, in the Public Baths, there was a casualty station. For the doctors and nurses, too, this was the night when the training of all the past quiet months was now put to the test. Dr Morton, a woman doctor at the Baths, has described one of the surprises of that night and the following months:

'When we were training the first-aid workers, we took a great deal of time explaining how they should be aseptic: how they should scrub their hands before touching any wounds, how they should take care of asepsis when putting dressings on. But the very first night of the blitz that just went by the

58

wind. What struck one was the tremendous amount of dirt and dust, the dirt and dust of ages blown up in every incident. Everyone came in looking absolutely filthy. Their heads were full of grit and dust, their skin was engrained with dust, and it was completely impossible to do anything much about anti-sepsis at all.' Yet, much to her surprise, almost no sepsis occurred in any of the cases that she followed up. It was all very rough and ready. 'In the Bermondsey baths, where we had our first-aid post, some of the bath attendants were using hose pipes to wash the people down. This cleaned their hair and gave them a good shampoo before we got going, and very grateful they were to get the grit out of their hair and their ears and their noses and so on.'

Another surprise of that night was the unexpectedly small number of casualties. Again Dr Morton says:

'All our knowledge of what to expect was taken from various books, mainly about what had happened in Spain. And I think it was a surprise to all of us, when the first Blitz did start seriously, how very few casualties there were. We had enor-mous numbers of shrouds sent round for us to use, and of course we expected gas. There was a general apprehension, an expectation of casualties which for people like myself, who are not surgeons—well, we wondered if we'd be able to cope, but in actual fact the whole thing was much more manageable than we had expected.'

But if the casualties were nothing like on the expected scale, many people were killed. In these last pages there have been several references to the Keeton's Road School. Mr Peters was a police sergeant at this time, at the Tower Bridge police station. The police, during these raids, carried out a multitude of tasks. On the evening of September 7th, Mr Peters was helping with the rescue work. Here is his story:

'The first major incident to which I attended was at Keeton's Road School. The people had been evacuated from Rother-hithe owing to the docks being well on fire, and some were taken into Keeton's Road School along with all their belongings and their families and food. Soon after ten o'clock a bomb fell on the school and I, along with a number of others, were ordered down. On reaching the school we entered by the playground. Fire had started going through some of the rooms. In one room I saw an A.F.S. man laying on a makeshift bedstead, and his face looked as if it had been skinned. A little further along I, with another officer, was searching amongst the debris and after a while my brother officer bent down and pulled something out. He thought it was a piece of bread. But it turned out to be part of a small child, the upper part, the upper limbs of a small child. This so upset us that we came out into the street. There were a number of bodies laying on the footway and in the road. I stood and watched these for a few moments. Eventually some of them stood up, and to my relief they were not all dead. But there were some of them who were dead.'

Thus did the Blitz come to Bermondsey. It was much the same in the neighbouring boroughs of Southwark and Deptford, Greenwich and Woolwich, and north of the river in Stepney, Poplar, West and East Ham. If I have reported at such length about this one borough, and indeed this particular incident of the evacuees from 'down town' and the Keeton's Road School, it is in the belief that the exact words, the frequent incoherence of the men and women who were there, can conjure up better then any outsider's description the confusion, the foulness and the agony of that night, among the crackling and whispering flames, with the bombers still droning steadily overhead—that hateful, unforgettable, rhythmically broken drone—and the bombs whistling down, and the rattle as loads of incendiaries landed on roofs or roadways, and, very occasionally, the crack of an anti-aircraft gun.

It was just as bad, that night, in the other East End riverside boroughs. In some it may even have been worse.

In Poplar, for instance, Mr Cotter, who was Deputy Chief Warden of the borough, has written:

'First, let it be said at once that it has been impossible to compile a complete record of the bombs dropped on the borough on that afternoon and night of September 7th and the morning hours of September 8th. In twelve hours, twenty-two of our thirty-five telephones were put out of action with the result that wardens were only reporting casualty-producing incidents either by runner or over some odd telephone that happened to be working. For instance, a stick of six bombs would fall in a Post area, two of them causing casualties and the other four creating more or less serious damage. Almost invariably, the warden confined his reports to the casualty incidents, with a mental promise to compile a complete list of other damage in the morning. Unfortunately, Sunday, September 8th brought a continuation of enemy activity and the mental promise was never put into effect. Throughout the first week or ten days, everyone was occupied with the task of locating and getting casualties to hospital; it was, I think, natural that many of the missiles were missed when a check-up was eventually put in hand. In addition, quite one-third of our members were themselves in difficulties; relatives had been killed or injured, homes had been totally demolished or so badly blasted that they were unfit for further habitation and alternative accommodation had to be found at once for wives and families. At ten or a dozen Posts, wardens were sleeping in chairs, cooking scratch meals and generally living a hand-to-mouth existence. All around them they saw friends and neighbours packing and preparing to move off into safe areas; never knowing what was to come, they decided, with very few exceptions, to stick and do their job.

'September 7th and 132 Incidents—a single night's bombing which reached the total suffered by more fortunate areas in five years of war. When, on the lines quoted above, one reckons the bombs which were not reported, the multitude of I.B., the missiles falling inside the Dock enclosures, and the number of bombs dropped in the huge Devas Street fire, the total for this area of some 2½ square miles must have reached the saturation point for the whole of London. From all outlying

61

parts of the metropolis, eyes were turned towards that Devas Street conflagration (the Dockside Fire) and tens of thousands of people wondered what was happening. They could not see stick after stick of bombs dropping into the flames and hurling burning wood, embers and showers of sparks hundreds of feet into the air; they could not see gangs of A.R.P. workers clearing earth from buried Anderson shelters and bringing the occupants, dazed and half-suffocated, out into the revivifying air which was, none the less, heavy with smoke and redolent of charred timber; they could not visualise wardens picking their way through debris and, since phones had gone, making their way hurriedly to Control to report fresh incidents; they could not imagine the A.F.S. crews, many of them literally receiving their baptism of fire, being hurled away from the blaze with hose and branches still gripped grimly in their hands; they could not see the Control staffs, perspiring, exhausted, foodless, endlessly ordering out fresh parties, nor could they hear the gasp of the telephone girl taking the air-raid message dealing with her own home.

'It would be impossible to relate fully the accounts of bravery and devotion to duty of members of all the Civil Defence services. Most of them were seeing violent death and wholesale destruction for the first time. At the rate missiles were falling and in view of the number of casualties on every side, there could have been no one who, at some time or another during that first night, did not estimate his or her own chances of survival; the obvious conclusion would be that their chances were pretty slim.

'In one way, our task was tremendously simplified by the exodus on September 7th and during the succeeding weeks. At 7 p.m. on the first day, during an 'all clear' period, a positive convoy of motor vehicles, filled with entire families and piled high with luggage, rolled from side streets towards Bow Road and East India Dock Road and proceeded westwards. Some were proceeding to friends in the more fortunate London boroughs, while others were definitely on their way

62

to the country for the duration. During the first few days, every available means of transport was used to remove the essentials for making a home elsewhere—crockery, pots and pans, and a few articles of furniture. Pony carts, hand-drawn barrows, perambulators and cycles with heavily laden carriers, all rolled out of the borough in a steady stream. At the Metropolitan Tube Station and at almost every bus stop, families burdened with suitcases and packages could be seen making their way out of the danger area; many of them no longer had a home and all they carried was the clothes in which they stood with perhaps an odd item or two salvaged from the wreckage.'

Poplar was a well-administered borough. Alderman Key, later the Regional Commissioner for Shelters, had organised the A.R.P. services with outstanding efficiency. It was also particularly fortunate in possessing as Chief Warden E. H. Smith, now an Alderman too and a winner of the George Cross. The writer has been told that it was Smith and Cotter who kept Poplar going during these terrible first weeks. They were out, all night and every night, visiting almost every shelter, present at almost every incident, an example to the other wardens and a visible sign to the public of Poplar that they were neither forgotten nor neglected. There were others, of course, clergymen, including the present Bishop of Taunton who was then a parish priest, doctors, the officers of the municipal administration and in particular the Town Clerk and his deputy. But Smith and Cotter were the men whom the people saw, and that tough and reliable pair kept Poplar's spirit from flagging. Alderman Smith is a Poplar man born and bred: he speaks the people's language, shares their political views, which are well to left of centre, but more important perhaps is, quite obviously and at first glance, a leader. He had been a regular soldier for many years, starting as a drummer-boy, and had the rare distinction of being awarded a battlefield commission in 1916. Cotter, a quietly-spoken and modest-mannered Irishman, a former officer of the Munster Fusiliers, was perhaps the ideal deputy for the rough-and-ready Smith. These two were Poplar, in 1940.

And the organisation, the A.R.P. service, that bore the imprint of their characters was in some ways a unique one. For one thing, it was entirely democratic. The West End and residential boroughs had a wealth of potential or actual leaders on which to draw for their Wardens' services. Poplar did not. Therefore they decided that the Post Wardens should be elected, not appointed. And this was done, by the people of Poplar, from 1939 on. In each post area, the warden responsible for the people's safety and protection was those people's own choice. During the Blitz the percentage of votes cast in these elections was far greater than in any municipal or general election before or since. Much was written during that war about the defence of democracy. Alderman Smith's A.R.P. service was a true example of democracy defending itself.

And the men and women elected by their neighbours and friends to the dangerous honour of patrolling the streets and controlling the incidents—the quaintly bureaucratic word invented to describe every sort of disaster inflicted by the enemy on the civilian population—were very conscious of the distinction that they had received and of the close scrutiny to which their behaviour was subjected.

Mr Cotter has described the attitude of the Wardens to their job, and to one another, in these words. (It should be said that one of the unwritten laws was that a Warden should not take shelter. He might, of course, go to an Anderson when off duty, or seek momentary safety from a stick of bombs in a brick street shelter, but the big shelters and the tubes were not for him.)

'What kind of people were our wardens? In Poplar we had a very rough-and-ready crowd indeed. If they liked you they probably called you "mate" irrespective of your rank; if they thought you were just passable they'd call you "mister", and if they disliked you they usually called you "sir". There was only one thing kept 'em together—they had a kind of discipline imposed by themselves, and that was the fear that their mates wouldn't think that a man was doing the job—they were afraid of their mates, definitely. We had one rather tragic case of a Warden, a good one too, indeed, who was by chance seen in a Tube shelter one night. He was with his wife. He went back to the Post the following morning with his usual cheery greeting: everybody refused to talk to him. They even took his name off the roster in the Post, and he was promptly sent to Coventry. We had of course to transfer him to another Post. The sad part of that story was that the man would never have gone into a deep shelter by himself. But his wife insisted he go along with her. And married men will know what I mean. . . .'

Poplar stood up to the tremendous ordeal of that first night. Its neighbour across the River Lea, West Ham, came near to cracking. There were many rumours current at the time about panic in the East End. For example, a country clergyman wrote in his unpublished diary, on September 11th: 'A Silvertown school, being used as a rest centre for the bombed-out, has been bombed with a death-roll of more than 400. How much longer can the East End stand it?' And, on the 12th: 'X, who has some wonderful stories and always seems to get hold of them long before anyone else, says that the East End has had enough, and wants to give in.'

Such rumours, which were very widespread, were undoubtedly in large measure put about by some of those refugees whom Mr Cotter had seen hastening away after the first daylight raid. It is hard to accept the fact that others may have more fortitude than oneself. But so far as they are traceable to any locality and incident, West Ham, and particularly Silvertown, would seem to be the source of origin. The great raid of September 7th-8th was not primarily directed against civilian morale, but it was the effect of the raids on morale that for months and years had caused the country and the Government the greatest apprehension. It is therefore worth seeing what did happen in West Ham and, so far as is possible, why. But first it is necessary to examine West Ham, briefly, for it was in some important respects an exceptional borough. What follows is largely taken from *War over West Ham*, a report prepared for the Fabian Society by E. Doreen Idle, and from Ritchie Calder's *The Lesson of London*.

West Ham is not part of London County, the eastern boundary of which is the River Lea, but is a county borough, in Essex, and is not therefore administered by the L.C.C. The opening of the Royal Victoria Dock, in southern West Ham in 1885, began a mushroom growth that in one generation was to change West Ham from an almost purely rural and agricultural community into what it now is. Its population in 1856 had amounted to 27,000, in 1886 to 180,000. The first serious attempts to deal with housing was The Royal Commission on the Housing of the Poor, 1890, but by that date almost all of West Ham had been built, as a slum. And, paradoxically, the various attempts at slum clearance and similar social legislation were, in some ways, to work against West Ham. For slum clearance in London proper drove many of the poorest people of London across the county boundary into West Ham, while the more sturdy citizens—stevedores, dockers and so on—moved further out, into East Ham and Barking. Also, being an extra-metropolitan area, many bye-laws concerning 'offensive trades' were much less strict than in the London boroughs: it was therefore popular for industries making manures, chemicals, soaps and other such concerns. In fact, West Ham stank. Those who could afford to leave did so. The docks, up to the war, relied heavily on casual labour. A great deal of this labour lived in West Ham, and there was chronic unemployment among the population which, in 1940, was estimated at some 260,000, about 50,000 persons being at that time evacuated or having for some other reason left the borough.

Not all West Ham was slums. The northern end of the borough, around Romford Road, contained, and still contains, many residential areas, the homes of what are now called the managerial class. But the southern end, by the river, was very bad. Canning Town, north of the Victoria and Albert Docks, and Silvertown, between those docks and the river, were the worst. A survey made in 1931 had shown that over 4.5 per cent of the inhabitants of West Ham lived more than three to a room. Conditions had scarcely improved during the years of slump, and a high proportion of this gross over-crowding was in these two areas. Silvertown, named after the firm of S. W. Silver & Co., which in 1852 brought waterproofing and the manufacture of rubber goods to this area, had, since the building of the Victoria, Albert and George V Docks, been virtually an island. In 1940 it contained about 13,000 people living in an area of rather less than one square mile, much of which was occupied by factories. The houses lay in narrow, crowded strips between the docks and the factories, dingy and squalid, many of them lodging houses for seafaring men and their women. Silvertown was not only physically difficult of access, its inhabitants felt themselves in other, subtler ways cut off from the rest of West Ham with its cinemas and schools and parks. Silvertown was thrown back on its own very slender resources for entertainment and recreation. West Ham as a whole contained the highest number of pubs per population of any borough in southern England.

Being a county borough, it was in a stronger position to argue with London Region and the Home Office than were the metropolitan boroughs. Before the Blitz its council had taken full advantage of this state of affairs. Since 1916 it had been a confirmed Labour Borough—it had returned Keir Hardie, the first Independent Labour Party member, to the House of Commons in 1892—and in 1940, fifty-seven of its sixty-four council members were Labour. Their seats were utterly safe and they themselves were therefore selected more for past services to the Party than for present energy. When they assembled at their Town Hall, up on the more salubrious, higher ground near West Ham Park three miles from Silvertown, they presented as fine a collection of municipal wheelhorses as was to be found in any local administration. Their average age was about sixty.

Many were pacifists, and thus had been reluctant to deal with A.R.P. matters before the war, and even before the Blitz. Their chief interest appears to have been in arguing that whatever had to be done should be paid for by the central administration. This was against the Government's policy in A.R.P. matters, but accorded with West Ham's policy in all matters. Before the war 42.6 per cent of West Ham's income came from Government grants. The result was a partial deadlock. Nor, it seems, did West Ham, before the Blitz, throw up any local man of the calibre of Poplar's E. H. Smith. There was a great shortage of Wardens. In one district, only four Wardens were less than forty years old, the remainder having an average age of sixty.

The Government shelter policy was less well suited to West Ham than to most of the other boroughs. The low-lying land made it almost impossible to keep Andersons and trench shelters dry, nor was dispersal attractive to the sort of people living in West Ham. The West Ham Trades Council agitated for deep shelters, one of its less heartening arguments being that the cost of such shelters per head of the whole population would not be greater than the cost of giving the people proper funerals. The Government replied by sending great quantities of shrouds to West Ham—as indeed to all the other boroughs—and all citizens were advised to make a will.

The missions and settlements did what they could, and the A.R.P. arrangements at the factories were far superior to those of the borough. But there were almost no full-time voluntary workers. For this the Council was largely responsible. It had had a violent reaction from its pacifist past, and now refused to employ pacifists in any of its A.R.P. services, thus depriving its people of the services of young men who, in other boroughs, did much brave and excellent work in Civil Defence rather than join the forces. The Council went further, and refused to allow pacifist organisations, such as the Friends' Ambulance

Unit or the International Voluntary Service for Peace, to function at all within the borough. The self-opinionated fuddy-duddies at the Town Hall even distrusted the Women's Voluntary Service. Miss Idle was told, even after the Blitz, that 'reactionary boroughs of course need the W.V.S. to work in connection with nurseries, libraries, etc., but not a progressive borough like West Ham'.

West Ham was, in fact, singularly ill-prepared for the horrors of September 7th. What it was like in Silvertown that night is described by Mrs Nancy Spender, who went down there with an ambulance.

'At 9.15 the call came through—they wanted one ambulance to go to Oriental Road. I was very lucky because I had a driver who was in the last war and was very experienced. I was the conductress. Well, we went off and we weren't allowed any lights at all, and the streets were absolutely pitch-black except when we got the full glare of the copper-coloured fire. On we went and I kept urging my driver to go faster. He said there was no hurry and we'd get there just as soon in the end. And sure enough two ambulances that raced past us had got themselves ditched on the pavement, and we passed them. Every mile or two we came across white-hatted officials who passed us on the way—we went on, and then after a bit we came to a sort of formation of ambulances, green buses, Green Line buses, all sorts of vehicles . . . and things, and we took our place and we waited. After a bit I asked the incident officer—Is this right for Oriental Road? Good gracious—he said —no. Oriental Road's in Silvertown. Well, we tried to get our ambulance started up, being old it didn't start, and we had to get four men to push us off. Well, we went on a bit and then I met a man, and I said—Is this right for Silvertown? And he said—Oh, that's about two miles further on—no good going there, it's entirely ablaze from end to end. Well, we went on and now we found we were completely alone, there wasn't a soul in any street. One minute we were going down a little pitch-black street, and on and on, and then eventually we

came to a sort of swing bridge into the Victoria Docks. And as
we went along the whole thing was absolutely one blazing
fire, I've never seen anything like it, you know, right across
the sky there was nothing but blazing things and everything
going up. As far as we could see everything was on fire—
great, red flames were going up and down the brick walls,
piles of houses all collapsed or on fire, warehouses like blazing
cathedrals standing up and then falling down, bricks going up,
bombs coming down, there was a most terrific muddle of fire,
everything reflected in the water. Then in the Basin, which was
just like a sheet of flame because it reflected the entire glow of
the fire, I saw two steamers completely on fire except for their
black funnels, which looked absolutely jet-black against everything else. Well, by now we were in a complete jam, there
was nothing but fire-fighting apparatus, ambulances, hosepipes,
the whole thing a complete and utter traffic jam, and we just
had to take our place in the rather narrow road and wait. We
waited there for about ten minutes or so, then my driver got
rather fed up and we edged our way along and got up to the
top; just as we were getting near the top, to see what was
holding everything up, a warehouse crashed right across the
road, and we had blazing stuff right across our roof and it was
impossible to go on. Well, then we were truly jammed—it
was very uncomfortable because about four feet away there
was a blazing patch of flame and a large pile of tar barrels
waiting to be caught. My driver said to me—Do you see what
I see? And I said—Yes, I do. And he said—Well, it'll be the
hell of a job to get out of here. However, we did manage to
turn, with people helping us and firemen pushing, we got
back and we went back along our tracks. The other ambulances
all shouted to us—You can't get through—and we said—
Don't we know it, we can't get through, but we know
another way. And they said—Wait for us—and I said—We
can't wait for you because we can't stop here, we're jamming
the roads—so we went on, and it was an absolute mercy that
no bomb hit the swing bridge because if it had we should have

all been trapped. However, it didn't and we edged along, on every side roofs fell in with the most terrific explosions, gas mains blew up, there were constant bangings of bombs and A.A. guns, but it was quite impossible to feel frightened because it was all on such an enormous scale. Every few minutes one of those blazing piles shot like a fountain into the sky. It reminded me very much of an eighteenth-century print of hot geysers in America, because of the fountains of stuff that jetted up and fell down with a crash. Anyway, we did get through and we got over the bridge and then my driver thought he knew another route. Well, we went on for some time and then we got blocked and we couldn't go through and we had to go back and take another fork, which we did. We went on for a bit more, past piles of burning stuff, and we couldn't get through again. Then he had an inspiration and he left the road completely and cut across the wharf. Now we were in a sort of maze of cinder tracks and little truck lines going here and there and nothing but hosepipes and fire people fighting the fires, everywhere there was nothing but hose-pipes. They were awfully good, and they gave us pushes to get over the worst debris. Then we came to a place that seemed to be a sheet of flame, but my driver said—Oh, I think this is nothing much, we'll get through this, and he put a terrific spurt on and we got through it and that was all right. Well, then we came to a whole group of firemen, all wearing masks, fighting one of the warehouses which was blazing, and I said to one of them—Anybody hurt here? He said—No, all dead, go on. So we went on, and then we came across a man completely distraught, his face absolutely black with soot—of course all our faces were black but we didn't notice it. He'd lost his wife and his mother and so we gave him a lift on the way—where to, I've no idea, but he wanted to come that way so he came, and we went on. Then we asked a man—Is this right for Oriental Road? Oriental Road—he said—that's absolutely hopeless, it's ablaze from end to end, you'll never get there. Well, we did, we went on and then left the worst of the fire behind us, and quite shortly we came to a little sort of deserted village, everything quite quiet except of course for the tremendous bomb racket which went on all the time, a little deserted village with two-storey houses and not a house had a roof, not a single house had a roof, just a little pub without anything on top of it, a lamp-post right across the road, enormous craters and in each crater there seemed to be a burning jet—gas main or something which had broken, the usual prams, stoves, anything across the road. We had an awful job to get by because the craters were so big and the road was so narrow and half the time we had two wheels on the pavement and two wheels over the crater. Then we came across another car, an ambulance car, also looking for Oriental Road, and he joined in behind us, and we went on for a bit and then we came to another road and there wasn't a single house standing—there was nothing, nothing at all except holes. Out of several of these holes little people popped their heads—exactly like a Chinese war film. I said—Is this Oriental Road? And they shouted—The ambulance? And I said—Yes, anybody hurt? They said—Over in the shelter. I said—Where's that? And they said—Under the arches. So then we tried to go on, and they said—Oh, you can't get your ambulance there, there's no possible road, you'll have to leave it. So we left the ambulance and I got out a stretcher and we went over to the shelter and put our heads in. I suppose there were about forty people there. I said—Anybody hurt?—and not a soul answered. So I said again—Anybody hurt?—and still nobody answered, so I went up to one woman and tapped her and said —Is there anybody hurt here?—and she said—Over there there's a mother and a two-day-old baby, they've both been dug out, and I think further up there's a boy with a very bad knee, he got dug out, he was buried up to his waist, but I don't know about the others. So I went over to the mother, she didn't speak, and I wrapped her in a blanket and put her on the stretcher, and I said—Is there a Warden here?—and somebody said—No, he was killed half an hour ago. So I got a couple of men, anyway, to help me, and we took her back on the stretcher, put her in the ambulance, then I came back again and collected the boy, with some help, and then we got back to the ambulance with him and after that I just filled the ambulance with as many people as I could cram in, about fifteen or sixteen. Still nobody spoke, it was all the most deathly silence, and I got in beside them this time, not beside the driver, and drew the curtains to shut out the ghastly glow, and deafen the noise a bit, and we drove off. About half-way back there was a most tremendous explosion and the whole ambulance left the ground and I thought—This time we've had it and the man has hit a crater—but he hadn't. It was a bomb which dropped in Liverpool Street Station, and we were very close then. Anyway, we got them all back and we got them all to hospital and we got back to our station, I suppose, about half-past one in the morning.'

Ritchie Calder went down to West Ham a few hours after Mrs Spender had left with her ambulance. He has described what he found in these terms:

'I sought out my old friend, "The Guv'nor", the militant clergyman, the Rev. W. W. Paton. I found his Presbyterian church in ruins. His pulpit still stood, but the roof and the front wall had gone. The streets all around were wrecked. They were poor "Dead End" streets, running down to the dock wall, but these heaps of rubble had once been homes which sheltered the families of the East London dockers—tough, decent folk who had deserved better conditions than they'd ever had in peace-time and who were having the worst in war. Some of these battered wrecks of bricks and rubble, with shabby furniture now reduced to kindling, had been the only homes which old pensioners had ever known. They had "married into them"; they had brought up their families in them; they had seen their children married out of them; and were eking out an ill-cared-for old age in them—when the bombers came.

'I found "The Guv'nor" at last. He was ashen grey with the

anguish of the night. He had been out in the raids, helping his people throughout the night. His lips trembled and his eyes filled with tears when he spoke of those of his friends who were dead, injured or missing. But his main concern was with the living. He was dashing round the streets seeking out the survivors whose homes had been wrecked.

'I went with him. We found many hundreds of them sheltering in a school in the heart of the bombed area. I took a good look at this school. From the first glance it seemed to me ominous of disaster.

'In the passages and the classrooms were mothers nursing their babies. There were blind, crippled, and aged people. There were piccaninnies, the children of negro firemen then at sea. There were youngsters whom I knew by name, like the red-headed impish "Charlie". Whole families were sitting in queues, perched on their pitiful baggage, waiting desperately for coaches to take them away from the terror of the bombs which had been raining down on them for two nights. Yes, for two nights! For the blitzkrieg had started in that fore-doomed corner on the Friday night before London had felt the full weight of it.

'The crowded people in the school included many families who had been bombed out already, on that first night. These unfortunate homeless people had been told to be ready for the coaches at three o'clock. Hours later the coaches had not arrived. "The Guv'nor" and I heard women, the mothers of young children, protesting with violence and with tears about the delay. Men were cursing the helpless local officials who knew only that the coaches were expected. "Where are we going?" "Can't we walk there?" "We'll take a bus!" "There's a lorry we can borrow!" The crowd clamoured for help, for information, for reassurance. But the harassed officials knew no answer other than the offer of a cup of tea.

'One mother complained that her children had been forbidden to play in the playground. The official could only say he was sorry and evade her questions. But he showed me the

74

answer. In the playground behind the school was a crater. The school was, in fact, a bulging, dangerous ruin. The bombs which had rendered these people homeless had also struck the school, selected by the authorities as their "Rest Centre". Note that the school had already been bombed at the same time as "The Guv'nor's" church had been bombed. So had the parish church which, because it was the favourite "church-wedding" place of the poor, was known as "The Cathedral of East London". So had other buildings and streets in a direct line with it. And then I knew, on that Sunday afternoon, that, as sure as night would follow day, the bombers would come again with the darkness, and that school would be bombed.

'It was not a premonition. It was a calculable certainty. These hapless people told me how the bombers had ranged over the Docks, shedding their bombs—one, two, three, four, then a pause as the 'planes banked in a tight turn and that remorseless fifth bomb, dropped each time on the same corner.

'All these hundreds of people spent another night inside the shelterless school. Some were taken to another school—providentially—although it was only the breadth of a street away! This was done to make room for a new flood of homeless victims of the Sunday night raids. During yet another night of raids and terror, the fourth in the school for some of the shelterers, the inevitable bomb hit the crowded building.

'The next morning I saw the crater. I saw the rescue men descending perilously into it, with ropes around them, saw them pause, every now and then, in a hushed painful silence, listening for sounds of the living; saw the tomb of whole families, of many of my "Dead End Kids". By then, two days after the coaches had been due, the survivors, mainly from that second school, were boarding buses. They were struggling for places as crowds clamber aboard at the rush-hour. I spoke to men, fathers of families, who had been cursing on the Sunday. They were speechless and numbed by the horror of it all now. They had been saved by the breadth of that road!

'An inquiry was started. It was found that the coaches had

been ordered on the Sunday all right. The drivers had been told to rendezvous at "The George" public-house in a neighbouring borough. The leader of the convoy thought he knew "The George". He did, but it was "The George" in a different borough. So the coaches just went home. Next day, coaches arrived at the school, but as the homeless were boarding them the sirens went. Local officials decided to abandon the transfer that day and attempt it the following day. The next day was too late.

'This tragedy was one of the first and grimmest lessons of London. About 450 homeless lost their lives in that school—a figure to be dismissed lightly by those who measure casualties in terms of Passchendaele or the Somme. It was the needlessness of the tragedy which made it so terrible.'

West Ham was left a desolate, despairing ruin, a great brick-and-rubble hulk half smashed by the first impact of the storm that was to continue to rage for many more weeks. In some areas the devastation was total, so complete that the army turned one part of West Ham into a training ground where the infantry practised street fighting among the ruins and the craters. In others people continued, living and partly living. Many of the small shops, which provided so much of the life in the poorer parts of the borough, had to close, since only food and drug shops were liable for repair under the Government scheme. There was a plague of flies as a result of a jam factory that had been bombed. The shops that remained were so dark, since boards had replaced the broken windows, that they became grim and forbidding places. The pubs suffered badly, and the cinemas were destroyed one after the other until, at the end of the Blitz, only two out of twenty-five remained open. What communal life there was took place in the shelters; but of this more later.

'After six o'clock a sense of desolation settles down on the place.' Miss Idle says she heard this, or a similar remark, repeatedly. And one man said to her:

'If there should be another Blitz, what have they done for us? *Nothing.*'

It was not easy to do anything for these embittered people, who revolted now without reason, even against measures designed for their own safety and comfort. Their attitude will become more apparent in the chapter about shelters. For outsiders, even if they could get past the senseless barriers erected by the West Ham Council, it was difficult in the extreme to help. Yet, despite all the rumours, there was no more panic than has been here described. There was bitterness, anger, even perhaps despair. But just as there were no leaders in West Ham to organise the defence of the borough before the Blitz—later the Rev. W. W. Paton was compelled by force of circumstances to take effective control—so there was no one to canalise this sensation of abandonment and misery into the sort of mass uprisings which Hitler had hoped his bombing would produce.

The night raid had been carried out by some 250 bombers of Air Fleets Two and Three, and they had dropped about three hundred and thirty tons of high explosive and four hundred and forty incendiary canisters on East London. Though these riverside boroughs suffered most, every part of London was hit, Victoria and London Bridge Stations so badly that they were closed for some days. How many millions of square feet of glass were smashed that night will never be known, but the streets were deep in it, so that the hurrying ambulances and fire engines made a weird sound, like the breaking of surf upon a pebbly shore. Gas pipes were hit, and all over London jets of pure white flame shot up from cratered streets.

The Government communiqué said: 'Fires were caused among industrial targets. Damage was done to lighting and other public services, and some dislocation to communications was caused. Attacks have also been directed against the docks. Information as to casualties is not yet available.'

The people had learned by now to read subtleties of meaning into the strangely laconic and non-committal prose of these official announcements. Everyone realised at once that a very heavy and murderous raid had taken place. Between five o'clock on the evening of September 7th and three o'clock the following morning, the German bombers had killed about one thousand Londoners, or over 5 per cent of London's total casualties throughout the Blitz. During the night raid, no enemy plane was shot down.

That evening Goering addressed the German nation over the wireless, even while his night bombers were setting out again for London. Amid threats and boasts and promises, he said:

'This is the historic hour when for the first time our air force delivered its thrust right into the enemy's heart.'

But if London is the heart of Britain and the Commonwealth, and was then, perhaps, the heart of all Western civilisation, where is London's heart? The docks were damaged, and much was burned, but they were not put out of action to any great extent. And in any case, can they be called London's heart? Or is it perhaps to be found in Whitehall, or St Paul's, or Piccadilly Circus, or the Elephant and Castle, or Buckingham Palace, or Oxford Street, or the House of Commons? Each of these was to be struck in turn in the weeks to come and London's heart, though it might seem to miss a beat—as it did on this first night—continued to pump the blood of resolution through the arteries of Britain and the free world.

Goering's metaphor was wrong. He had not struck at the heart, but rather at the hide of this great, grey city which sprawls, shapeless as a whale, about its river. His darts had hurt. The pachyderm had winced and shifted. But what had he achieved? A child dismembered in Bermondsey, a timber fire in Poplar, a plague of flies in West Ham, a blazing gas pipe in Chelsea. Multiply that a thousand times, and it is still not a great wound, let alone a mortal one, to a city the size of London. But it was a wound.

CHAPTER FOUR

THE NEXT DAY, Sunday the 8th, had already been appointed a day of national prayer. (Lord Haw-Haw, the British traitor who spoke on the German wireless, once suggested that since these days of national prayer seemed to have no efficacy, the British Government might consider arranging for Aleister Crowley to conduct a Black Mass in Westminster Abbey.) It was also a day of extreme tension, rumour and activity. The issuing of the code-word 'Cromwell' on the evening before had led many people to believe that the invasion had actually begun. In some of the eastern counties soldiers blocked the roads, and the Home Guard sounded the tocsin by ringing the church bells. Stories were soon on everyone's lip of German bodies washed ashore on the Isle of Wight, of the sea being set ablaze by the R.A.F., of a great naval battle fought in the Straits of Dover. As a topic of conversation in the country lanes, on the way back from matins that morning, the invasion that had not happened was a keen competitor of the Blitz that had. Human imagination, when totally unfettered by reality, can always well outbid the truth.

In London, at least outside the stricken boroughs, rumour also had a great day. The authorities were naturally anxious to prevent sight-seers and other curious individuals from entering the docks area, and these were at once sealed off by the police, while the firemen continued to fight the conflagrations—which were all under control by the time darkness fell —and the Civil Defence organisations attempted to deal with the first, monumental chaos. Luckily enough, though the sun was shining over London, there was considerable low cloud over the French coast. This, combined presumably with the normal needs for rest and overhaul of the German crews and their planes, was responsible for the fact that there was no daylight raid on London that Sunday, though a number of enemy bombers were over the southern counties.

The resources of London's fire brigades were stretched to the full. Indeed, on that morning there were no more pumps available, and London Region had to call on the neighbouring regions to supply additional fire-fighting equipment, though for the time being the handling of this equipment was left to the Londoners. It was not until forty-eight hours later that the Home Office Fire Control called in reserve crews from several towns within reach of the capital. However, exhausted and grimy as they were, the firemen did manage to get the tremendous dock fires under control. During the previous night that great red glare in the blacked-out sky had seemed to threaten that nothing would be left of the docks, of the East End, and even perhaps of the City as well. But by day it was soon apparent that although the damage to warehouses, and to the streets behind the docks, was very great, the docks themselves were not mortally hit. The German newspapers announced hopefully that London was no longer a seaport. This was quite untrue. London, even throughout these next few weeks, continued to be the world's busiest, as it was the world's largest, port. It is one thing to burn huge stacks of timber and other commodities in the dock area: it is quite another to put the dock installations themselves out of action. And the great proportion of the docks remained at all times open and working.

But if the docks were to continue to function, there must be dockers to unload the ships. And those dockers must themselves have somewhere to live. It was the damage to property that confronted the authorities with their immediate biggest problem once the fires were under control. Those authorities had of course realised that many houses would be destroyed by the enemy's bombs, but they had simultaneously over-

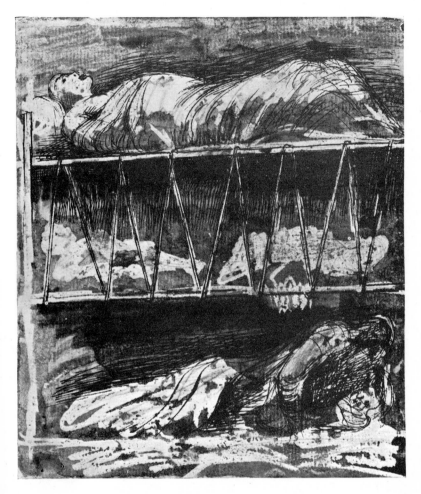

UNDERGROUND SLEEPERS, PICCADILLY

estimated to a fantastic extent the number of people who would be killed or so badly hurt that they must go to hospital. They had, apparently, more or less equated the two, and it was roughly assumed that the amount of houses left standing after the bombers had gone would contain enough living space to house the survivors. It was of course realised that this would not take place entirely automatically, but only the sketchiest arrangements were made.

In the first place the problem of dealing with the homeless was handed over to the boroughs and made the responsibility of the poor law authorities. Their directives laid down that they were to organise feeding stations and temporary shelters of some kind for the homeless. They were not entitled to requisition buildings for this purpose: they were expected only to look after the homeless citizens of their own boroughs: they were not encouraged to look after them for long: and they received almost no financial or other special assistance from the central Government in carrying out these instructions. Supplies of such items as blankets, stocks of food, crockery and so on were either non-existent or inadequate. The theory behind this apparently callous policy, or absence of policy, was based on the general misapprehension of what the raids would be like.

It was hoped that after the sharp, short raids, probably by day, that were anticipated, the homeless—after a brief visit to a rest centre where they would be given a cup of tea, identity papers if theirs had been destroyed, and perhaps a minimum of financial assistance—would either go back to their bombed homes and put them in order, or would find alternative accommodation for themselves with friends or relatives. A Government circular stated that 'a small residuum' might have to be officially billeted. It was believed that these people would only be in the rest centres for a few hours. There was therefore no need to make such centres comfortable, sanitary, or, apparently, even safe. Indeed it was considered wiser not to do so, since this might make the people want to stay in places

81

that were intended for no such purpose. The result, of course, was that when the bombing began the homeless were taken to buildings like the Keeton's Road School and the school in West Ham described in the previous chapter.

The question of voluntary evacuation was even more intractable in view of the Government's directives to the boroughs, and the psychological background created by the failed evacuation of 1939. Homeless, shocked, penniless people might—and did—pour out of the bombed boroughs, but they were not anyone else's responsibility. The poor law authorities, inevitably not the most open-handed of men, quietly administering their 'spikes' in happier localities, could hardly be expected to devote their inadequate stocks of food and clothing to destitute strangers, when their own people were likely to be in the same condition within days or even hours.

This problem of the homeless, the bombed-out, was to affect large parts of London and many of the great provincial cities in the weeks and months to come. But it appeared in its most acute form immediately, on September the 8th and during the next twenty days in the East End riverside boroughs. It was the problem of those people whom Mrs Spender has described, sitting silently in their shelter in Silvertown, too stunned even to answer the voice of the ambulance girl.

What was to be done with them? A proportion fled, in any conveyance or even on foot, from the next night's terror. Five thousand are said to have trekked out nightly into Epping Forest where they slept in the open air and, regrettably enough, were occasionally treated as felons by the lucky inhabitants of the respectable, adjoining suburbs. Many spent the night on Hampstead Heath or in Greenwich Park. Others went even further afield. For nearly two months several hundred 'unauthorised evacuees' were living in the Majestic Cinema in Oxford, eating, sleeping and, to the disgust of the burghers of that ancient and unbombed centre of learning, even copulating among the cinema seats. A visitor to one such cinema—it may have been the same one—described it in a contemporary Mass

Observation bulletin as follows:

'I slept the night in the cinema. It is lit by six large lights; four of these are turned off at 11 o'clock, the other two remain on all night. Firemen and nurses patrol the cinema throughout the night, the nurses tucking up children, fetching water and milk, and so on. Each family takes a small piece of ground as their own province. Some are in the orchestra pit, and are given a little privacy by the curtains in front of it. But the majority sleep in the gangways and between the seats. There are perhaps 800 in all in the cinema. All are provided with blankets and palliasses. These they park somewhere and put their belongings (mostly a change of clothing) on the seats nearby. When it is bedtime the men take off their coats, the women their overalls, and lie down. The gangways become crowded, people lying very close to one another. Between the seats there is perhaps an average of one person to a row of ten seats. Here and there is a baby in his pram. There is no noise during the night, except of babies crying. Nearly every mother has a small child, and as soon as one cries, three or four others start too. It was quite impossible to get more than ten minutes uninterrupted sleep.'

But a person named Lady Patricia Ward, who wrote in a national newspaper, seems to have worn spectacles of another colour when visiting this cinema:

'The East End loved it. They settled themselves down each night, on rugs and cushions and blankets along the corridors; in the daytime they sat in the tip-up seats and sent their children to play in a disused ice-rink at the back of the stage . . . and wasn't it a lovely, bright place, almost like a palace? So they told each other.'

It is not hard to imagine what some of these unfortunate people may have told each other, if they happened to read Lady Patricia's article.

There were tens of thousands of these unfortunate refugees roaming the countryside. By September 14th almost a quarter of the population of some badly hit boroughs had gone.

Reception arrangements in the country were inadequate or non-existent. One country rest centre greeted the bombed-out with a large notice, stating: BEHIND EVERY SOCIAL PROBLEM IS REVEALED THE HIDDEN HAND OF ALCOHOL. Profiteering was rife. Sixteen guineas a week was demanded and obtained for a Cotswold cottage, eighteen shillings for a tiny bedroom in Hertfordshire, eight-and-six for a wretched dinner at a West Country hotel, and money then was worth more than twice what it is today. It was not until September 18th that the Ministry of Health took preliminary steps to meet the conditions that had arisen, and to organise this new evacuation or flight. On September 24th mothers with children of school age were declared eligible for evacuation, under the state scheme, from eight of the worst-hit boroughs: on October 7th this was extended to all the County of London. But on November 1st there were still over 250,000 children in the capital.

Attempts had been made to find the bombed-out alternative places to live in the city itself. For example, on September 9th the town clerk of Stepney, on his own initiative, arranged that a thousand or so people be evacuated by river steamer from Wapping to Richmond and other towns up-stream which had agreed to find them billets. On September 11th the Minister of Health, Mr Malcolm Macdonald, promised that on the following day buses would be sent to Silvertown and all who wished to leave that desolate place, whether homeless or not, could do so. In fact only 2,900 persons, out of an original population of some 13,000, accepted this offer which, they had been assured, would not be repeated.

West End billets for these people were not very popular. They believed that they would be treated as pariahs, and on occasions they were. For example, a rich family in Belgravia, with a large house, had a bombed-out family from White-chapel billeted on them. The rich put the poor in the servants' quarters—that is to say, under the eaves and nearest to the bombers—and refused to let them shelter in the basement where they themselves slept. The refugees preferred to return to Whitechapel. Such cruelty was undoubtedly the exception, but tales of this sort travel fast. They travelled extremely fast in the East End, and once the full measure of the terror had been faced most of the inhabitants of those boroughs who were still there preferred, whenever possible, to remain among their own battered, broken streets, even though their homes had gone. But where were they to sleep and eat and wash? That was the problem that had to be faced on September 8th.

The homeless were not only those whose homes had been destroyed, but also the people who were forced to leave their houses or flats because an unexploded bomb had landed nearby. The nuisance of the UXB, as it was called, was one that had not been fully foreseen, and in retrospect it is questionable whether this weapon was not treated with exaggerated caution. The Germans did drop a few delayed-action bombs: impact started a fuse which exploded the bomb hours, or very occasionally days, later. These were expensive contraptions, and it is estimated that of the bombs dropped by the Germans less than 1 per cent were of this type, nor of course were all of these effective. On the other hand, according to Professor Peter Danckwerts, G.C., who dealt with UXBs for the Port of London Authority, about one in ten of the bombs that were dropped on London were duds. A few of these were capable of going off if roughly handled or even if a heavy vehicle passing nearby caused the ground to quake. Their effect could therefore be identical to that of a delayed-action bomb. The large majority, however, were simply big, ugly, metal objects, to be removed by the sappers or the navy.

But the authorities decided that all UXBs should be treated as delayed-action bombs, and to begin with it was ordered that all premises within six hundred yards of such a bomb must be immediately evacuated and the roads within this area closed. This turned out to be quite impractical. A few hundred UXBs, skilfully placed, would have put all central London out of action, and by late November there were no less than 3,000 of these unpleasant objects waiting to be dealt with in

London Region alone. Nevertheless, though decreasing the danger zone, the Government continued with its policy whereby all UXBs were to be regarded as delayed-action bombs. From a purely military point of view it would undoubtedly have been wiser to treat them all as duds, unless they were actually ticking, and risk the very occasional explosion. The saving in time and in trouble caused by evacuation and traffic diversions would have been enormous. On the other hand the people might then have complained that they were not being properly protected.

In any event the Government's decision concerning these nuisances served vastly to increase the numbers of the homeless. Since people evacuated on account of UXBs expected soon to be able to return to their homes, they were naturally not very interested in finding alternative accommodation, even of a temporary sort. And since they were often ordered from their homes at the shortest notice, or prevented from entering them on their return from work or after a night in the shelters, they too often arrived at the Rest Centres as destitute as the truly bombed out. Finally, since the bomb disposal crews were quite hideously overworked, the temporarily evacuated were often a charge on the public assistance authorities for days on end. This was a major contributory cause to the congestion in the Rest Centres.

John Strachey, in his book of reminiscences about the Blitz in Chelsea, *Post D*, describes an early encounter with a UXB in terms that will be familiar to many. This incident apparently took place on September 14th, and 'Ford' is Mr Strachey's name for himself. He was returning from the country to his London flat: the street names are fictitious:

'Ford asked the conductor if the bus would get back on to its normal route. The conductor said, "I've no idea". As they seemed to be diverging farther and farther Ford got out and began walking home. He passed two more newly wrecked houses, upon which rescue or other work was going on. He turned down James Street, a nondescript sort of street that he never remembered having walked down before. It took him into Gage Street, which he walked along into Marlow Square.

Two or three Air Raid Wardens were walking about rather busily at the far end of the Square. Where his own street, St Hilda's Terrace, began he found a rope barrier. As he came up to it two wardens stopped him. "You can't go past", they said in chorus. "Unexploded bombs in Bedford Court." Ford immediately felt determined to go to his house. He said, "But my house is only two doors down. It's really in Marlow Square. Surely I can go there."

"Quite impossible", said one of the wardens.

"But I *must* get a toothbrush."

"Do you want to risk your life for a toothbrush?" said a lady warden.

Ford said, "Who wouldn't?"

His facetiousness was not encouraged. Another warden came up. Ford recognised a Miss Sterling. Miss Sterling, he vaguely knew, was "his" warden, in the sense that she lived only a dozen doors away, and had come round once or twice to enquire whether they had a stirrup pump, if their gas-masks were in order, and so on. He appealed to her. "Oh, Miss Sterling, I only want to go home just for a minute to get some things."

The other wardens repeated, "Quite impossible".

Ford thought of the two old ladies who lived in the basement and "did for him".

"But what about Miss Team and Miss Aird?" he said. "Have they been evacuated yet?"

Miss Sterling said, "They haven't gone yet."

"Then it's perfectly absurd", he replied. "Of course I must go back and help them to pack, and to get my own things." Without waiting for a refusal he stepped over the rope barrier. As he went he heard the other two wardens blaming Miss Sterling for letting him go.

At home the two old ladies were packing in a fluster. "Oh, Mr John, we've got to be out in three minutes. Wherever shall we go—whatever shall we do?"

Ford said, "We'll find somewhere for you."

Just then the sirens went again. Miss Aird dropped the string bag into which she was stuffing a half-eaten joint. Her hands fluttered. They began to hear gunfire.

Ford went upstairs and began throwing clothes into two big suitcases. He hadn't finished when the front-door bell rang. He opened it and found Miss Sterling standing on the doorstep. She was not facing him, but was looking, with a detached expression, down the street towards Bedford Court. She said, "Mr Ford"—she spoke very slowly—"Mr Ford—I don't think—I don't *think* there are any D.A. bombs at all."

Ford was considerably puzzled. He said, "Don't we have to go, then?"

"I don't think so."

"What did you say about 'D.A.' bombs?" Ford asked.

"D.A. simply means delayed action."

"But do we have to go or don't we?"

Miss Sterling looked worried (as Ford was to find it often did when pressed).

"I'm not *sure*; but I don't think so", she said.

"But shall I tell the old ladies to stay or go?—They're in a state already."

Miss Sterling said, "I think I would". She turned away. He saw her begin to walk towards Bedford Court. He interpreted her last sentence to mean that he should tell his old ladies to stay.

He went down to the basement and said, "We needn't go —yet, at any rate." Miss Team said, "Oh, but Mr John, shall we all be killed if we stay and those bombs go off?"

"Well, don't unpack and I'll go and see."

Ford went out and turned towards Bedford Court, opposite which, he remembered, was an A.R.P. hut. The gunfire, he noticed, had become heavy and there was a drone of engines. In the hut he found several wardens. They, too, appeared to be packing. He noticed one, with two stripes round his arm, who seemed to be in charge.

"I want a ruling, please", Ford said. "Are there, or are there not, delayed-action bombs in Bedford Court? And do we or do we not have to evacuate from 39 St Hilda's Terrace?"

The striped warden said, "Oh yes, there are some D.A.s all right. We're just evacuating now. 39? Let's look." He got out a large-scale A.R.P. street map. "Yes", he said. "I'm awfully sorry, but you're six doors within the danger area. You've got to go."

"Isn't that rather a borderland case? Can't we even come back and get things when we want them?"

The striped warden became entirely human. He said, "Well, it's at your own risk, but personally I should."

Ford said, "Let me get this clear. I don't at all want to get killed: and I mustn't let the two old ladies, who do for me, get killed. If, in your view, our house will be wrecked if and when these bombs go off, we certainly won't go near it."

They looked at the map again.

"No, I don't think so", he said. "It's just my guess, of course, but I think that all that would happen is that your windows would go and that sort of thing."

"All right, then. We'll all go now, but we shall come back and get things when we want them."

Ford left. He went back to 39. He felt that the local A.R.P. Services had given him a clear-cut and rational ruling, which was satisfactory. It was now half-past nine in the evening. The raid was definitely noisy; the light was beginning to go. He told the old ladies that they would have to go, after all, and went on filling his suitcase with his own clothes.

Miss Sterling came back. "You'll have to go, I'm afraid", she said. "It was only a rumour about there not being bombs, after all."

Ford said, "I know." He asked her where the old ladies could go. She said she had already arranged with the people three doors from her at 52 Marlow Square to take them in. He saw that Miss Sterling attended to the things that mattered. Ford told the old ladies, and they started off down the road to 52.'

In the East End, the two old ladies would probably have had to go to a Rest Centre. Professor Titmuss, in his official history entitled *Problems of Social Policy*, has a great deal to say about the conditions of those centres as they were in those early days.

They were usually in schools. The standard diet, provided for children as well as adults, consisted of bread, margarine, potted meat or corned beef, with an occasional bowl of tinned soup. There was frequently no crockery or cutlery. On September 12th one such centre in Bethnal Green had two spoons and a blunt knife. In another centre it was impossible to open the tins of soup because there was no tin-opener. There might be a few blankets, but usually no other bedding— or indeed beds—for the bombed-out, who often arrived wearing only their night-clothes. Sometimes there were not even enough chairs. In a previous chapter Dr Morton has described the all-enveloping filth that was thrown up by the bombs. The bombed-out were almost always extremely dirty, but most of the Rest Centres had inadequate washing facilities, or none at all. Sanitary conditions were little better. Some of the Rest Centres soon became quite disgusting.

A Red Cross worker described a particularly bad one in a report which she sent to Lord Horder at the time, and which he forwarded to the Ministry of Health. It had been an elementary school, in Stepney, and each September night the floor was crowded with some two or three hundred homeless people, lying on blankets, mattresses and piles of clothing. They had ten pails and coal-scuttles to use as lavatories. 'By the middle of the night these containers . . . overflow so that, as the night advances, urine and faeces spread in ever-increasing volume over the floor. The space is narrow, so that whoever enters inevitably steps in the sewage and carries it on his shoes all over the building . . . the containers are not emptied until 8 a.m. By dawn the stench . . . but I leave that to your imagination.' These people were provided with seven basins to wash in, but no soap or towels.

90

Another social worker, also quoted by Professor Titmuss, wrote as follows:

'The picture of the rest centres in those early days is unforgettable. Dim figures in dejected heaps on unwashed floors in total darkness: harassed, bustling, but determinedly cheerful helpers distributing eternal corned beef sandwiches and tea— the London County Council panacea for hunger, shock, loss, misery and illness. . . . Dishevelled, half-dressed people wandering between the bombed house and the rest centre salvaging bits and pieces, or trying to keep in touch with the scattered family. . . . A clergyman appeared and wandered about aimlessly, and someone played the piano.'

Voluntary social workers soon arrived to do what they could, and they did a great deal. The various charitable organisations distributed large quantities of blankets, clothes and food; and those admirable women, the spiritual daughters of Florence Nightingale, who always appear at last to sort out the chaos when the male authorities have almost given up in despair, soon got to work. Many of these were trained social workers, nor did they accept the rigid bureaucratic methods of the overwhelmed public assistance administrators. 'They raided school feeding centres and took away cutlery and crockery without permission, they bought food out of a variety of charitable funds, they appropriated babies' nappies and clothes . . . and one at least fetched to a centre administered by the public assistance committee coal which belonged to the local education committee.'

Not all the people who thus turned to in those early days were trained social workers, though these undoubtedly bore the main weight of the work.

In West Ham, in those first days, there were no canteens, mobile canteens or communal feeding centres. In one Rest Centre there was no food available for a great many people save sardines, hard biscuits and meat roll. A pie-shop keeper, with the appropriate name of Cook, came to the rescue. His shop had been burned out, and with it all his cooking equipment. But he collected some old drainpipes, caulked them together with dough, and mended his oven. Next day he sold 2,700 dinners, consisting of celery soup, meat pie, potatoes and bread. He charged 4d. per meal and, according to Miss Idle, not only fed the hungry but even made a profit for himself.

In Islington there was a red-faced, loud-voiced, middle-aged woman who for years had made her living selling beet-roots from a barrow in the market. She simply marched into the Ritchie Street Rest Centre and took charge. She found milk for the babies, bedded them down with their mothers and gave them each a powder, the ingredients of which are lost to history. However, this powder sent them all quickly to sleep. She then gave the remaining beds and benches to the oldest and feeblest people there, and by the time that night's raid began her whole household, consisting of 103 persons, was asleep or dozing. In the morning she organised washing, bathed the babies, swept the floor, and supervised breakfast. She left at eleven, presumably to sell her beetroots. In the evening she returned. As Professor Titmuss has said: 'She made one rest centre a place of security, order and decency for hundreds of homeless people.'

And, of course, after a little while the Government and the L.C.C. stepped in. The worst period was in middle and late September when the population of the Rest Centres rose to some 25,000. Thereafter the figures fell, billeting was properly organised, and the centres themselves, now made decent and run with tolerable efficiency, reverted to their intended role. People no longer lived in them, but simply went there for a meal, a wash, an issue of clothing if necessary, and above all advice.

But on September 8th it was to places such as those described above that the bombed-out, and those evacuated because of UXBs, had, in many cases, to go.

The first ten days of the Blitz, from the afternoon of Saturday the 7th until the late afternoon of Tuesday, September

17th, was the most intense phase of the Battle of London. It was also the critical, though not quite the final, phase of the Battle of Britain. The German strategy which prevailed throughout those days, and which was abandoned at the end of the period, is therefore worth a glance, since it profoundly affected London's ordeal.

It has already been made clear that Goering's strategic objective, since September 6th, had been to get the R.A.F.'s Fighter Command into the air by attacking a vital target—London's docks—and to destroy the fighter planes as a preliminary to the invasion. He had only a few days in which to do this. The transports and the army were at their embarkation stations in the Low Countries and France, but it had been agreed among the German leaders that the invasion could not take place until air supremacy, at least over the Channel and the south coast of England, had been won. On the other hand the German navy had stated that the week beginning September 21st was the last practical date for the operation in that month, while the weather in October would probably be too bad. Furthermore the masses of shipping could not be left indefinitely in the Channel ports, a sitting target for R.A.F.'s Bomber Command. Since ten days were considered the minimum between receiving the final orders for 'Sealion' and the actual landings, this meant that Hitler must issue those orders on September 11th. That is to say, Goering had four days in which to destroy the R.A.F. He himself seems to have thought that this would give him adequate time. His pilots were bringing back such wildly exaggerated claims of their successes that he believed Fighter Command to be even nearer the end of its reserves than it actually was. He apparently reckoned that three or four more days of heavy fighting would see those reserves exhausted and the battle won.

A subsidiary objective during this week of battle was the destruction of the docks. As already stated, had he continued to attack the R.A.F. directly—that is to say, the sector stations —it is just possible that he might have won the day. But this choice of a secondary, and simultaneous, objective produced the state of affairs that is known, in German, as 'riding two horses at once'. The horses tend to move apart, and the rider to fall between them. This is a cardinal, perhaps *the* cardinal, error in military affairs. It might be all very well for Goering to speak of destroying the R.A.F. by going for the docks. For his subordinate commanders, it inevitably produced a schizophrenic state. What, they may well have asked, were they supposed to be doing, wrecking the docks or downing the R.A.F.? The *Schwerpunktprinzip*, that tactical and strategic axiom whereby maximum effort is applied to the enemy's weakest vital point, went by the board. Among the German archives we can detect the note of vacillation and even of petulance.

The War Diary of the German Naval High Command stated, on September 7th:

'. . . the Armed Forces High Command intends to bring about the complete destruction of London's harbours, docks, industries and supplies by means of continuous air attacks, and so hasten the decision.'

And the next day, after the first successful attack, the Luftwaffe informed the Navy:

'The attacks will be continued until the destruction of harbours, supplies and power stations is complete.'

No mention, it will be noted, of preparing the way for 'Sealion'. On September 8th they attacked the docks by night, and on the 9th by day and again by night.

On the 10th, that is the day before Hitler was to make his decision, the Naval War Staff noted, with a certain comprehensible irritation, that whereas they would be ready to carry out their allotted task on D-day, September 21st, it did not look as though air supremacy, particularly as far as the R.A.F. bombers were concerned, would be achieved by that date. After all, Fighter Command was still very far from defeated. And the Naval Staff went on, somewhat sourly:

'It would be more in the sense of the planned preparation

for Operation "Sealion" if the Luftwaffe would now concentrate less on London and more on Portsmouth and Dover, and on the naval forces in and near the operational area, in order to wipe out any possible threat from the enemy. The Naval War Staff, however, does not consider it suitable to approach the Luftwaffe or the Fuehrer now with such demands, because the Fuehrer looks upon a large-scale attack on London as possibly being decisive, and because a systematic and long-drawn-out bombardment of London might produce an attitude in the enemy which will make the "Sealion" Operation completely unnecessary.'

On the 11th, air supremacy being still, as Goering thought, almost within his reach, Hitler postponed making his decision for three more days, which meant a postponement of D-day until the 24th. On that afternoon one hundred bombers attacked London, and the Luftwaffe considered that they had won a victory. There was little action by day on the 12th, but on the 13th and 14th they again bombed London against what appeared to be rapidly diminishing opposition. The Luftwaffe therefore asked Hitler for yet a few more days' grace, and this he again granted. The final decision would be taken on September 17th, with D-day now the 27th. It could not possibly be delayed beyond that day. The Luftwaffe made ready to fight their decisive battle on the following day, Sunday the 15th.

Meanwhile on the 14th an important conference, so far as London was concerned, took place at Hitler's headquarters. The relevant documents, together with those already quoted, can be found in Brassey's *Naval Annual* for 1948.

Admiral Raeder, who was by now blowing very cold on the whole 'Sealion' plan, decided that Hitler's alternative plan of defeating England by bombing London should be given every support. He submitted a memo to his Fuehrer, stating:

'Air attacks on England, particularly on London, must continue without interruption. If the weather is favourable, attacks should be intensified, without regard to "Sealion".

The attacks may have a decisive outcome.'

In fact his attitude was now quite the reverse of that apparent from the entry in the Naval War Diary four days earlier. No longer was it a question of asking the Air Force to support the Navy in its hazardous cross-Channel venture. Rather is it: 'Let the Luftwaffe get on with it, if they think they can win the war that way. After all, they *may* be right. And in any case, it lets us out.' This somewhat pusillanimous memorandum was the subject of a conference that same day.

At this conference, Hitler began by saying that he would not call off 'Sealion' just yet, since the air battle of the previous day had gone well for the Luftwaffe. The possibility of an October 'Sealion' was discussed without much enthusiasm on anybody's part. Finally Raeder got the conversation around to the bombing of London. The report of the meeting says that Raeder '. . . supports the view of the Chief of the General Staff, Air, that the attacks on targets of military importance will not suffice to produce mass psychosis and large-scale evacuation since the residential areas are some distance from the docks, etc. The Fuehrer however wishes to reserve the deliberate attacks on residential areas as a final method of pressure and a reprisal for British attacks of this nature. Raeder points out in this connection what a small area the port and industrial sections cover in proportion to the gigantic area occupied by the residential part of London.'

The Luftwaffe, setting off on the morrow to fight the battle, was thus suddenly offered yet a third horse—the creation of mass psychosis by terror bombing—to ride in addition to the two on which it was already so awkwardly perched. A fourth, the knock-kneed and spavined old reprisals nag, was being held ready to be pushed into the circus ring as well.

But apart from that, Raeder's rather officious interference with air strategy was remarkable for another reason. The bombing of the docks was a classic operation of its sort. So far as creating mass-psychosis went, nothing that the Germans ever did to Britain came nearer to achieving this end (though even that was not very near). Had the Luftwaffe continued to pound the East End it is conceivable that a demand for surrender might have been made by its unfortunate populations. Though this would certainly have been at once and firmly silenced, the fact was that the rough division between rich and poor was beginning to be confused with another rough division between the safe and the bombed. If continued and reinforced by skilful propaganda, the division might have produced a nasty rift in the British nation. Why, then, bomb the 'residential areas', whatever they may be?

Furthermore it was tactically senseless. Almost every bomb falling in the crowded East End caused death and destruction, for that part of London has few open spaces. On the other hand, London as a whole is the least built-up city in the world: of London County, only twenty-two per cent was built up at that time, while Greater London as a whole consists of no less than ninety per cent parks, streets, playing fields and so on and only a tenth is houses. Thus even as pure terrorisation, the bombing of the 'residential' areas offered less rewards than the continued bombing of the docks and the East End. Presumably Raeder, busy with his tide tables and his flat-bottomed barges, had scarcely had the time to examine in all its complexity the problems facing the German Air Staff. This, however, did not cause him to hesitate in expressing his views, nor Hitler from largely accepting them.

After this conference, still on the 14th, Keitel, who now and throughout the war was Hitler's glorified secretary, issued a directive, stating:

'The air attacks against London are to be continued, and the target area is to be expanded against military and other vital installations (e.g. railway stations). Terror attacks against purely residential areas are to be reserved as an ultimate means of pressure, and are therefore not to be employed at present.'

The last sentence is more or less meaningless. The first spelled at least a measure of relief for the docks and the East End. The Luftwaffe bomber crews were no longer limited in their objective. Once over London, they were bound to be somewhere near a railway station. At night particularly it was only to be expected that they would prefer to unload their cargo with all speed, rather than hang about among the ack-ack shells, looking for 'military' targets. This directive gave them clear authority to do just that. And they took it. Henceforth, though the East End continued to be heavily bombed, the central and western boroughs received their nightly tonnage too. From then on the load was borne by London as a whole, not just by the East End. And this meant a psychological trump card thrown away by the Germans.

On September 15th the Luftwaffe set out in full strength, and with a minimum of tactical manoeuvre, to sweep the rest of Fighter Command out of the skies. The battle raged all day and resulted in a great victory for the R.A.F. This was the last big daylight battle, for on September 17th Hitler cancelled Operation 'Sealion'. And this, together with the expansion of the German bombers' London target, marked the end of the first phase of the Blitz.

The second phase, lasting until early November, involved almost no daylight bombing. The night bombing, which was heavy, was not concentrated against any particular area but was directed against London as a whole. The East End's worst agony was over.

The British defences against the night bombing during this first phase of the Blitz were both slight and ineffective. There were two forms of active defence: the night fighters and the anti-aircraft guns.

The anti-aircraft gunners had long been the Cinderella of the army. After the First World War this branch of the service was scrapped altogether, and in 1920 the establishment of both A.A. guns and searchlights was nil. It was re-created, but it seemed a hopeless job. In 1926, during combined exercises with the R.A.F., guns, firing from permanent emplacements at targets flying on a known course, at a known speed, and at a height that was ideal for the gunners, scored only two hits out of 2,935 rounds fired. It is hardly surprising that the report on this fiasco stated that the chief effect of A.A. fire must 'still be regarded as mainly moral'. Only in 1934 was it again considered possible that A.A. guns might actually shoot down enemy planes. When it came to re-equipping the army in the 1930s, however, this dubious arm was very low on the priority list. In early 1938 the total A.A. defences of Great Britain consisted of 100 guns and 800 lights, when 216 guns and 1,056 lights were recognised as the minimum establishment for the defence of London alone. In October of 1939 General Pile, who had succeeded General Alan Brooke as G.O.C. A.A. Command some months earlier, spoke of his command's 'terrible inefficiency'.

It was not only guns and searchlights that were in short supply. During the first year of the war A.A. Command got the dregs of the call-up. Out of twenty-five recruits sent to one battery, one had a withered arm, one was mentally deficient, one had no thumbs, one had a glass eye which fell out whenever he doubled to the guns, and two were in the advanced and more obvious stages of venereal disease. Out of 1,000 recruits sent to the 31st A.A. Brigade, fifty had to be discharged immediately, twenty more were mentally deficient, and a further eighteen were below medical category B2. Of the useful recruits many were young soldiers, too young to be sent overseas, who were not infrequently transferred to other branches of the artillery once they were old enough and trained. Meanwhile the Command was drained of experienced officers and N.C.O.s who were sent to the B.E.F. Many of these returned, *via* Dunkirk, but usually of course without their guns.

This was the Augean stable which General Pile had to put in order. When the bombing of London began, A.A. strength for the whole of Britain was approximately fifty per cent of the heavy and thirty-three per cent of the light guns as envisaged in the pre-war programme. Most of those guns, and the methods of firing them, were, according to Pile, 'technically entirely unfitted for dealing with any but the bomber of twenty years earlier'. Their fire was controlled by sound-locators and the Fixed Azimuth system. In London a complicated and expensive Fixed Azimuth apparatus had been installed before the war, when it was realised that full radar defence would not be ready in time for the impending battle. 'Information from a geometrical layout of sound locators was passed through an ingenious computing apparatus in a central control room, and was from there conveyed to the guns. But it was based on our old assumption that the enemy would fly on a straight course and at a constant height and speed, and as the information depended on sound (with its consequent inaccuracy), and as the cumbersome machinery produced only a small volume of fire for a large number of guns, it failed lamentably.'

Furthermore, during the first few days of the Blitz, the gunners had to identify the planes as hostile before firing, since British night fighters were also operating over and about London.

The result of all this was that during the nights of September 7th, 8th and 9th there was only the occasional banging of an anti-aircraft gun to be heard in London, an insignificant noise among the crash of bombs and the steady, broken drone of the bombers. Indeed, only ninety-two 'heavy' guns were in position when the Blitz started, and the German bomber flew usually above the ceiling of the lighter A.A. guns. The people, in their shelters or in the wretched Rest Centres, felt again that nothing was being done to protect them. During these three heavy raids only four enemy planes were shot down out of more than 600 bombers that had bombed London by night. By the night of September 9th-10th it seemed, not only to the public, that Anti-Aircraft Command was almost a total failure.

That night, General Pile says, 'it was obvious to me, sleeping in my bed, that our system was no good. I became both angry and frightened at the same time, and lay awake the rest of the night thinking how to deal with this business.'

Next day he held a conference and determined that,

regardless of all previous theories, in the next night's raid he would fire off every gun he could at the enemy planes. He had been bringing in guns from the provinces and the ports for the last two days, and he now had 199 barrels at his disposal. Later that day he summoned the commanders of every gun position in London, together with their Battery, Brigade and Divisional commanders, to the Signals Drill Hall in the Brompton Road, where he addressed them personally. He said that every gun was to fire every possible round. Fire was not to be withheld on any account. Guns were to be got to the approximate bearing and elevation, and then fired. R.A.F. night fighters would not be operating over London and every plane was to be engaged immediately, without waiting to identify it. 'What in effect we were doing', he says, 'was to use our predictors, with all the information we could feed into them from any source, to engage the enemy by predicted fire from all the guns that could bear on any particular target. It was in no sense a barrage, though I think by that name it will always be known.'

That night the barrage opened up, and its roar was music in the ears of the Londoners. The results astonished Pile, the London public and apparently the German pilots too, who flew higher as the night went on. Many of them, seeing the twinkling shell-bursts in the sky ahead, jettisoned their bombs on the southern and eastern suburbs and turned for home.

This new method of firing was scarcely more effective in destroying enemy planes than the old had been, and until the arrival of radar sets on the gun sites very few night bombers were shot down. But as a morale-booster for the people on the ground, its effect was incalculable. Though it is certain that during these first weeks ack-ack shells and shell fragments killed many more English civilians than German airmen, the noise of the guns not only went some way to drowning the noises made by the enemy, but also gave Londoners the impression that their own people were hitting back at last. They even, rather touchingly, collected the lethal, white-hot shell fragments which throughout that winter clattered and sparked into their streets. These lumps of gashed steel are still to be seen on many a mantelpiece.

So far as the Germans went, the very fact that the sky was full of bursting shells strongly discouraged the bomber crews from pin-pointing their targets. The consequent dispersal was of course very much in the interests of the defence. The Civil Defence services of individual boroughs were not swamped by concentrated attack, for the suffering and damage was more widely, which means more thinly, spread.

Those experts who had said, fourteen years before, that anti-aircraft fire was primarily concerned with morale were proved to have prophesied with a curious accuracy, at least so far as the night raids of these first few weeks went.

There was, as usual, the delightful eccentric who objected. The council of one suburban borough wrote complaining that the vibration of the guns was cracking the lavatory pans of the council houses, and would A.A. Command please be so good as to move its barrage elsewhere? While a gentleman sent a letter to General Pile saying: 'Dear Sir, As a citizen of London, I think the anti-aircraft defence of London is the biggest scandal since Nero. . . . Why, you don't understand the meaning of the word barrage. . . .'

The strain on the gunners was very great. Many of them were raw recruits, living in crude dugouts they themselves had built beside their gun-sites, often deep in mud, often half-full of water and half demolished by the blast of gun and bomb. One battery arrived from the Midlands twenty-four hours after receiving its movement order and was firing within three quarters of an hour of being ready for action. For ten hours they served the guns. They then boiled out the guns. They had half an hour's sleep before the day raid began, and the same men took post again. This went on for eight days, at the end of which time they were almost unconscious at their guns for lack of sleep. On the ninth day they were relieved by soldiers who had had no more than basic training.

The guns, too, suffered. The gun barrels were wearing out, and twice Pile attempted to cut down on the firing. But Churchill immediately noticed the decrease in the nightly din, and that most sensitive politician knew exactly what the barrage meant to the population of London. He telephoned through at once to demand why all the guns were not firing. They fired, and they went on firing so long as the intensive Blitz on London continued, even though General Pile reckoned in late October that at this rate he would have no 4·5s left in two months and no 3·7s in four. But by then the Blitz was about to move elsewhere.

Night fighters, in those early days, were even less successful than the anti-aircraft gunners. Group-Captain John Cunningham was to be the most successful night-fighter ace. Before the winter was out he, usually with Squadron-Leader Rawnsley, his navigator, was to shoot down more than a dozen enemy bombers. But all that came later. He has described the acute frustration of those early weeks, to this writer, in these words:

'The September to November period was the most depressing for night fighters. We had mainly Blenheims in our squadrons then.' On September 7th there were, in Southern England or the Midlands, five squadrons of Blenheims, a flight of night-fighter Hurricanes and another of Defiants. 'The Blenheims had a very inadequate form of radar. Most nights we were able to hear the aircraft going over our airfields before we got into the aeroplanes to take off. But having started up, and got into the air, we were seldom if ever able to see them. The radar wasn't working well enough to enable us to get contacts and close in that way. On the very few occasions when the searchlights did illuminate the enemy aircraft, you were usually in the wrong place or not high enough, and by the time you got near the target the searchlight would have gone off it, or the aeroplane would have flown away from the searchlight region. So one was left with a feeling of almost complete helplessness. But in October the first Beaufighters arrived in squadron. . . .'

The story of the radar-directed night fighter belongs later in this book.

While awaiting the arrival of the new night fighters and above all of the new airborne radar sets and ground installations which would enable the night fighters to close with the enemy, many expedients were tried, all without success. One was the use of single-seater day fighters by night. This proved both expensive, owing to the number that crashed on landing, and unsuccessful, though a few kills were recorded on the rare occasions when the moon and cloud produced an almost daytime clarity. But every single day fighter, and its pilot, was needed for the day battle, at least during the first weeks. This experiment was soon abandoned. Others were tried. Squadron-Leader Rawnsley, in his book *Night Fighter*, has written:

'The authorities tried all kinds of ingenious and even fantastic schemes, and a vast amount of thought and effort was expended on a fallacy. We now knew where the solution lay; but how could we, on our past showing, expect them to put all their eggs in one black and as yet unproved basket?

'The fallacy lay in their deep-rooted and understandable conviction that our failure was due simply to our inability to see another aircraft in the dark. We knew well enough that there would be no difficulty about that if—and this was the important point—we could be brought into the right position relative to the aircraft we were pursuing, going at the same speed and in the same direction. But first of all we had to be placed in the right position to make full use of our own radar.

'But other schemes were brought into play and we were beset with such things as airborne searchlights, showers of magnesium flares, airsown minefields dangling on parachutes, and other menaces to our own defensive fighters. Some of these schemes were good enough in theory, but the practical difficulties were too great. And they all missed the most essential point of all: to get the fighter into a position where it could make an attack.

'It was said of one very new pilot on one of his first night patrols that he suddenly saw an airborne searchlight projected horizontally out of the darkness at his own level without knowing what it was. He immediately lost all faith in his instruments and dived straight into the ground!

'Another source of amusement for us was the correspondence columns of the more irresponsible newspapers. There we read of people who wanted anti-aircraft guns mounted on balloons; of the idea that bombers should fly above the raiders and drop sand into their engines; and there was even one who suggested forming up a hundred obsolete aircraft in line astern, each trailing a thousand feet of cable, to fly across the track of the raiders.

'Fortunately for all of us the sponsors of the radar-equipped night fighter were not side-tracked.'

The night-fighter pilots did not, at this time, enjoy the immense prestige and popularity that the Spitfire and Hurricane pilots had won in the Battle of Britain, and that they themselves were to acquire in the coming months. Squadron-Leader Rawnsley has told this writer the following anecdote of the period:

'I'm afraid we weren't very proud of our performance in those early days. We had the feeling that we weren't doing our stuff, that we were letting the public down. And most of us were Londoners. When we went home on forty-eight hour leave occasionally, we were only too glad to get back to the comparative safety of the aerodrome. I remember one of our air-gunners who went home and went to his local pub. They were giving him a good time on the strength of his Air Force uniform when he inadvisedly let drop the information that he was not in bombers but in night fighters. He was immediately met with the rejoinder: "Oh, you are, are you? And where were you last Saturday night when they made that hole across the road over there?"'

The day, or rather the night, of the radar-directed Beau-fighter was to come later.

The last big daylight raid on London took place on September 18th. By then the night bombing was no longer limited to the docks and the East End and, though this was of course unknown, Hitler had postponed 'Sealion' at least until next spring. The bombing henceforth was to be almost entirely by night and was to be directed against the whole of London, with the admitted purpose of destroying the capital of the British Empire and producing such misery and distress that the populace would compel the Government to sue for peace. Before going on to discuss the next phase of the battle, the phase when the shelters were the centre of it all for London's millions, and which lasted until November 13th, a brief summary of the Luftwaffe operations against London during those first twelve days might suitably end this chapter. The night figures, taken from *The Defence of the United Kingdom*, are derived from German archives.

Sept. 7th **Day** Over 300 bombers bomb the docks and riverside boroughs.

Night 247 bombers drop 335 tons of H.E. and 440 incendiary canisters, mostly in the dock area.

Sept. 8th **Day** Little activity.

Night 171 bombers drop 207 tons of H.E. and 327 incendiary canisters, again mostly in the dock area.

Sept. 9th **Day** Of 200 bombers sent against London, 90 bomb the metropolis.

Night 195 bombers drop 232 tons of H.E. and 289 incendiary canisters. Target, the docks and the East End.

Sept. 10th **Day** Little activity.

Night 148 bombers drop 176 tons of H.E. and 318 incendiary canisters. Target, the docks and the East End.

Sept. 11th **Day** Heavy attacks on London and Southampton. The R.A.F. lose 29 fighters to 25 enemy planes shot down. The Germans count this a victory.

Night 180 bombers drop 217 tons of H.E. and 148 incendiary canisters. Partly due to the A.A. barrage and partly to orders received, there is less concentration on the dock area.

Sept. 12th Day   Minor raids.

Night Only 43 bombers over London, dropping 54 tons of H.E. and 61 incendiary canisters.

Sept. 13th Day   Minor raids.

Night 105 bombers drop 123 tons of H.E. and 200 incendiary canisters.

Sept. 14th Day   Heavy daylight raid on London. 14 R.A.F. fighters destroyed for a similar number of German planes shot down. Goering believes that victory is at hand and Hitler postpones his 'Sealion' decision for three more days.

Night A light raid on London by 38 bombers dropping 55 tons of H.E. and 43 incendiary canisters.

Sept. 15th Day   More than 200 bombers escorted by some 700 fighters sent against London. 60 enemy planes shot down by the R.A.F. for the loss of 26 fighters. This marked the defeat of the Luftwaffe's attempt to secure air supremacy and thus meant the end of 'Sealion'. This victory is annually celebrated as Battle of Britain day.

Night 181 bombers drop 224 tons of H.E. and 279 incendiary canisters on London.

Sept. 16th Day   Minor raids

Night 170 bombers drop 189 tons of H.E. and 318 incendiary canisters on London.

Sept. 17th Day   Minor raids. Hitler cancels 'Sealion'.

Night 268 bombers drop 334 tons of H.E. and 391 incendiary canisters on London.

Sept. 18th Day   The last big daylight raid. 70 bombers sent

against London, in three waves. 19 shot down
by the R.A.F. for the loss of 12 fighters.

Night The heaviest night raid on London yet. 300
bombers drop 350 tons of H.E. and 628
incendiary canisters.

There were two famous incidents during this phase, which
have both been very adequately described elsewhere. One was
the unexploded bomb that buried itself under St Paul's
Cathedral on September 12th, close to the Southwest Tower.
It was eventually, and after immense trouble, dug out on
September 15th by Lieutenant Davies of the Royal Engineers,
who was awarded the G.C. The details are given by the Dean
of St Paul's, Dr Matthews, in his book *St Paul's Cathedral in
Wartime*.

The other was the deliberate bombing, in the late morning
of the 13th, of Buckingham Palace. King George VI and
Queen Elizabeth had a narrow escape, which is graphically
described by Sir Winston Churchill in the second volume of
his war memoirs. This incident was given considerable
publicity, and it undoubtedly heartened the people in the East
End to know that their perils were being shared by the highest
in the land. In a curious way, this knowledge was almost as
good for morale as the anti-aircraft barrage.

A third incident of this early period of the Blitz is a curious
and rather sad little event which, though much talked about
at the time, was not fully reported in the English papers. This
was a Communist demonstration at the Savoy Hotel.

Reference has been made earlier to the 'Deep Shelter
Controversy', which began well before the war, and which
continued into the Blitz. Phil Piratin, the Communist M.P.,
and a Mr 'Tubby' Rosen, also a Communist and the head of
the Stepney Tenants' Defence League, decided that the present
misfortunes of the East Enders made this a suitable time for a
demonstration on this subject. The place they chose was the
Savoy Hotel, and their reasons for so doing were two-fold.

The Savoy has, and had, an underground banqueting hall.

The hotel management turned this hall into a large air-raid shelter for the use of its customers and clients. This shelter was divided into two: one part was used as a restaurant, with a dance floor and a cabaret during the earlier part of the evening, later being transformed into a dormitory: the other was permanently equipped with beds, and was partitioned by curtains into men's quarters, women's quarters, married couples' areas, with even a special corner for the notorious snorers. It was all most comfortable, and, being under eight floors of ferro-concrete, extremely safe. Indeed, in the restaurant it was not even possible to hear the nightly raid outside. It is, of course, customary for expensive hotels to do all they can for the comfort and convenience of their patrons, and, in its air-raid arrangements, the Savoy lived up to its usual high standards. So, incidentally, did the other great London hotels. But the Savoy was the nearest to the East End. It was also the rallying point of the American correspondents in London. A demonstration there could be sure of achieving maximum publicity.

On the evening of September 15th, as dusk fell, a group of people gathered in the gardens outside the Embankment entrance to the hotel. Among them were several women, one in an extremely advanced state of pregnancy. A few minutes later the Alert sounded, as it was then doing each evening at about this time, and the well-drilled party, estimated by the manager of the hotel at approximately one hundred, converged on the hotel entrance, pushing the pregnant woman in front of them. They informed the porter that they demanded shelter. The porter was in something of a quandary; but since he could obviously not physically repulse a woman who looked as though she might give birth at any minute, he let her in. The others followed, some standing about in the hall, others making their way into the small bar that had been fixed up for the American journalists. Certain English journalists who were also in this bar were not at all taken aback by this influx, since they had received advance information of what was planned.

The manager now arrived on the scene. He found himself in a most embarrassing situation. Although there were no bombs falling as yet, he could hardly eject all these people into the street without appearing excessively callous. On the other hand, his first responsibility lay with his clients. His shelter had sufficient accommodation for them, but if it were thrown open to the public, it was obvious that within a night or two it would be completely filled with people who had no connection with the hotel at all. In that case the hotel might just as well go out of business. Furthermore, were not the pilots and other people who sought an evening's relaxation at his hotel entitled to it?

He therefore asked the police what he should do. The police were ambiguous. They could not, or would not, throw the demonstrators out. On the other hand, if the hotel staff ejected them, and they then made a demonstration outside, they could and would be dealt with by the police. Neither then nor at any other time did the manager succeed in discovering whether he was obliged, by law, to admit anyone demanding shelter to his converted banqueting hall.

It was a situation to test the tact of even the most tactful restaurateur. He dealt with it most adequately. He had the demonstrators—who, he has told me, were so awed by the Chaldean splendours of the hotel that they soon forgot to shout their slogans, despite the promptings of their leaders—led down into the dormitory part of the shelter. This was empty at that early hour. A few made their way into the restaurant, where the cabaret was going on. The diners were watching Vic Oliver, and most of them never noticed what was happening, even though some of the interlopers asked quite loudly why Vic Oliver should be at the Savoy and not in an air-raid shelter in the Commercial Road. Nobody seems to have answered this rather easy riddle.

About fifteen minutes later the All Clear sounded, which was unusual at this time and a stroke of luck for the manager, since he could now quite clearly insist that these people, who were not the hotel's customers, must leave. They left, but hung about in the gardens outside, awaiting the next Alert. However, by the time it sounded arrangements had been made, and Piratin, Rosen and their flock were escorted to another shelter, a deep public one a hundred yards or so away. And that was the end of that, nor was the demonstration repeated either here or at any other hotel.

As they had known it would be, the news was immediately flashed to the United States and from there to Germany. The German press made great play of it, and printed long paragraphs describing infuriated mobs of East Enders storming luxury hotels and being shot down by the police. Similar rumours were current in England. But in fact it was only a very damp squib of a demonstration. Even so, it was the most spectacular one of the Blitz. That is surely striking commentary on the morale-breaking effects of bombing. All that was achieved on the lines that Hitler had hoped was this little fizzle, which was not even spontaneous, arranged and carried out by his Communist allies.

CHAPTER FIVE

DURING THE autumn months and those of the early winter the heaviest night raids took place when the moon was full, or nearly full. The heaviest for September was on the 18th, when 300 bombers flew against London, and the heaviest for October was the 15th, with 410. Never before had the inhabitants of a great city been so conscious of the lunar phases, for though the 'bomber's moon' was dreaded, it brought with it at least the minor advantage of making the blackout slightly less unpleasant.

People in London were very conscious of their city during those weeks. For years, perhaps, men and women had walked along streets grown so utterly familiar that their eyes consciously registered nothing of the architecture about them. Nor, indeed, is there much beauty in most of London to be observed. But now, when each dawn revealed new gaps in the well-known rows of house-fronts, people looked with awareness, even with the wonderment of love, at their old streets and squares. After all, this might be the last time. And on these moonlit nights the façades and roof-line, which had seemed so utterly dependable and safe, and which were now revealed to be so vulnerable and fragile, were transformed. With no lights to reveal the grime and dullness of the city office building, no advertisements to shout the banality of the chain store or cinema, with the vulgarity of the brash hotel and the tedium of the endless surburban streets hidden in shadow, enormous London, beneath the bomber's moon, acquired the poignant beauty of mortality.

This writer remembers walking, on one such night and

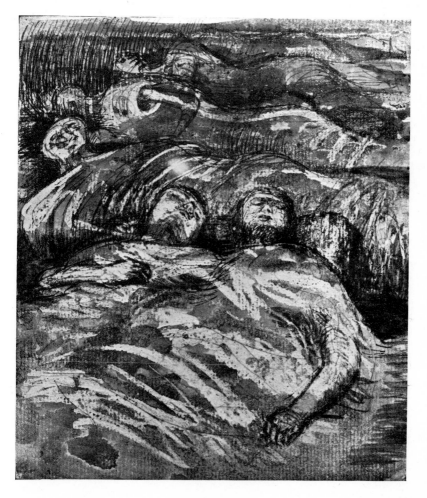

TUBE SHELTERERS

before the raid began, from Ludgate Circus through the blacked-out City. St Paul's in the moonlight seemed almost white, or at least not its usual sooty black, colourless perhaps, its loveliest of domes a great uncoloured bubble against the ominous sky. The City was a strangely broken horizon of roofs and chimney-pots, with blank, bright windows. The Baltic Exchange was magical, the huge empty offices of the insurance companies in Leadenhall Street romantic and pitiful too, for insurance was something that belonged to another age. From Trinity Square the Tower of London seemed suddenly less massive, its yard-thick walls less brutal, as the sirens began to wail and, almost immediately, the distant guns to shoot. We walked down Tower Hill as the guns came closer and the sky shook to the drone of the engines overhead. We pushed open the door of the pub called *The Tiger*, and then the heavy blackout curtains within, and entered the bright fug of the almost deserted public bar, with its wooden tables and its dartboard and the advertisements for mineral waters and bottled beers and biscuits upon the walls. Outside, where the Tower lay with its atrocious history beside the oily river, the first bombs were screaming and whistling down.

'The best nights for visibility', a former German bomber pilot has told this writer, 'were moonlit nights after rain, particularly if the moon were not too high in the sky. Then, with the shadows cast by the buildings and the moonlight reflected from the damp streets and squares, London below us was as clear and readable as a map.'

What was life like for the millions who lived in, on and beneath this moonlit map? It is of course quite impossible to generalize about a city the size of London, but nevertheless certain impressions of those early days have been confirmed so frequently by all sorts of men and women that they seem to have a general validity.

People became extraordinarily friendly. City life in normal times is one long series of attempts to avoid unwanted contact, to preserve an element of privacy even amidst the jostling crowds at rush-hour or in the pushing throng that fills the theatre foyer between the acts. The English, and I speak here of the middle classes, have always been extremely sensitive in the matter of privacy. The Englishman does not like his neighbours to know what he is doing: he even prefers his neighbours not to know who he is. This fact, presumably connected with puritanism, leads him to live behind locked doors and curtained windows, to avoid conducting his social life in public—the façades of most clubs, and of all pubs, are impenetrable to the eye of the passer-by—even to regard dining in restaurants as, somehow, faintly raffish. The occasional exception who attempts to break down the wall of reticence between himself and his neighbours is regarded as at best a nuisance, at worst a dangerous lunatic. A mumbled 'good-morning' on the doorstep, a non-committal banality about the weather in the lift, these are considered perfectly adequate acknowledgment between people who have lived, for years on end, within feet of one another. Anything more might encourage these strangers to cease being strangers, and heaven knows what might not happen then.

This reticence went very quickly. Hitherto men and women had associated with their equals for valid reasons of friendship, common interests, because they were related, because they had been at school or in the army together. Now they associated automatically with their neighbours. The Wardens at the Post, the women at the canteen or the first-aid station, even more so the people in the air raid shelter, all were the inhabitants of the same few hundred square yards of brick and stone. In peacetime, and even before the Blitz began, they may have had very little in common. Now they had a greal deal: the unexploded bomb behind the baker's shop, the fire at No. 32, the officiousness of Warden Snooks, the shocking way the blackout regulations were neglected at the joinery works. There was much to talk about; above all there were the bombs. Everyone had his story, and if other people's were obviously less interesting than one's own, it was at least worth listening politely while awaiting one's own chance to tell. Contact was established.

Once it was established, and it was discovered that these strangers were not dangerous interlopers eager only to pry into one's private life and to take advantage of any chink in one's social armour, acts of friendliness became easy. There was plenty of scope for them in the unnatural chaos caused by the Blitz, whether it be helping to put out an incendiary bomb on a neighbour's roof, or lending a hot-water bottle to a mother with a sick child in a shelter, or just telling the postman the new address of the bombed-out people next door. People joined together to form fire-fighting parties to protect their streets, to mend each other's broken windows, to store each other's furniture, and even carry out elementary building repairs to one another's houses, to look after children. When the gas went, the lady of No. 12 would cook on the electric stove at No. 14, and when the electric cable was cut, this would be reversed. Men, and even more women, who had never been there before would now meet in the pub on the corner for an encouraging glass after a bad raid, every detail of which would then be discussed with keen interest and even enjoyment.

This relaxation of social reserve spread. People talked on buses. A friend of this writer, who had been quite badly knocked about in a raid, went next morning to a chemist's in Piccadilly famous for its pick-me-ups and asked for a double. An extremely crusty and purple-veined old Edwardian, a complete stranger visiting the chemist's for the same purpose, said:

'Have it on me, old boy.'

People shared taxis with strangers invisible in the blackout, talked to others in the protective doorways of houses, were granted more than a cursory and embarrassed 'thank-you' by women to whom they surrendered their seats in the crowded tube or bus. One evening I was dining with a girl in a small restaurant when the raid grew very noisy and the building shook badly. An elderly gentleman, the only other diner, invited us to his nearby flat in a large, safe, ferro-concrete block. We spent several hours examining his remarkable collection of Greek gold coins and drinking his excellent brandy. We have never met before or since.

In the East End, since privacy was never easily obtained among the crowded tenements, neighbourliness was not such an innovation. The poor have always tended to look after one another.

Mrs Itzinger, who was a charwoman in a Bermondsey mission, has described this aspect of life at that time in these words:

'It was a good three weeks after the Blitz started, and sometimes we had no gas. And then we'd come home and we found we had no water. And we used to have to run round all the places where the roads were up, and perhaps there'd be just a little trickle running right through and we used to ask the man that was there whether it was all right to drink. And he says: "Oh, yes!" So we used to get a bucket and take a little mug, and put it in and fill the bucket up. And then there'd be another poor old soul come along, and she says: "Is the water all right, ducks, do you think it'll be all right? Do you think we'll be able to get our dinner in the oven in time, before the gas goes off again?" And I used to say: "Oh yes, dear, don't worry." So she says: "I don't know, every time I start to get me dinner in the oven, so the blessed warning goes—" And she says "—off goes the gas again, into the shelter again, and then we come back again—" And then she says: "—and there's the dinner all spoilt, and if you'd happened to forget to turn the gas off, well", she says, "your dinner was absolutely done for", she says, "and bang's gone your rations again."

'Anyhow, we fiddled it out and we got on all right again. So we got over that day. And we'd start work again, the warning go again, back to the shelter again and somebody'd say: "Where's Mrs so-and-so? We ain't got our regulars here." Then another one would say: "Well, I wonder if she was safe?"

Then Mrs next-door'd say: "Oh, I think she's quite all right. Oh well, let's go round and see her, let's come round to her house and see if she's all right, and if she's not ready, well, we'll get her ready, and if she's got the children there, well, we'll get the children ready as well."

'And then we got safely in the shelter again, and everything was all quiet that night, we was all right and the children asleep all right, and then just as we were coming out in the morning, up goes Moaning Minnie. Back in the shelter you'd go again, and the women'd say: "Oh bless me, what time we going to get to work this morning?"

'Well, we get to work and you're absolutely tired and as soon as you get to work up goes the warning again, down goes the bucket and pails, into the shelter, you're downstairs again, upstairs you come again, and then the boss'd say: "How much work you done?" Then when you turn round and tell him you've been up all night, he says: "Poor old souls, but still, never mind. I suppose it's the Lord's wish that we've got to carry on, like this. But still, it won't be for ever." And we used to say: "No, but if it was for any longer we wouldn't put up with it." '

In East Ham an organisation came into existence called MAGNA, the Mutual Aid Good Neighbours Association. Its first purpose was to provide fire-watchers, volunteers who would stay awake and above-ground and deal with incendiary bombs as soon as they fell and while they were still quite simply extinguished. After a time this organisation, based on groups of fifty houses, became somewhat more ambitious and took to repairing its members' damaged homes. It would have spread to West Ham, but in that unfortunate borough it came into collision with the Borough Council, which disapproved of any such scheme on the grounds that it was likely to affect the interests of the permanent officials. It was also opposed lest it infringe the Trade Union rights of the building trade. But in less doctrinaire areas of London this and similar schemes of self-help flourished quite spontaneously.

In those parts of London where the classes mix, class distinction, if it did not actually vanish, was very much ignored. It is hard to persevere in looking down upon, or resenting, a man who night after night is sharing the same dangers and doing exactly the same work as yourself. Even in the suburbs, where social status and apparent respectability are so cherished a talisman, the impact of the bombs inevitably caused a mingling. A former Warden in Ilford has told this writer of how he would go into houses, to which he would not normally be invited, in order to wake up the next shift of voluntary Wardens. Front doors would be left open, and he would walk straight into that holiest of inner chambers, the marital bedroom, to summon the husband to his Post. He has described the easy relations which then existed between all sections of the community within his borough, and even with the evacuees from the East End. Though he has added, sadly enough, that this ended, almost overnight, in 1945.

The relationship between employers and employees was also on a sympathetic footing which, in some cases at least, was new and surprising, while in others hitherto unspoken loyalties were given a chance of self-expression. The staff-manager of a big hotel has told how cleaning women, arriving half an hour late for work, would apologise: it was not their fault, their houses had been blasted. And, he said, they were clearly quite sincere: they were truly sorry to be late at work. The clerks at the offices of a huge metal combine in the City were deeply distressed when their building caught fire, and risked their lives saving small personal items that belonged to the chairman from his threatened office. A girl who was in a bombed restaurant, but was unhurt, went to work next day: 'It was not till later in the morning that the tension broke. I was standing in my chief's office with some papers he had called for when I suddenly started to cry. The pent-up emotion burst and knew no bonds, my tears were uncontrollable. I was sent home. . . .'

It may be that people clung to their work as to a stable,

understandable link with the realities of the past in the insane and incomprehensible present, but it is also true that human relationships were suddenly much easier. For the men and women who worked in the munitions factories, or had other jobs connected obviously and directly with the war, there was the added incentive that by sticking to their jobs, and working as hard and as long as they could, they were striking back at what was now their own, personal enemy. This served to counter-balance to a great extent the inevitable interference with production caused by the bombs and by transportation difficulties. Far from inducing people to flee from their places of work, as the Germans had hoped, the bombs, in London at least and for the majority, had quite the opposite effect. Figures for absence from work during this period are only fragmentary, nor are there adequate pre-war figures for purposes of comparison, but neither the Government nor the managers were at any time worried by absenteeism in the London region.

Let it be repeated that these remarks about friendliness and the breakdown to social reserve are generalizations to which there were many exceptions. As already stated, the active Communists did their best to spread ill feeling and to intensify class hatred, and they met with a certain success, particularly in the early days when almost all the bombs were falling in the East End. The Fascists, too, exploited the misery of Stepney and such boroughs for their own immoral purposes. Anti-semitism was their strongest card, and they did their best to play it. Pre-war anti-semitism had been quite marked in the East End and, indeed, was the only emotion to which the Fascists could appeal in that area. A very large proportion of the small shops were in Jewish hands: the Jews thus became automatically creditors with all the popularity that that entails. Furthermore, their numbers had been greatly swelled by the influx of refugees from Hitler's Germany, and although most of these unfortunate people had been interned if they were men, there were still a lot of foreign women about. Finally, the Jewish shopkeepers, though often very poor, were not usually as poor as their neighbours. Many had cash and were thus in a position to pay for taxis to take them away when the Blitz began or to arrange for comparative safety within London if they stayed. They tended to be more timorous, and more noisily timorous, than their neighbours. They would crowd and push into the shelters, occasionally bringing with them prams which contained valuables but no baby, talking loudly in foreign languages, and in general arousing strong feelings of xenophobia among their ill-educated fellows. In such circumstances, the Jewish house-owner who tries to collect the rent after his property has been damaged is automatically castigated as 'a Jew', while the Jewish doctor who works for long hours, unpaid, looking after Jew and Gentile alike, is simply regarded as 'a doctor'.

Fascist attempts to exploit such feelings, with the slogan 'THIS IS A JEWISH WAR' scrawled upon walls, met with very little success. Many people seriously feared that the misery and anger in the East End would find its outlet, as in so many other countries, in a pogrom and anti-Jewish riots. This, thank God, never happened. It would have been too atrocious to think of refugees from Hitler's Germany being beaten up by Englishmen while Hitler's bombs rained down indiscriminately on both. This, at least, was one of the many horrors which had been anticipated, and which London was spared.

Work, then, continued almost normally, or as near to normal as was possible during the Blitz, but the problem of sleep, or rather the lack of it, and the resultant, cumulative exhaustion might have been expected to have very serious effects. Figures compiled by Mass Observation show that during the night of September 11th-12th, that is to say the night on which the A.A. barrage opened up, about one third of London's population got no sleep at all, and approximately another third slept for less than four hours. Four nights later two thirds of London's population were still getting less than four hours sleep per night. The women, being more timorous than the men— a far higher proportion of women took shelter—got considerably less sleep than their menfolk, though they often managed to catnap during the day. Rather surprisingly, this absence of sleep, which it must be remembered continued for weeks on end, does not seem to have worried most people unduly. One reason may have been that the noise that kept them awake was chiefly the sound of the guns, and, as stated earlier, that was accepted as a reassuring noise, almost as an antidote to the noise of the planes and the bombs which made many people extremely frightened. Three reactions, recorded by Mass Observation on September 12th, are characteristic:

"I must say that though the noise was awful last night, we were all relieved to hear it—the louder it was, the greater confidence we had. Made us feel safer.'

'I didn't mind so much because it was our guns, and we can get used to that. No one in the shelter was afraid. They like the guns better than the bombs, I can tell you.'

'You can't sleep with the guns. But it's a good sound. We shall have to get used to it.'

In an attempt to enable the people to sleep, the Government issued free earplugs, via the Wardens' Service, but despite much publicity—including a photograph which purported to show Winston Churchill asleep with earplugs plugged in—these never caught on. The almost universal explanation as to why they were not used was: 'I like to hear what's happening.' When it is realized that during the Blitz fear was intimately connected with noise, this makes sense. To block out the real noise was to open the way to all the fears of which the imagination is capable.

There are, fortunately, other aspects to life beside work and sleep. One very important one is food, and another is entertainment or relaxation. A third, at least in the great cities, is transportation.

In normal times over a million people move into central London to work each morning and travel back to their homes each evening. During the Blitz, while the total number of London's inhabitants had decreased by well over a million, this scarcely affected the rush-hour traffic, since a great many people who would normally have slept near their place of work now moved out nightly. For example, between 12,000 and 15,000 working-class people from eastern and south-eastern boroughs went each night to Chislehurst, and slept in the caves there. North of the river there was a similar trek out to Epping Forest. The man living in a wealthier district who was fortunate enough to possess, or who could borrow, a cottage—or a room in a cottage—in the country would probably send his wife and children and go down there himself, if not every night, at least as often as he could. Perhaps as high a proportion as one third of those people who lived in the more expensive blocks of flats had moved out by late September, and for sixty miles around London, in a great semi-circle to the north-east, north, west and south-west, there was soon scarcely a room to be had. The villages were bulging with commuters. The nightly exodus was enormous.

The transportation available was less than normal and, of course, liable to repeated interruption. Every single main line terminus was out of action at one time or another, and after heavy raids several were frequently out at once. The tubes worked remarkably well, but they too had bombs, or un-exploded bombs, on their lines while, as will be seen, many tube stations suffered direct hits. There were not a great many private cars at that time: many had been requisitioned, and petrol was rationed. The buses ran, particularly in the central areas, with remarkable regularity though frequently making lengthy detours because of cratered roads or, again, because of UXBs. In the suburbs, in the very beginning, they simply stopped when the warning went, and the passengers were ordered to a shelter. This, however, did not go on for long. But the bus queues were endless.

An American, Basil Woon, described a trip into London from Shepperton, which is some twenty miles west of the flat he had in Bloomsbury during the early days of the Blitz. He and his wife went to catch the bus connecting with the

8.35, but there was, as usual, an Alert that evening, and the bus did not arrive. So they walked the two miles to the station, almost running the last few hundred yards. The 8.35 arrived at 10.35. There had been an 'interruption' on the line. At Kingston the guard announced that the train would go no further. They went out into the darkness, still some fifteen miles from Central London, and groped their way to the bus stop. After a longish wait a blacked-out bus loomed up, headed for Kew Bridge. They took it. There were bright fires over London. At Richmond tube station they got out, to take the Southern Line. There was a train, but it was only going to Barnes. So they tried the District Line. Here there were two trains, one to Earl's Court and one to Broad Street. Though neither station is anywhere near Bloomsbury, Broad Street is beyond it, and Mr Woon assumed that this train might stop at King's Cross. The train pulled out at 11.30 and, after half an hour, stopped somewhere on the line. They remained in it until one o'clock, mostly under the seat, and then got out to find themselves near Islington, which was in flames. They walked home, arriving at twenty past five.

This suburban journey of over seven hours duration at an average speed of under three miles an hour was not, of course, typical, but on the other hand it was certainly not unusual. Almost everyone who commuted into London during this period made at least one such journey. And even when the journey went comparatively smoothly, it was all excessively and exasperatingly slow. To stand in a mammoth bus queue or to sit in a packed and motionless train for three quarters of an hour or more is hard enough on the nerves at the best of times. To be thus forcibly immobilised while the light fades and the certainty increases that the bombers will soon be over is more than infuriating. Yet somehow or other the trains and tubes and buses moved this great mass of people into and out of London daily.

The food situation was, in general, good. Rationing ensured that everyone had a basic, if dull, sufficiency and it was not yet as stringent as it became later in the war. The distribution of food stocks was carried out with great competence by the Ministry in question and only very rarely were there mistakes made, and people left without food, as happened in some of the dock areas in early September. And this competent distribution of food, and its sufficiency, undoubtedly contributed greatly to the remarkably high morale of the Londoners. They were tired and they were often frightened, but at least they were not hungry. Had they had to go through the Blitz on the rations of 1944, and after the exhaustion of five years of war, they might have proved far less resilient. That is perhaps why so many people say today that they found the flying bombs far worse than the Blitz.

If food was adequate and, in general, well distributed, many other items rapidly became very hard to find. A typical minor horror of the war was that decent toilet paper became rapidly unobtainable. A major one for many people was the difficulty in buying cigarettes. Just why cigarettes should have become so essential a part of twentieth-century warfare, it is hard to say. Almost any volume of officers' letters from the 1914-18 war is full of references to tins of Gold Flakes gratefully received, while the privates actually sang about their Woodbines and the matches to light them with. It was the same in the Second World War, and Field-Marshal Montgomery's pleasant habit of handing out cigarettes to the troops certainly contributed more to his rapid achievement of popularity in the Eighth Army than did the two cap badges in his beret. Indeed, so automatic was the gesture of reaching for a cigarette during a halt on the march, during a pause when digging, during a lull in battle, that it is hard now to imagine what, say, Henry V's soldiers did with their first five minutes after Agincourt was won.

During the Blitz, though cigarettes did not disappear, they became hard to find. They were not rationed, but shopkeepers rapidly put them under the counter and would sell only to their regulars, or sometimes at black market prices. Meanwhile a host of hitherto unknown brands of cigarettes appeared on the market, with weird names which even now I dare not repeat for fear of the libel laws. These fags were often quite disgusting. Some were made of an almost non-inflammable, flannel-like tobacco. Others were so dry and badly packed that when held vertically all the tobacco ran out of the bottom end. Others again used to hiss and crackle like miniature fireworks. And even to buy these horrors it was often necessary to visit a score of tobacconists, or to queue. The cigarette shortage was a real hardship to many during these months.

Drink, another near-essential in times of danger and protracted strain, was not so hard to find, though spirits were soon difficult to obtain by the bottle. The pubs had plenty of beer, but there was a shortage of glasses, and some publicans asked customers to bring their own. The restaurants and hotels had plenty of wine, particularly German wines of which large stocks had been bought in anticipation of the war: the rapid collapse of France had taken the wine-importers, too, by surprise, and French wines became rare and very expensive.

With the cinemas all closing by nine o'clock at the latest, what entertainment there was in the East End was to be found in the pubs. It was not much. A Bermondsey man has said: 'When the Blitz started, the trade in the pubs absolutely dropped to nothing. You used to see the habitual drinker pop into the pub for his quick pint, but as soon as he heard a bomb drop he was out back again into the shelter. I know two or three publicans, after the Blitz started, that would have willingly given their pubs away to anybody that wanted them. One publican has told me that during the Blitz his customers would remain in the house until the warning went, and then dash out. He, of course, would have to remain on the premises, and one evening he turned to look at his optic and found that the bombs had caused him to drink one whole bottle of whisky on his own—much to his surprise.' And well he might, standing there alone among all those mirrors and bottles, particularly since there was a curious rumour current in the

East End that pubs were more likely to be hit than houses. (This arose probably because a bombed pub is more of an eye-catcher than a bombed cottage: but it may be something atavistic, connected with thunderbolts and the evils of drink.)

In Bethnal Green a shelter warden has said: 'They always had a little courage on Saturday night. If you came early, six o'clock was the usual time, Mum and Dad would leave the kiddies with some of the relations that didn't drink or didn't want a drink, and of course Mum and Dad would go out. They'd go very near the shelter to the little pub, and of course if Hitler was a little bit kinder, and he'd let them have an extra one, of course they'd come back merry and bright.'

Later there were entertainments of a sort inside the shelters, as will be described in the next chapter; but to begin with, these few rapid drinks at the local were almost the only relaxation available in the East End. For those who did not enjoy this, and perhaps particularly for young girls in the East End, life was drab and dreary indeed. One East End woman, a girl at the time, has said, with pardonable exaggeration: 'From 1940 to 1945 there was just no such thing as theatres or dancing or cinema. We all just finished working, the sirens went, we had some tea and went straight to the shelter, and there we just talked or read and listened to the bombs falling, and hoped we'd still be there the next day. The next day just go to work and the same thing over again.'

The West End preserved a night life of a sort. One by one the theatres closed, partly because it was difficult to run them, but chiefly because attendance fell to almost nothing. Only the Windmill Theatre stayed open throughout. As is well-known, the Windmill Theatre, whose slogan since those days has been 'WE NEVER CLOSED', is a non-stop revue which relies to some extent for its evergreen appeal on young comedians, many of whom have later become stars, but principally on a great many beautiful girls who dance in elegant costumes noted for flamboyance or brevity, who sing, or who pose, far up-stage and motionless, in the nude. It, too, suffered heavy financial loss in the early days of the Blitz, though the determination of its owner, Mr Vivian van Damm, to keep it open at all costs was well repaid by the enormous publicity his theatre received. But here, too, the audiences sank to negligible proportions. A former Windmill girl has told this little tale of the Blitz in its early days:

'The air raid sounded and to our amazement the entire audience got up and left, with the exception of one man sitting in the middle of the front row.' Since they still had an audience, the show went on. 'At the end of the show we were all very curious to know why this very brave man had sat through, and we asked the stage manager if he knew. He said: "Oh, yes, the little man asked the front of the house manager, on his way out, why the entire audience got up and went. And he had the greatest difficulty in explaining to him that the air raid warning had gone." Because, you see, the poor man was stone deaf.'

Presumably he had not gone to the Windmill to enjoy the comedians' jokes or even the singers' songs.

Later the theatres began to re-open, some at mid-day—such as the Arts Theatre, where ballet was performed—some in the afternoon or early evening. There were mid-day concerts between the now bare walls of the National Gallery, and these attracted large crowds. The unbombed cinemas were also mostly open in the daytime. But the evenings were inevitably bleak, besides being dangerous.

The attitude of the authorities towards entertainment generally had been a somewhat ambiguous one. When the war first began all theatres had been closed and, for all intents and purposes, all sporting events cancelled by order of the Government. One reason for this was the fear of crowds collecting and the consequent dangers should air raids occur. However, this puritanical decree also undoubtedly appealed to that segment of Britain which regards gaiety as sinful at all times: for such people it is presumably even worse to enjoy oneself in wartime than in peacetime. Mr Winston Churchill, as he then was, was emphatically not of this persuasion, and he brought pressure on his Cabinet colleagues to relax regulations which in any case were obviously futile during the phoney war. With the collapse of France and the imminence of invasion the cry for more austerity was raised again. It seemed to many people genuinely shocking that nightclubs should be open while men were dying. A number of them were therefore closed by the police. This attempt by the Metropolitan Police, however, to prevent anyone not eating in an expensive restaurant from securing a drink after 10.30 or 11 o'clock proved, as usual, a labour of Sisyphus. The result was simply the opening of many more smaller, and often less reputable, clubs. A girl who was then much about the West End has said: 'One phenomenon was the way the small drinking clubs suddenly popped up everywhere. They all had very fancy titles like "The Stars and Stripes", "The Canadian Maple Leaf", Czech names and Polish names, and they all sold atrocious liquor. They were, in fact, clip joints.'

Some provided a convenient evening perch for the street-walkers who could now only promenade their beats in the afternoon. All of them did a thriving trade, particularly as the Blitz went on and people grew less nervous of going out at night. After all, there were few other places for the soldiers and sailors and airmen on leave, many of whom were from the Colonies and Dominions, to go. Even the most enthusiastic amateur of *poses plastiques* cannot sit in the Windmill Theatre indefinitely.

The comforts provided by the big hotels have already been described in the previous chapter. Those with shelters were crowded each night. The same girl, quoted above, has said: 'The best place to be caught in a raid was in a big hotel—preferably the Grosvenor or the Dorchester—they laid things on in style in such places. The shelterers were taken care of. I remember I used to go a good deal to a night club called the Coconut Grove, and in that place the management very kindly allowed most of their staff to bring in their immediate relations.

But then they found that that corner was flea-ridden, so they had to clear everybody out and clean it up.' Other restaurants and nightclubs provided a special 'get-you-home' taxi service for their patrons—taxis being extremely scarce during raids, of course. In fact an evening's entertainment was a problematical business, and there was little telling where it would end up. In Basil Woon's published diary of the September period, *Hell Came to London*, he writes, on September 18th: 'You can dance, dine and sleep at Hatchett's, Hungaria, the Lansdowne, the Mayfair and Grosvenor House. When a girl goes out for the evening these days she brings her pyjamas and make-up with her. This has led to some interesting situations, and it certainly gives the girls an excuse for not getting home till morning.' Some people, with simple tastes, remember London leaves during the period of the Blitz as times of splendid gaiety.

They were the young. The girl who went to the Coconut Grove has said: 'The war was still reasonably new. It was exciting, a terrible thing to say, but it was. After all, when you're twenty-three years old a stimulus is a stimulus. There was a good deal too much drinking. On the other hand I was scared stiff of bombing, and I don't mind admitting it. I wasn't terribly afraid of dying, but the thought of being maimed, losing legs and arms and eyes, was frightening and horrible.' And another girl, of the same age but of a very different social class, living in Holborn, has said: 'It gave me excitement—I mean it's an awful thing to say, but it did, it gave me a lot of excitement, the raids I mean, they went on for about four hours, didn't they? Those nights used to go on about four or five hours continually bomb-bomb-bombing, I mean. And then of course in the morning the girls used to come in, I used to make them some tea, and they said: "A shocking night!" So I said: "Oh yes", I said, "but I'm still here. It's perfectly all right." '

For the middle-aged, in the suburbs, life was not gay and the excitement, one may fairly assume, was not appreciated.

Croydon, once a country village, has long been swallowed up into London. It is, in general, a most respectable suburb, streets and streets of those small houses whose owners take great pride in the appearance of their front gardens and of their cars. For those whose lives fall either in the central city or the country, it seems, above all else, dull, these miles after mile of little, neat houses, often pretentiously named. There is a wide belt of them around London, around most of the great cities of the Western world. In them live the men who do the dull clerical work of our civilisation, dull, safe jobs in banks and other offices. They are not vocal, for their sons who are go elsewhere. But Croydon, too, was bombed and heavily. Here, in the rather stilted, somewhat pretentious and yet extraordinarily characteristic prose of a local, anonymous writer, printed in the borough's official *Croydon and the Second World War*, is a description of Croydon under its share of the bombs, when all those houses, so similar to the passing motorist, so very personal to the people behind the black-out curtains, were the almost anonymous targets for high-explosive and burning phosphorus.

'A clear evening, with some clouds indeed, a high wind chasing smoke-like clouds across the disc of a moon nearing the full in the eastern sky. One walked along the road on the ridge, where the pleasant villas, homes of a seemingly contented race of people in days of peace, now slept in that fateful quiet which is characteristic of days of war. Only an hour ago, or even less, the last red flush in the west ended a troubled sort of day. The planes in their arrow formations had filled the sky for hours with that rolling, throbbing, which is the sound of high battling speed. . . . In the sunlight, with a blue dome above, the manoeuvres and spinnings of the planes, enemy or friend, were not so dreadful; they had sometimes a beauty, as of glistening dragonflies when the sun struck them into silver.

'But at night?

'Here all was expectant silence. All the windows were curtained or shuttered; some with the rather pathetic trelliswork of adhesive paper over them, which would never save them from the blast of the Teutonic bomb. All, too, seemed so silent, for in this November time night came almost immediately on the heels of mid-day. Dusk closed in savourless, inexorable; the streets unlighted, the traffic noises weird, heard queerly and insistently, as if they infringed the natural, the lawful, silence. Noises, too, that were sometimes mis-interpreted. A motor bus starting up was very like the noise made by the onset of the siren. An electric train which had rattled past retreating into the distance and, one could not help feeling, into the safety of it, did so with a hum that mocked the sound of the heavy enemy bomber. A time of acute sense, when the wind made its own contribution to the speech of a distrait earth and worried the listening ear. Other sounds, whatever they were, seemed intrusive, interrupting the task —which was to listen, listen. Behind these houses were people; one here, two or three there, but all more or less lonely; because in these days few dared to visit. The fear of being caught in the dark, and unsheltered, outweighed even the fear of being trapped ratlike in the house. Friends rarely met now; sometimes hurriedly in passing in the day, with a smile and a word of cheer; for our resilience has been wonderful; we awake thankful and almost immediately try to encounter life as it was. It never is as it was, but "new every morning" is the attempt to make it so. Night falls like a shutter on a brilliantly lighted shop window—only in relative contrast, we mean, because our towns are not brilliant these days. . . . Anyhow, at dusk the shutters fell; people gathered in anxious crowds or knots at the bus stops, eager to get home. There was little of the erstwhile eager rush to pictures, concerts, restaurants or those homes of the sociables which all towns usually possess. A few soldiers and their girls—it may be a few hardy civilians —went to such of these places as found it possible to function with gravely reduced attendances and takings. Most went home. Home, too, on this November evening soon after four. How brief is the unlighted November afternoon—but we have already said that. Going home—to what? To the certainty that within an hour they will be sitting, or lying, or crouching, listening, wondering, hoping and, perhaps, praying: because a daemonic force has loosed on us the ugliest, most vicious, cowardly and indiscriminate form of assault.'

This is one man's picture. Mr Gerard Kealey, who also lived in Croydon at this time, has described Blitz life there in slightly less grim terms:

'One's social life continued more or less normally. We invited friends for coffee, if not for dinner—dinner was more difficult because of the food situation—but I do recall friends coming in for coffee. Possibly we indulged in a game of chess. If a raid came on during such visits, then often our friends stayed on, and we seemed to drink innumerable cups of tea or coffee throughout the long hours of night, until the All Clear sounded, which was usually in the early hours of dawn. We still went to the local cinema, although the difficulty was that you had to walk some mile and a half, because the buses were so infrequent, even if they ran at all at night. There was the usual difficulty of getting home, and one was inclined to dodge from shelter to shelter—the shelter of people's porches, I mean —to avoid the falling shrapnel. However, it was always worthwhile. There was the excitement of seeing something different and experiencing some new emotion apart from the bombs. I remember the cinema seemed to be well attended—it must have been, otherwise they wouldn't have kept open.'

Once again, it must be stressed that generalisations about Londoners are inevitably tentative in the extreme. However, it does seem that while the disasters, dangers, minor discomforts and irritations were much the same for all except the very rich —and many of those who had chosen to remain in London accepted them voluntarily, by joining the Civil Defence services, or, in the case of women, the ambulance service—the young found a considerable stimulus in the excitement, and even a sense of freedom: in most young people there is a happy streak of anarchy. For the middle aged it was a dreary, exhausting, but just tolerable ordeal. It was the old who suffered most, since for them adjustment is always more difficult. Dr Morton has said:

'Very adequate provision was made for young children with their mothers to be evacuated, but there was no official Government scheme for old people. For the time being, at the beginning of the Blitz, the old people stood it very well, but gradually they were the first to show the strain of the prolonged bad nights, the prolonged bombing, having their windows broken, their ceilings down, and all the discomforts of the Blitz. As the winter months came on, the voluntary organisations did their best to try and evacuate the old people privately. We at the Bermondsey Mission opened a house down at Brighton. . . . It's the old people who first feel the strain of these things.'

For young, middle-aged and old alike, one of the more unpleasant official forecasts was proved totally incorrect. This was the expected psychological effects of the raids. It will be recalled that the Government's medical advisers before the war had anticipated several million cases of acute neurosis or hysteria. Though the Government did not accept those figures, mass neurosis was certainly expected. In fact, quite the contrary occurred. During the Blitz the number of persons with neurotic illnesses or mental disorders attending clinics and hospitals actually declined. There was no increase in insanity: there were less suicides: drunkenness declined by over 50 per cent: there was less disorderly behaviour in public: and only juvenile delinquency increased, which increase can be largely attributed to the break-up of family life.

These facts are obviously, like most statistical reports on civilians during this period, questionable in detail. But the general picture is perfectly clear. There was no increase in neurosis then, nor has there been any subsequent, or delayed-action, increase recognisable to the doctors which can be attributed to the Blitz. Indeed, the contrary seems to have been the case. And is it not possible at least that this relaxation of nervous tension is connected with the relaxation of social rigidity described earlier in this chapter, to the friendliness of people towards one another during the Blitz, the feeling of excitement among the young, of being so very alive, of the sweeping away of social and sexual barriers? This is all most unscientific and literary: but at least, unpleasant though it was, the Blitz not only did not drive the people mad, but apparently kept quite a number of them sane.

CHAPTER SIX

THE PICTURE that we have of the Blitz, more perhaps even than that of roaring fires, of collapsing buildings, and of aeroplanes throbbing high in the night sky, is a picture of great communal shelters, of men and women in ungainly attitudes sleeping in huge vaults and under sombre arches, on tube platforms, in the long, thin, pipe-like tunnel of the then uncompleted Liverpool Street extension.

In fact comparatively few people went to such shelters, which were only some of the many forms of shelter available. Though the figures were higher for the public shelters during September and October, by early November—that is to say, while the Blitz in all its intensity was still going on, and when the first shelter census was taken—more than half the population never went to shelters at all. Of the 40 per cent who did, 27 per cent, or again more than half, spent the night in their private domestic shelters of which the Anderson was the commonest type; 9 per cent slept in public shelters, that is to say in the brick street shelters, the large underground shelters and the arches: while only 4 per cent went down into the tubes. Yet it was the tube shelterers whom everybody in London saw, sleeping or dozing on the platforms while the underground trains pulled in, the passengers alighted, and then, with a rapidly diminishing rumble, the trains vanished again down their black tunnels. The incongruity of large numbers of people leading their intimate lives in this most public of places was striking in the extreme.

This may not be the only reason that the shelterers, and particularly the tube shelterers, have remained so clear in public memory. At least a contributory one is that their strange slumbers were recorded by Mr Henry Moore in a series of drawings which immediately attracted great attention, and which were probably the only major works of pictorial art to spring directly from the Blitz. In any immensely complicated and heterogeneous series of events and overlapping situations, an artist will tend to see and portray one aspect. If he is a great artist, the aspect that has caught his eye, and that he has recorded, will become for posterity the visible reality of this mass of confused and often paradoxical events. It may be a single picture; it may be a series. Thus the Napoleonic occupation of Spain had a thousand facets. Yet because Goya saw and recorded the shooting of hostages and the cruelty of starving brigands, our vision of those years is inevitably connected with, perhaps based on, the brutality, the ferocious glee, of scarecrows about camp fires. In 1940, had some other great artist been interested in, say, flames and smoke, or the nature and texture of rubble, that image might have been the dominating one. As it is, when we think of the Blitz we see again those pathetic, lump-like and yet breathing figures waiting hollow-eyed or in their public sleep.

Yet they were, as stated, a very small minority. Most people who remained in London simply went to bed, at home. They probably modified their arrangements, shifting their beds downstairs, under the stairs if that were possible, when their home was a house. In a block of flats people would move away from the windows, and might have mattresses in the halls or corridors where there was no danger of flying glass. If theirs was the type of house with a basement, they would probably sleep there, having perhaps first reinforced it with beams or double walls and even, occasionally, steel struts, often with their most valuable possessions and irreplaceable papers beside them. For most of the middle classes, this was the full extent of the precautions taken. Furthermore, a sort of pride, or even of snobbery, developed about sheltering in public. And there can be little doubt that many people, who would secretly have preferred to go down and down into the deepest of tubes, were held back by the fear of losing face, for to do so would have meant the admission of another fear; and they had been trained since childhood to believe that the fear of death, though natural enough, is one that must never be displayed.

When houses, as opposed to office blocks, were bombed there were almost always people to be dug out of the rubble, alive or dead, by the rescue services or found in perilous situations on upper floors. These were, of course, the people who had not taken shelter. Mr Miles Mordaunt, who was in the Borough of Holborn, has said:

'There had been a raid warning on for a couple of hours, but we'd got used to that sort of thing and hadn't taken any particular notice. There'd been no gunfire in our immediate neighbourhood or any sounds of bombs falling. Very soon an anti-aircraft battery in a public park no great distance from us, perhaps a mile, started firing wildly, and shortly afterwards we heard the drone of planes sounding pretty well overhead. This was followed by the usual assortment of noises of falling bombs. It seemed extraordinarily varied. Although people very quickly became expert in identifying various types, I never did achieve any expertise in this matter. They all sounded as if they had been made very clumsily, and came down like old tins of corrugated iron, making weird flapping and shaking sounds in the air. I think it was discovered afterwards that the Germans had deliberately put screamers and banshee sounds into them for no other reason than to worry the civilian population.' This is not quite correct: screaming bombs had already been used against ground troops, both in Poland and in the French campaign. A number were dropped on London. 'When we'd had a few bombs fairly close, as far as one could judge from an indoor listening post, we decided to go out into the street and look. We went out into the road and looked up and down. A neighbouring street appeared to have turned into a river of red fire, because there was a very strong glow coming up from it on to what we slowly realized

137

were not low rain clouds, but smoke clouds billowing and rolling along the tops of the houses.

'As we watched there was a shattering explosion in the street, and the front of one house disappeared, leaving it like a series of super-imposed stage sets, with the various rooms and their wall-papers all starkly shining in the red light. At about the third floor one room stood out very sharply, for the white tiling—it was a bathroom—caught the light. We heard some wild calls, but it was impossible to tell where they were coming from at first. We walked towards the scene, and probably because the white tiling caught our eye, we looked up again, and could just make out a figure that seemed to be stuck to the wall. We found out afterwards that a man was holding a towel-rail in one hand, and standing precariously on a ridge consisting of about half a tile and the bit of cement holding it to the wall.

'Before we could get there the fire brigade were on the scene. The man was rescued and complained bitterly that he'd been left up there for days, as he thought, and had had a nightmare time screaming, when he thought nobody would come to his assistance. In fact the fire brigade was very efficient. I admired the way they had a turntable up there, or a long ladder, in no time and picked the man down. It was of course no concern of ours, they got him away to hospital, and he no doubt has lived happily ever after. But at the time he was a very angry man, and the Home Office were compelled eventually to have an enquiry into his complaint. Having observed the facts myself, I never afterwards paid much attention to the reports of anybody who'd been too close to an explosion. They were usually, to say the least of it, highly subjective, if not wholly nightmareish and imaginary.'

Mr William Sansom tells the story of a Westminster man who arrived home very late, and did not realise that the house in which he lived had been sliced in two. He climbed up the stairs and, luckily for him, went to bed in the half-a-bedroom that still stood. He was brought down by ladder.

The tales of people dug out of collapsed houses are innumerable, and some are quite astonishing, people being not infrequently pinned down by rubble and beams or furniture for days on end and surviving; others being dug out only to die of shock or of internal wounds when safely in hospital. There were many very weird escapes. One that I was told by Alderman Smith, G.C., the former Chief Warden of Poplar, seems to me worth repeating.

A pretty and extremely respectable Poplar girl was taking a bath when her parents' house was hit. By some fluke, and the effects of bomb blast were often extremely odd, the tub was tipped upside down, with the girl still in it, and thus provided her with shelter from the mass of bricks and rubble in which she was buried. The rescue men dug a shaft from the top to get the buried person out, and when they lifted the tub off her were not unnaturally surprised to discover a beautiful, naked, uninjured girl. Her reaction was one of acute embarrassment: East End girls are very modest. Warden Smith found a flannel nightdress in the rubble, filthy but still better than nothing, and this she gratefully put on at the bottom of the shaft. She was then hoisted up it by means of a block and tackle. Unfortunately on the way up her grimy nightdress caught on a nail or a long splinter, and when she emerged at the top of the ruin she was once again as naked and pink as Venus rising from the Cypriot sea. This time Warden Smith gave her his greatcoat. But so acute was her shame that, as he rather ruefully remarked, not only did she lack the courage to return him his overcoat, but to this day she always crosses to the far side of the Bow Road when she sees him coming towards her.

The most widely used domestic shelter during the Blitz was the Anderson. (The Morrison, a table-like affair of steel and wire mesh, which was erected in downstairs rooms and which, like the young lady's tub, could support the weight of a small collapsed house, only began to be distributed in the spring of 1941, and therefore played an insignificant part during the big Blitz.) The Anderson fully lived up to expectations.

It was never intended to be able to stand up to a direct hit, but it was able to withstand the blast from a 500lb. bomb bursting in the open as near as ten yards away, and on many occasions those small shelters did even better than this. Alderman Smith has said:

'I have seen an Anderson on the edge of a crater, where the people in that Anderson shelter were quite okay, not even touched, but if they'd walked out of the front of the shelter they'd have got into a crater which was about twenty feet deep. So you can realise how near they was to catching a nasty knock.

'I've also seen an Anderson shelter where a bomb had dropped quite near, the place was afire, and two women and two kiddies was in this here shelter. So you can understand what we felt like when we got on with the job. The National Fire Service put their hose on the top of this here shelter, and in a very, very short time we had the emergency door down. We got these people out of the shelter, and today I see them walking up and down the road in this borough. But every time my missus opens the oven I think about that shelter. They'd have only had to stop there a little while longer—and without the co-operation of the Fire Service—and I'm sure they'd have come out like a rabbit comes out of your stove on a Sunday.'

One of the disadvantages of the Anderson was that, being half buried, and being embanked with earth, it was very liable to fill with water. People did their best to arrange drainage, but this was not simple, and the firemen, in addition to their other, very intensive duties, had to spend a lot of time pumping Andersons dry. Nor were they easily warmed in the winter nights. Another disadvantage of the Anderson, as opposed the communal shelter, was a psychological one. Every crash and roar was audible to the shelterers, and during the raids it soon became apparent that noise was the prime cause of fear. But taken all in all they were extremely successful. Even an Anderson, however, could become a deathtrap.

Hartland Way, by Addington Golf Course in the southern suburbs, is a street of pretty, gardened villas. On September 11th a Royal Air Force fighter crashed into two houses. The petrol from the wreck caught alight and poured, blazing, into a shelter where a young wife with two children and a woman friend had taken cover. They all died.

The brick street shelters, originally intended for passers-by or for the inhabitants of tenements and flats without the space for the erection of Andersons, and given the inelegant name of 'communal domestic surface shelters', did not enjoy either popularity or a good reputation. This was largely the fault of a Ministry of Home Security clerk and his superiors. Late in 1939, in order to economise on cement, which was in short supply, the Ministry issued an instruction that when building surface shelters lime should replace cement in the ratio of 2:1 in the mortar used. This proved satisfactory. But in April of 1940 the Ministry issued new instructions which were so badly worded that many borough engineers took them to mean that mortar consisting of lime and sand only should now be used. In July the Ministry issued new instructions in which it made plain that ungauged lime mortar must not be used, but no reference was made to the earlier, ambiguous instructions. Thus the brick and concrete shelters built between April and July were left unfortified until the bombs actually fell, whereupon some of them collapsed. The most common disaster was for the roof, a concrete slab, to be lifted by the blast of a nearby bomb and then to crash down again on the brick walls which, being insecurely mortared, would collapse, crushing the shelterers. The solution, which was rapidly carried out, was to build a second, outer wall and also to enlarge the flat concrete roof so that it overlapped the sides and could move a few inches one way or another without falling off its supports.

The brick and concrete shelters, in addition to their unfortunate history, were in some ways the most uncomfortable of all. They lacked the privacy of an Anderson since they held some fifty people, but they did not provide the measure of communal relief to be found in the huge, popular shelters. Also they looked flimsy, and people feared that their flat roofs were conspicuous from the air, and that the German airmen therefore aimed at them deliberately. This was, of course, pure nonsense, but was nonetheless quite widely believed: in some streets the shelterers tried to hide their shelter by covering the flat roof with branches. They were, at least to begin with, cold and damp and dark. Later stoves were provided, and electric light. Hooligans used to steal the bulbs and use the shelters by day for activities quite unconnected with civilian defence. So the shelters had to be locked, but since they had to be easily and quickly available it was not enough simply to give the key to the local warden. Glass panels were built into the doors, as is often seen with fire-fighting equipment in hotels and other public buildings. In an emergency the glass panel could be broken and the door opened from the inside. The hooligans often broke the panels, stole the bulbs and carried on as before. The brick and concrete street shelters were never popular, and in those parts of London where other forms of shelter were available they were usually left almost empty. I remember dodging into one during a very heavy raid on Chelsea. There were two old women seated in it, beneath the feeble light of a blueish bulb too dim for reading and knitting. They both looked utterly wretched. And well they might.

The only other type of Government-sponsored shelter, at least in the beginning, was the trench shelter. These were usually in the parks. Many had been dug with almost panic haste during the Munich crisis at the request of the Home Office. To begin with they were simply holes in the ground, but during the following winter the boroughs were told to make these crumbling trenches into permanent shelters, four foot deep, capable of holding 10 per cent of their populations. They were lined and roofed with concrete or steel and were provided with closed entrances, but were not fitted with duck-boards, seats or sanitary arrangements. They thus came to resemble narrow surface shelters, half underground and with earth floors. With the outbreak of war in 1939 this programme was accelerated. Large orders were placed for pre-cast concrete trench linings, but these proved unsatisfactory: they not only let in water, but buckled when the raids actually began. These somewhat primitive shelters were supposed to be small, in accordance with the Government's policy of dispersal, and, like the street shelters, to hold about 50 persons each. Many, however, were considerably larger. Duckboards and benches were installed in some, but not all, of them before the Blitz began. They were more popular than the street shelters; the people felt safer underground and the trench shelters had three feet of earth on top of them. Also they were believed, erroneously, to be warmer. When the Blitz began, they were many people's first choice.

Mr Shepherd was an air raid warden, and he has described these shelters, in Bethnal Green, as follows:

'I speak of Victoria Park trench shelters, knowing them very well indeed. As Post Wardens we were always encouraged by our Chief Warden, Sir Wyndham Deedes, to add the personal touch to the shelters by going and visiting them ourselves. Which we did. And the experience when the Blitz first started was something one can never get out of one's mind.

'The first night of the Blitz the park trenches, which held about fourteen hundred and fifty people, was packed from end to end. It was packed so tightly that the Wardens couldn't get through the trenches themselves, but just had to go to each entrance to see that things were just so. But as the Blitz went on various people went away—evacuation—they went to other shelters, and it became a little less troublesome. But I feel that the people that kept to these trench shelters were real courageous, because I have known the time when the water has been well over the duckboards. Almost ankle-deep they've had to sit there, with their feet in the water because there was no room to put them up on the forms. I know various people that had frostbite, and they suffered quite a lot of agony before the arrangements were made for fires and bunks to be put in.

'Incidentally, it was adjoining a barrage balloon site, and these particular trenches were bombed completely round, they had bombs on every part of the shelter but there was no damage done to any individual, no injuries, no nothing at all.' These trenches were not lined with the unfortunate pre-cast concrete slabs, but with steel or ferro-concrete. 'They were a mixed crowd and there was Jewish people, English people, Irish people, but there was a wonderful spirit, and although they had all that to put up with in the first place, they never failed to do what they could for people that were less fortunate.

'Then of course, we had the alterations made to the trenches.' This was, however, not until early in 1941. 'We had fires and bunks and it was wonderful to see how comfortable people made themselves on those bunks. Some of them would be there from six o'clock in the evening till the next morning— in fact, some of them stayed there all the next day. Their husbands, when they came home, came to the shelter and found the dinner on the little fire being kept warm for them.

'We had quite a number of bad bombings, and later we had nurses and doctors stationed in the shelters, and they certainly worked wonderfully well. There were hundreds of tragedies taken into the trenches, and they worked like Trojans. The wonderful part about it was that Jews and Gentiles, all turned out trumps, doing everything, walking backwards and for-wards round the shelters to see what they could do for those that were injured.'

Then there were what the authorities called 'self-chosen' shelters—basements, cellars, arches and other underground places which were, or looked, safe. Some of these had been officially designated as shelters by the boroughs and were strengthened and equipped with blast-proof entrances, anti-gas protection and so on. Others were simply taken over by the people for a number of reasons: because they had been used as shelters in the First World War: because they looked

FALLING BUILDINGS
The City, 30 December, 1940

safe: or for quite illogical reasons of mass psychology. Very big buildings, such as railway stations, gave an often quite illusory impression of safety for reasons of size alone: a cellar on a hillside might seem safe, because its entrance was underground, though the greater expanse of the cavern was covered only by one thin roof. These improvised shelters varied enormously, from the utterly safe vaults of huge modern office buildings to the deathtraps that many railway arches proved to be. Some were clean, warm and comfortable, others indescribably filthy and squalid. It usually proved impossible to eject the shelterers from these places, no matter how unsafe and insanitary they might be. The boroughs, and particularly the East End boroughs, thus found themselves in a quandary. Should they do their best to make these unsafe places as safe and as clean as possible? This would seem to justify their continued occupation. On the other hand, could they leave their people in filth and squalor? The answer in most cases seems to have been to leave these improvised shelters uncared for, to begin with, in the hope that the people would move out of them. When they did not do so, and the public outcry became too great, there was a Government enquiry and the outcome was that the boroughs did what they could to improve conditions.

In Bethnal Green many sheltered under the railway arches. Mrs Rennie says:

'I first started the part-time warden work in 1939, when they was issuing out the gas-masks and things, and I volunteered to fix on the gas-masks and things, but they said I'd be more needed in the shelter, which was quite true, and as soon as the Blitz started I donned my helmet and out I went. And the first thing that met my eyes was the people as they staggered into the shelter, fighting to get in, who should get there first, and the deplorable state of the shelter when I went in. They had issued some sanitary arrangements, which wasn't very good, and that hit you in the face as you walked in. And there was people, partly dressed, sleeping on sacks and old coats, and there was water oozing down the walls, which was very inconvenient.'

In Bermondsey Dr Morton says:

'The tendency was, I think, to find their own form of shelter and go to it, and then always go to the same kind of shelter. Often it was very inadequate shelter, for instance in the arches, and we had some really bad incidents there. It wasn't a safe place, because the arches are very thin at the top, but in the 1918 war they'd sheltered there, and they wanted to shelter again. We had some nasty incidents in the railway arches. They're just honeycombed with passages, and we didn't even have a plan of them. Until they put up blast walls we had bad incidents there, but they felt safe, and I think the salient thing with all the people was that where they thought they were safe, and felt safe, they were safe. You see, everybody had their own kind of burrow.'

But when the arches were hit, these big incidents were horrible. She says:

'Though we might get more casualties in a number of isolated incidents, the thing that really shocked the whole neighbourhood and set people talking and feeling worst were the bigger incidents, such as the Stainer Street Arch (which is under the tracks by London Bridge Station) and the Druid Street Arch. Large numbers of people were killed, sometimes whole families wiped out. Bermondsey is a very small borough, and most people know one another in it. The people have lived there for years and years. They don't come to Bermondsey to live, they've always lived there. It's a little corner of London, and news of tragedies like that just shook everybody. It was on everybody's lips, everybody was shaky after it, and there were more people deciding to evacuate.'

Mr Austen, G.M., was a warden:

'We went down there, to Stainer Street. The warden goes in first. When we got in it was all upside down, the people laying on the floor, wounded and killed. It was filthy with the blood and one thing and another. And it stunk. There was money,

146

too, bags of it all over the place. And we had a job because the lights were out and we had to do it with our torches. You see, he'd dropped a bomb, they reckoned it was over the pub—the pub facing—and they reckoned when the people came out of the pub the light guided the aeroplane and then they dropped it on the railway. There was no fire. It was simply—blasted. We felt sick with the smell of it, and we brought some of the people outside and sent them to hospital.'

To digress for a moment from this matter of shelters, the remark about the light from the pub attracting the bomber's attention is an interesting example of a myth that was widespread during this period. A German pilot has commented as follows:

'Painstaking observation of the black-out regulations was in Germany, too, based on the belief that bomber pilots needed only to see the most minute speck of light in order to dump their bombs on to it. This was, of course, nonsense. Neither a single light, nor a group of lights, was of any help in navigating a plane, if there was nothing else to be seen. In any event London's approximate position was easily detected, even from very far away, owing to the concentration of searchlights. There were a number of recognisable searchlight positions, with groups of massed lights, which our more experienced bomber crews soon learned to use as navigational aids. If they did not expose, and we wished to establish our location more exactly, we would attract their attention, and make them illuminate, by briefly switching on our navigation lights, or firing tracer, or shooting off our guns at their supposed sites. This usually succeeded in drawing their light. Taken all in all, the black-out was extremely thorough in England during this period.'

Indeed, just because it was so unpleasant, people ascribed immense virtues to the black-out, or rather immense perils to its neglect, which dangers were sometimes mixed up with vague and sinister suspicions about 'signalling to the enemy'. In Soho, owing to a wiring fluke, a neon advertising sign suddenly went on during a raid. Because the police and Wardens were not quick enough for their tastes, an angry crowd broke a plate-glass window and smashed the neon sign themselves. On at least one occasion this public fear of lights was indirectly responsible for a tragedy. In Croydon it had been customary to disperse the L.P.T.B. buses at night, but the public objected that the inevitable use of lights, when cleaning them, might attract raiders. They were therefore returned to their depot. When the depot was hit, with the buses tanked up ready for the next day's work, the result was a holocaust. A brave ambulance man, Mr H. Lock Kendell, entered the depot, while a fireman played a hose on him. (The water, he says, came almost scalding from the hydrant.) He succeeded in rescuing several trapped bus drivers and conductors, but fourteen were killed and forty badly burned. This is surely a curious example of the delayed-action effect of a senseless panic, in this case the fear of light. Throughout London at this time it was not just the Wardens who enforced the black-out regulations. An unscreened window would draw immediate shouts, or on occasion brickbats, from passers-by. The public even protested—according to the official publication *Front Line*—when rescue workers, digging out buried persons, used flares or too many torches.

To get the people into the proper shelters, and to discourage them from using the undesirable ones, many expedients were tried. Compulsion was not successful. Persuasion produced better results. In Poplar, in order that the people might be encouraged to use the more suitable shelters, the Council had the clever and original idea of organising open-air dancing in the parks during the fine autumn evenings. The music was relayed over loudspeakers attached to gramophones. When the warning went the dancers and spectators could be easily directed, by loudspeaker, to the proper shelters in or near the park. Order was preserved, chaos avoided and, perhaps equally important, the people tended to arrive at the shelters in a comparatively good humour.

On the other hand, a direct hit on a surface shelter, or a trench shelter, with heavy casualties, would naturally cause much loss of faith in such edifices. In Chelsea, for instance, a reinforced trench shelter in a children's playground, serving a block of working-class flats, was hit in an early raid. The roof cracked and caved in, stunning but not killing five occupants. Simultaneously a water main near that end of the shelter burst. The stunned people were drowned. The inhabitants of that block inevitably lost faith in their shelters and went elsewhere, with considerable bitterness.

It is hardly surprising that in the East End, when the people saw the badly-built street shelters collapse, some preferred to crowd into quite inadequate vaults and cellars.

In West Ham the public took over a great cellar almost as soon as the raids began. It had no adequate ventilation, no sanitary arrangements, and the stone floor was quite unsuitable for sleeping on. People brought in boards, plywood, even newspapers to lie on. However, it was so crowded that there was not even room to lie: they had to squat. Sanitary conditions rapidly became unspeakable, and the dangers of disease great. Nevertheless, by the end of October nothing had been done: no flooring laid, no drainage or lavatories installed, and all the mayor could think to say was that these premises were not recognised as a public shelter.

The most notorious of these great shelters was the Tilbury shelter, which was actually part of the Liverpool Street goods station, off the Commercial Road, Stepney. The story of this shelter is a complicated one, and has a political aspect, in that the Communists led the agitation to occupy it and, when it was occupied, claimed this as a triumph. It was later visited by the Russian Ambassador, and the shelterers sang the *Red Flag* enthusiastically. The whole business caused a lot of head-shaking in Whitehall.

The Tilbury shelter, too, had been used in the First World War. Part of it, cellars and vaults, had been taken over as a public shelter for 3,000 people in the Second World War.

The other part was the loading yard of a huge warehouse, below the level of the Commercial Road, but not of the side roads. Above it the massive warehouse was supported on great steel girders, which looked safe enough. There were large loading bays, piled with food and flanked by roads and a railroad line. There were outside walls.

Mr Ritchie Calder, who visited the Tilbury shelter in the early days, has described it in these words:

'When the official shelter was crowded out, those in charge of the other parts allowed the people to use it, on compassionate grounds. The result was unbelievable. Estimates of the numbers using this expropriated shelter varied, but on a wet night when I was there, extra people came in from their domestic shelters which had flooded, and the shelter wardens calculated that in the two halves there were over 14,000 people.

'People queued up from midday, waiting for the gates to open at four-thirty in the afternoon. Service men on leave kept places for their families out at work. Unevacuated school-children were "proxies" for their relatives. Old folks in bath-chairs, cripples, children in perambulators, and men and women of every age and condition lined up, oblivious of daylight sirens and even dog-fights overhead, because if they took shelter they lost their places in the queue and their "option" on their favourite sleeping-spot for the night. When the gates were opened the police linked hands to stem the rush down the slope, but it was like holding back a stampede of buffaloes. Usually a way was made for the aged, and for mothers with perambulators and young children (although the police got wise to the fact that some were getting priority for perambu-lators which contained not babies, but the family valuables). Sometimes women and children got crushed in the rush.

'At night, it presented a scene unequalled by anything west of Suez. One had to pick one's way along the roads between the recumbent bodies. Until the Ministry of Food intervened and had the cartons of margarine and the other food stuffs removed, people slept in the bays, beside or on the food. To begin with there was practically no sanitary provision, and the filth seeped into the blankets or was spread by trampling feet. Cartons filled with margarine were sometimes stacked up to form latrines.

'Every race and colour in the world were represented there —Whites, Negroes, Chinese, Hindus, Polynesians, Levantines, East Europeans, Jews, Gentiles, Moslems, and probably Sun-Worshippers were all piled there in miscellaneous confusion. Seamen came in for a few hours between tides. Prostitutes paraded. Hawkers sold clammy fried fish, which cloyed the fug with greasy sickliness. The police broke up free fights. And children slept.'

Strange as it may seem, some people from the West End used to go sight-seeing to this and other such shelters, even as before the war they would make up jolly parties to visit Chinatown or do a riverside pub-crawl in Wapping. Needless to say, slumming of this sort was not at all popular with the shelterers singing their songs of solidarity in Stepney, and at least one party of sight-seers was quite roughly handled before being ejected. But for those whose tastes ran to such spectacles, there was plenty to be seen, and smelt, in the tubes, for the trifling cost of a ticket.

The Government's policy of keeping the tubes free of shelterers failed almost at once. The people simply bought a 1½d. ticket, went down below, and remained there. To turn them out into the raids would have needed not only a huge police force but also a callousness which was not greatly in evidence at this time.

Mr Sidney Toy, the celebrated architect, was a member of the voluntary watch that protected St Paul's during this period. On November 8th, 1940, he was on duty at the Cathedral, and he came in that evening from Epsom to stand watch. He has described his journey in these words, which Dr Matthews quotes in his book about St Paul's in wartime:

'Tonight my journey to St Paul's was varied and protracted. I arrived at Epsom station at 7 p.m., prepared to take the first train going to any of the stations in London. At 7.30 p.m. I boarded a train said to be going to London Bridge, though I had doubts as to its final destination. At Peckham Rye the train came to a stop and all the passengers were turned out on to the platform. It was pitch dark and raining heavily; I had neither raincoat nor umbrella. Groping my way down the stairs and through the dark passages of the station I got out into Rye Lane; the street was dark, dismal and deserted, and there were no buses. I made my way towards Peckham High Street; after a considerable time of waiting I saw a tramcar going westwards and boarded it; the conductor told me that he did not know where his destination was likely to be—it all depended upon events. However, the tramcar took me to the Oval where I took the Underground to London Bridge. Going down to the Oval station I had to pick my way along a narrow path bordered on either side by people lying prone: men, women, boys, girls, babies, lying three deep on either side on mattresses and blankets spread out on the floor. Down in the station the platform was crowded with people from end to end about five deep, only a narrow pathway at the edge of the platform, two feet wide, being reserved for circulation. Here were people of every conceivable character, appearance and age—thousands of them. The largest number were lying on mattresses and other bedding material; others were raised on one arm or were sitting up; others again were marching up and down the pathway at the edge of the platform. Young girls, having to all appearances the time of their lives, formed the bulk of this last section. All the stations we passed through were similarly crowded. The train had its windows covered with opaque or black-out material and when it stopped at a station and the doors were opened from the centre the effect was remarkably like that of a stage when the curtains are raised. Here was a stage, brilliantly lighted, and packed with humanity in all stages of animation; and here was no histrionic display but intense reality. Having arrived at London Bridge I walked to the Cathedral.'

A Canadian girl has said:

'It wasn't, in those early days, considered quite *de rigueur* to go into the tube, but I was a fearful coward, I hated the bombs, and I went in the tube. I remember once, after a particularly bad raid, patting the walls of the tube and thinking: Bless you, I don't care how long I'm in London, I shall always feel grateful to the good old London tube.'

An English girl had a contrary reaction:

'I only travelled through them, you know, from one place to another. I used to see the people arriving, I mean they used to arrive about five o'clock, half past five or six at night, with their bundles and their bits and pieces. And I think of the whole war it was the most *demoralising* and *depressing* sight I ever saw, because to see people in this country . . . I mean, one reads and knows about refugees from other countries, the sort that comes up against it, but you never expected to see your own people doing that. And it was a terrible thing to see them swinging on those hammocks, the children and mothers and fathers and all. It was terrible.'

The reference to hammocks might be taken to be Cockney poetic licence for the wire bunks erected later in the winter. But in some tubes at least there were hammocks, slung between the rails over which the trains run during the day: and in those hammocks children slept: there was also almost everything else.

The Canadian girl, now Mrs Blair-Hickman, has said:

'Down on the platform there was a wonderful couple who were Belgian, and they used to bring with them a complete double feather bed, with all the trimmings, sheets, blankets and what have you. Furthermore they undressed, and each night they made up their bed, got in, and went to sleep like a truly married couple. Mr Hitler wasn't going to separate those two.'

The number of people using the tubes for shelter reached its maximum in late September—according to the London Passenger Transport Board's publication *London Transport*

Carried On, on September 27th, with 177,000 people in the Tubes—and then gradually declined. During raids in the winter and spring the number averaged something over 100,000, on raid-free nights between seventy and eighty thousand. Not all these people slept in the seventy-nine active tube stations used as shelters: disused stations such as South Kentish Town, Museum and City Road were especially opened as shelters; trains no longer ran through the Aldwych branch, which was largely given over to shelterers; while the then uncompleted Liverpool Street extension, running through Bethnal Green to Stratford and Leytonstone, was one vast, elongated shelter holding an estimated ten thousand people.

In the beginning it was all confusion. Since the Government had informed the L.P.T.B. that the tube stations were not to be used as shelters, but had not had the heart to eject the shelterers, the arrangements were excessively makeshift. The system, if so it can be called, in the early days was that shelterers were allowed into the tubes after four o'clock in the afternoon, but not before. Therefore, to be sure of obtaining a place, women would start to queue outside the tube stations, or would send their children to queue for them, as early as ten o'clock in the morning. The gangs of youths who used to make a spivish living selling places in theatre queues, now turned to these more vital queues since there were no theatres open. They would do the queuing, would dump bundles of rags to mark a 'reserved' place on the platform, and would sell these places for varying sums, half a crown being considered an excessive but not exorbitant charge. The transport officials and the police, meanwhile, did their best to keep at least part of the platforms clear for travellers by painting two white lines, one eight feet and the other four feet from the platform's outer edge. Until half past seven, the shelterers were not supposed to cross the eight-foot line. After the rush hour, and until half past ten, four feet of platform were kept clear for travellers. At half past ten the train service was discontinued, the lights dimmed (at the request of the shelterers) but not extinguished, the current cut off in the electric rail. The shelterers, who had hitherto in some cases passed a social evening with cards, sing-songs and banter, now had the whole station to themselves, and usually settled down to sleep all over the platforms, in the passages, on the escalators, some actually between the rails. They were turned out very early next morning.

In September an investigator from Mass Observation prepared a careful report on the Holland Park Tube Station, one of the smaller stations in a generally residential area of western London. It consists of two platforms, about one hundred yards long by five yards wide. The platforms at that time were bare, except for three benches and two lavatories—one for men, one for women: a recent addition—on each. What the observer saw may be summarised as follows:

Most of the shelterers were working-class people, from the neighbouring streets, though some had travelled from other parts of London in the hope of securing better places in Holland Park than could be found in their own more congested areas. The men were usually dressed in their normal working clothes, as were the older women, though many of these had on very old, laddered stockings and rubber shoes. A large number of the younger women wore trousers or siren suits. At bedtime the men took off their coats, while the women lay down as they were.

Each family or group had reserved its patch of station, one member having come down early, in some cases as early as two o'clock, and put down bedding or other goods to stake out a claim: the other members arrived later, after work. By five o'clock it seems that all the best places were taken, and by the time the investigator arrived, at seven, the only place left was at the bottom of the emergency stairs. By eight, when the last comers turned up, there was no place down below at all: they therefore camped at the top of the emergency stairs, underneath a glass roof. (This, of course, was considerably more dangerous than being out in the streets.)

Most of the shelterers were regulars and knew their neighbours. Greetings were exchanged, and news of the situation down below. 'Hallo, Joe, you won't get anywhere tonight. They've been down there since two this afternoon.' 'Excuse me, but weren't you the people who lent me a cigarette last night?'

By seven the people on the platforms were settling in. Some of the children were already tucked up for the night. Many people were eating sandwiches, chocolate or fruit, or drinking beer and tea out of thermos flasks. Others were talking and reading. All were surrounded by blankets, pillows and suitcases. There was little laughter and gaiety, but a great deal of talking. Almost no attempt was made to pass the time in an interesting manner. Two groups of people were playing cards: here and there people would be reading magazines in a half-hearted manner: there were almost no books in evidence: most just sat and talked, or did nothing at all.

At about nine the adults began to settle down for the night, most lying on one blanket, with another over them and a pillow for their heads. Some slept in a sitting position, with their backs to the tunnel walls. It rapidly became impossible to move about for sprawling bodies. One policeman and one shelter marshal, who were on duty, had tried to keep a passage-way clear, but once the people were lying down they more or less gave up.

There had been considerable grumbling earlier in the evening about the system of 'booking' space. This, of course, was on the part of those in the passages and on the stairs, who were annoyed that others should have annexed the best spots by two or three in the afternoon. On the other hand, an announcement posted on a board, stating that from the following Wednesday shelterers would not be admitted to the tube before seven in the evening, caused even more annoyance. One or two people grumbled loudly and continually. A woman could find nowhere to sit save the stairs, and installed herself in the middle of them. She complained in a loud voice of unfair treatment, but nobody took any notice of her. When a policeman told her to move to one side, so as to keep a gangway clear, she began: 'I'm a ratepayer, I pay my rates as good as anyone else, I can sit anywhere I like.' The policeman again told her to move. She started to shout at him. The policeman just stood and looked at her in silence. At last she moved. The same argument about being a ratepayer was used by a man who wished to sleep in the middle of the stairs, thus completely blocking them.

At intervals during the night a man would go upstairs for a breath of air. When he came down again, he would tell what was happening up above, and this would spark off prolonged discussions. One man, for instance, said: 'There's a fire over the Bush way.' This led to various theories concerning where the fire might be—the White City, an aeroplane factory, the guns on 'the Scrubs', and so on.

About five, while it was still dark and the raid was still going on, people began to leave. These were mostly men, postmen and labourers who presumably had to get to work. By about a quarter past five whole families were leaving, most of them apparently to go home and get a few hours' sleep in bed before starting the day's work. The lifts were not working, and they all went up the emergency stairs. Some, on reaching the top and hearing the guns still firing, decided to go back down. This caused confusion, since others were coming up, and as yet more people were still trying to sleep on the stairs, there was soon a confused and solid mass of people milling about. At twenty to six the All Clear went, and the confusion on the stairs was thus sorted out. By six o'clock there were only about half a dozen groups left on the platforms. By seven they were completely empty, and the mess of papers and fruit left behind had all been cleared away by the porters.

In the Liverpool Street extension there was no compulsion to leave, and in the early days some people stayed down there for weeks on end. This was the 'deep-shelter mentality' which had caused the Government such fear and anxiety before the war. It was, however, the exception. Most people only used the tubes for sleeping, and went off to work as usual each morning. There were, however, families who, being bombed out or for some other reason, made the tubes their homes, which of course they had to vacate during the daytime. At London Bridge Station there were 134 such families alone, consisting of 350 people. It must have been inconvenient and uncomfortable, but it was certainly very cheap, with no rent to pay, no overheads for light or heat, food later provided at cost price from canteens, and medical attention available free on the premises.

That it was uncomfortable is certain. Among the minor inconveniences were a plague of mosquitoes which haunted the tubes that winter, refusing to hibernate owing to the warmth engendered by all those packed bodies: the winds which howl, now hot now cold, through the tunnels (later the shelterers requested that the ventilator fans be turned off after 10.30, and in many stations this was done): the lice which caused the medical authorities considerable anxiety: the stench of human excrement from the tunnels, before lavatories were installed: and, of course, the hardness of the stone platforms, and the crowding. No matter. The tubes were believed to be, and in many cases were, safe. The people crowded down into them, and within two weeks of the opening of the Blitz the Prime Minister, being as always a realist, was demanding why the other Ministers still maintained that they should not be used as shelters. Almost at once the first steps were taken to make them as decent and as comfortable as was possible in the circumstances.

But only the deepest ones were safe. This the people failed to realise. The result was that they crowded into tube stations which were later hit, with numerous casualties. On successive October nights, Trafalgar Square Station was hit (seven killed), Bounds Green (nineteen killed, all but three of them Belgian refugees who occupied one end of the platform, a pathetic colony), Praed Street (eight killed) and, worst of all, on October 14th, Balham.

The Balham tube station roof is some thirty feet below Balham High Road, and between the road and the tube is the usual intricate tangle of water mains, sewer mains, electric light and telephone cables and gas conduits. These were smashed. Water from the mains and sewers ran into the tube station, where about six hundred people were sheltering, first a trickle, then a torrent, finally a river three feet deep bringing with it tons of sand and rubble. There was a stench of commercial gas. A motorman, employed by the L.P.T.B., has described what he saw in these words:

'It was about 8 p.m. I was standing on the platform talking to people when there was a terrific explosion above the station and at the same time one of the platform lamps "arced", and that put the station in darkness. When the station went into darkness panic started; it was bad panic. I said to them: "It will be all right; we will have a light on in a few minutes."

'There were a lot of women and children, including my own wife and two children, and I was talking to them. When I was saying we could soon get a light, I didn't realise that the tunnel had collapsed. Then there was a smell of gas, and the children were shouting out for their gas-masks. I got my torch and flashed it up and saw water was pouring down in torrents.

'I thought it was time something was done to get these people out. I went back and opened the emergency hatch. I got the people more disciplined and they filed through the escape hatch in single file. It took some ten minutes to pass them through the hatch—about seventy or eighty of them. I told them to come up the escalator, to wait in the booking hall, and the rescue squad came along and took my torch and I had to manage without one.

'All this time water was pouring in and I was up to my knees in water. Soon it was like a waterfall. In about five minutes all the anti-suicide pits were full. The water went up to about the second stair of the escalator.'

Seven years later, according to Mr Charles Graves, this motorman still had scars on his hands caused by people tearing at them while he was trying to draw the bolts of the emergency hatch.

Above the station a bus-driver had been driving his red double-decker towards Vauxhall. There were eight of those multiple flares called 'chandeliers', the almost certain precursors of bombs, hanging in the sky overhead as he reached Balham High Road. The bomb fell twenty-five yards ahead of his bus:

'My bus began prancing about like a horse and the next thing I knew I was lying in a shop doorway. I picked myself up and was taken to Ducane Road for first aid. My conductor had been laid out. . . . After leaving the first aid post I decided I must go back to the bus, but as I approached it, I said to myself, "it's O.K., somebody's moved it." But when I came nearer I saw to my horror that only the roof was protruding from the crater in the road.'

A man who went down into Balham Tube Station through the emergency exit to see what could be done has described what he found in these words:

'I crawled through the emergency exit and shone my torch and had a shock when I saw a mountain of ballast, sand and water washing through a huge hole at the north end of the platform. The emergency exit is very small—you have to stoop to get through it. The water was about two feet deep in the lower booking hall. I crossed it, and went through the emergency exit at an angle, crawling up the ballast. Very noisy it was, with a hissing of gas and water washing down. As it poured through the tunnel it washed past me, like a river, from right to left. It was like the sand and pebbles at Brighton on a very rough day. . . .'

This was one of the worst. But many other tube stations were hit. At St Pancras, a bomb went through 47 feet of solid ground, at Holloway 45, at Bounds Green 32. Moorgate Station was burned out on the night the City burned, December

29th, and the heat was so intense that glass and aluminium melted to form pools. On January 11th a bomb caused the roadway to collapse into the Bank Station subway, while the blast travelled down the demolished escalators. Many people were killed, being either crushed or blasted to death. A train was entering the suddenly darkened station at the moment the bomb fell. The blast knocked the driver's hands off the controls; the automatic brake worked, but not before several people, who had been blown off the platform, were run over. The death-roll was one hundred and eleven.

But the deep tubes, at least, were safe.

The attitude of the Government, and hence of the boroughs, to the whole shelter problem underwent two major changes during the first few weeks of the Blitz. One was dictated by what was happening under ground, the other by events on the surface and in the sky.

The policy of dispersal had proved a partial failure so far as central London and the East End were concerned. The big, commandeered shelters and tubes existed. If the people were not to be ejected—and this was not a course that was seriously advocated—something must be done to minimise the dangers which had led the Government to oppose mass sheltering from the beginning. There were three main dangers: that to physical health, in the form of epidemics: that to mental health, in the form of progressive demoralisation, hysteria, absenteeism and all that was contained in the phrase 'deep-shelter mentality': and, closely connected with the latter, that of large incidents involving heavy and shocking casualties.

As early as September 14th, that is to say just one week after the heavy bombing started, the Minister of Health and the Minister of Home Security appointed a committee, under the chairmanship of Lord Horder, whose frame of reference was to enquire into 'the conditions of air raid shelters used for sleeping purposes, with particular reference to health'. The Horder Committee, working with what must be almost record speed for such enquiries, made their initial recommendations four days later.

The Horder Committee regarded overcrowding in the 'self-chosen' shelters as the main danger. It therefore advocated an intensive publicity campaign to persuade the people to remain in their Andersons and their communal surface shelters, and also advocated that these should be made more attractive: the Andersons should be provided with bunks, entrance curtains and light: the communal surface shelters should be assigned to specified residents 'who should be entitled to regard them as their own (and who, if there are doors, should be provided with keys)'. These suggestions, which were carried out to a certain extent in some of the boroughs, do not seem to have persuaded many people to leave their 'self-chosen' shelters. As already pointed out, the motives that had led them to the arches and cellars were emotional, not logical. On the other hand, they probably helped to prevent more people from abandoning their Andersons and street shelters.

The Horder Committee suggested that the boroughs examine all the 'self-chosen' shelters and attempt to find more of similar type to relieve congestion. The boroughs should then approve such shelters which reached a decent standard of protection and hygiene. This was done, and gradually took effect: though as has been seen, people in West Ham were still crowding into a shelter at the end of October which did not reach the minimum standard in these matters, and which therefore could not be scheduled.

It was proposed that the boroughs pool their shelter resources, a purely administrative matter, that the factory shelters not in use at night be opened to the public, and that 'the possibility of using the Tube system for shelters during the night be considered'. This last suggestion was already long out of date: the problems in the tubes were almost the same by then as the problems of the other 'self-chosen' shelters, that is to say, crowding and an absence of hygiene.

The aged, the infirm, the bedridden and as many young

children as possible should be evacuated. By early November 4,000 of the former had been moved from London shelters to hospitals in the country and more were going. Tens of thousands of children went, some with and some without their mothers.

The four final recommendations were all of a more positive nature, and were also carried out. Shelter marshals were appointed—whole-time paid officials, both women and men—with duties defined by the Regional Commissioners. They formed part of the Warden Service. The local authorities were told to install the necessary sanitary equipment and to arrange for the disposal of sewage and the cleaning of the shelters. The Medical Officer of Health and his staff were to make regular inspection of the shelters. And finally First Aid Points should be provided in the large shelters and for groups of smaller shelters. A subsequent recommendation that these Medical Aid Posts should each have a small sick bay was also carried out so far as this was possible.

The question of ventilation and heating was gone into. This was a difficult one to solve, since the two were to a certain extent contradictory. But stoves and fans were installed in many shelters. To reduce the dangers of infection, shelters should be, and were, sprayed regularly with a cheap antiseptic, sodium hypo-chlorite in aqueous solution.

Such, then, were the basic medical recommendations. They produced results which astonished the doctors. There was no influenza epidemic, no diphtheria epidemic, no great increase in respiratory diseases such as tuberculosis. In fact the health of the shelterers does not appear to have suffered at all during the months spent in the stuffy, crowded arches and tubes. Indeed the provision of First Aid Posts, each with a trained nurse and many with a doctor as well, enabled the shelterers to have immediate medical attention for maladies and indispositions which in many cases would otherwise have gone unchecked. Within a few weeks, too, the necessary sanitary arrangements were installed.

Body vermin were a problem, but this too was handled with remarkable speed and success. The basic method was to segregate the verminous and a special shelter called the Hungerford Club, equipped with baths, bunks, and a plant for decontaminating lousy clothes, was installed at Charing Cross: the lice were passed on to laboratories, such as that of the School of Hygiene and Tropical Medicine, to help in the research against louse-carried diseases. The lice, in fact, were kept at bay, though not, of course, eliminated. Scabies, on the other hand, spread rapidly through the shelters, but this unpleasant parasite is not a disease carrier.

The morale factor in the shelters was in some ways more difficult, in others easier, to tackle. The first problem was to provide a modicum of comfort. Heat and light were laid on quite rapidly. But when towards the end of the year the installation of wire bunks began, a surprising amount of opposition was met from the shelterers themselves. These bunks, three-tiered wooden frames (later replaced by metal frames, since the wood harboured lice), of which the centre one could be raised so as to make them into seats when not in use as beds, occupied considerable space. A shelter, or a tube platform, equipped with bunks could not hold as many shelterers as one without. This meant that in the crowded shelters a number of people would have to go elsewhere. A ticket to a bunk was allotted to each shelterer. The result on occasion was anger, amounting to rebellion.

In some East End shelters the shelterers, having become accustomed to sleeping on the floor, quite refused to use the bunks. Opposition became at time so strong in West Ham, according to Miss Idle, that it was necessary to call in the police, the fire brigade and the full complement of wardens to handle the disturbances.

In Bethnal Green, the log of a Warden's Post has the following entry, for Friday, January 10th, 1941:

'Today has been a very busy one the shelter; problem has become very difficult, a round-robin was handed to the Post to be forwarded to Mr Miller, to the extent that these people did not want any bunks in their compartment of the shelter, as they were quite satisfied to sleep on forms, the matter is being considered by the emergency committee.' And on January 14th: 'Another round-robin was handed to Mr Miller today protesting against bunks in shelters.'

The motives that inspired this apparently senseless revolt against bunks and the 'ticketing' that went with them were confused. One, as stated, was a conservative dislike of change: the people had become accustomed to sleeping on the ground or benches. Another was the break-up of what had become small shelter communities, when the installation of the bunks necessitated the departure of some shelterers elsewhere. A third was the disorganisation to communal life caused by the bunks themselves: their physical presence made card games, dancing and so on more difficult. A fourth was a down-to-earth dislike of regimentation and of authority in general. Hitherto the shelterers had been able to do more or less as they pleased, but now order was being applied and they were being told where, and even when, they must sleep.

The atmosphere in the shelters varied of course greatly from district to district, and even from shelter to shelter. Thus in Bethnal Green one former shelter marshal, a woman, tells this story:

'I used to try hard to get the children into their bunks for their night's rest, but it was very difficult, because all the crowds of adults sitting there talking and laughing would keep the children awake. So I hit on a scheme to have a penny raffle a week off of every one of the people that was in the shelter, which they quite agreed to do. And with these pennies I used to go and buy all the cheap little sweets that I could get. And I used to say to the kiddies: "Now, come on, the first one of you which is undressed and in bed gets a nice sweet!" And there used to be such a scramble for them all to get into their bunks to see who would be the first one to get their sweet! And perhaps this sweet was only just a little tiny toffee, or a liquorice allsort, or something like that, but they used to be thrilled, and they'd get into their bunks, cover themselves up, have their sweet and go to sleep.'

Another Post Warden, a very small woman also in Bethnal Green, has said:

'In one of my shelters unbeknown to us they moved in a piano, and of course the first I heard of it was that they'd all come out of the pub and it was a proper bedlam. They said it was like Barley Fair over there. They was singing and dancing, and they said: "You'd better come over, Doll, because you know the people and you can deal with 'em." Well, I will say this. I grew up with some of these people, and rough as they was, they didn't make it too hard. But I had a nasty one among them now and then. I could handle them. But my shelter wardens, they couldn't do nothing with them. They moved the piano once, and it came in again. Finally it got so bad we had to get the Town Hall to do something about it. Because people did want their rest, and up to a certain time, yes, you're allowed a singsong, like you was in an ordinary house, but when you went into the early morning it had to be stopped—and let other people get their rest. . . . Because if you got a bad night in the shelter you didn't feel as if you could work next day. Oh, I might tell you we had some lively times, mouthorgans in one, the piano in the other. . . .'

In yet a third Bethnal Green shelter, the shelter warden, a man, has said:

'The only entertainment we had was the Church used to come in there and hold a service, but then that had to stop because the kiddies used to come in there eating potatoes and hot dogs, running around, some fetching their homework in, making stools for the shelter, so that fell off.' This seems to have been an argumentative shelter. 'Yes, there was Belgian Jews, Russian Jews, all nationalities, and my job, well, I couldn't understand a word they was saying. And there'd be a little argument going on, I used to go round and ask if there was anyone could speak their language. By the time I got back to them there'd be another little argument started a little way along, then I'd start all over again.'

But still, the bunks were installed and the tickets issued—in the tubes, for sleeping space on the platforms as well for the bunks—and thus by the end of the year, or at least early in 1941, a certain order was established. People had their homes above ground, with their Anderson shelter to sleep in, or they had a bed, their semi-permanent property, down below ground. And in this underground half-world, there were gradually installed some of the amenities of war-time civilisation, with canteens, medical attention, even entertainment and culture of a sort. In Bermondsey, amateur actors toured the shelters, with a production of Chekov's *The Bear*, while the shelterers in the Swiss Cottage tube station produced their own magazine entitled *The Swiss Cottager*. In some boroughs the indefatigable and admirable ladies of the W.V.S. organised sewing bees and lectures. South of the river the soldiers of 167 Coy, Pioneer Corps, engaged on clearing rubble, soon had a concert party going, which performed in the shelters six nights a week for thirteen weeks. And here we are moving away from the purely indigenous relaxation, of which the pack of cards and the Bethnal Green mouthorgans are perhaps the archetypes, into more sophisticated forms of entertainment, sent down to the shelterers from above.

Library services were organised, four thousand 'Penguin' books being provided for the West Ham shelterers alone. Not everywhere were religious services made impossible by hot-dog-eating children, and in Bermondsey we learn that they were appreciated by many, though care was taken not to offend or irritate the irreligious, for a contemporary document says: 'Wherever possible the services are conducted in places where only those who wish for a service need come.' The large shelters had film shows, and the authorities took advantage of this most popular entertainment to insert a short public health film in each programme. By January of 1941 the London County Council were holding more than two hundred classes in the shelters, on such subjects as current affairs and dress-making. P.T. classes were planned for the boys and girls. Anarchy, in fact, was well under control. Dartboards were supplied, and darts leagues organised, shelter *v.* shelter. The Council for the Encouragement of Music and the Arts (the fore-runner of the Arts Council) sent people into the shelters with gramophones and albums of classical music. It was the job of the person who worked the gramophone, we are told, to 'explain the meaning of the music and the circumstances in which it was written'. (Is this the origin of the B.B.C. Third Programme's curious habit, whereby it gives its cultured listeners a brief résumé of the plot of *Faust* or a potted biography of Mozart before the music is played?) Once this campaign for the entertainment of shelterers was in full swing, it went to great lengths. No London shelter seems to have rivalled the Bristol shelter, where in late 1940 there was a non-stop variety programme going on for twenty-four hours per day. On the other hand welfare services of an elaborate sort were organised. After the Blitz was over, but while the shelters were still in use, we read of parties of shelterers being taken around the Zoo, or driven off to the Serpentine for a swim.

The welfare of the tube shelterers, since they were the most obvious unfortunates, was very thoroughly looked after and owing to the efficiency of the L.P.T.B. they were well cared for. Indeed, of all the hundreds of thousands who sheltered in the tubes, only two persons brought successful legal actions against the L.P.T.B. for negligence, one being a gentleman who had had the misfortune to swallow a drawing-pin embedded in a currant bun purchased at an L.P.T.B. canteen.

It may be said, then, that at least by early in the new year the chaotic condition that had existed in the shelters and tubes when the Blitz began had been reduced to order, and that a very great deal had been done, and done most successfully, to safeguard the physical health and spiritual well-being of the shelterers. The shelters had become dormitories, and as such were moderately satisfactory: as shelters, however, many of them were still far from safe.

This amelioration of the conditions of the tubes and large shelters was in itself a change of Government policy, dictated by the nature of the raids. Throughout October there was a raid on London every night: only on two nights did less than sixty planes bomb the metropolis: and usually these raids lasted from dusk till dawn. These were conditions very different from those envisaged before the war, when the shelter policy was laid down against the expectation of short, sharp raids killing many thousands of people. Instead there was this steady, all-night pulverisation of London's buildings, with far fewer casualties than had been expected. (In October almost 5,000 tons of high explosive were dropped on London, causing fatal casualties at the approximate rate of one per ton dropped, while only 6,343 people were detained in hospital. When it is realised that at no time were there less than 120,000 beds available in London hospitals for air raid casualties, it is seen again how enormously the fear had surpassed the reality.)

On the other hand, there seemed then no reason why this steady pounding away at London should not continue indefinitely, for months and perhaps for years. Sir Winston Churchill has written: 'Our outlook at this time (October) was that London, except for its strong modern buildings, would be gradually and soon reduced to a rubble-heap.' The R.A.F. and A.A. Command were still shooting down almost no enemy night bombers, and though great, and justified, hopes were placed in the radar equipment which was about to be issued both to the night fighters and to the guns, it was always possible that the Germans would find an answer to this defensive weapon.

Indeed it was expected that the bombing would get worse. When the Blitz started the Germans had few big bombs. In 1940, 99 per cent of the bombs dropped weighed 250 kilograms or less, the 250-kilo and the 50-kilo high explosive bomb being the standard models. It was against bombs of this size that the pre-war shelter programme had been designed. But heavier bombs were on the way. The R.A.F. were thinking of making larger bombs, and it was assumed, quite correctly, that the Germans were doing likewise. Indeed, a few 1,000-kilo and a very occasional 2,500-kilo bomb were being dropped, as well as quite large numbers of mines attached to parachutes. In general a 1,000-kilo bomb does far more damage than four of 250-kilo each, and a 2,500-kilo bomb is worth much more than fifty weighing 50-kilo, provided the engineering problem of making all the high explosive explode simultaneously is overcome. It was clear that the Germans realised this, since one reason for their dropping expensive 500- or 1,000-kilo sea mines against land targets was their shortage of heavy bombs (as these mines exploded on impact, without burying themselves, the radius of blast was very great: on the other hand, being ill-fused for use against land targets, some 20 per cent of the 4,000 dropped failed to explode). In fact all the evidence pointed towards an indefinitely continued bombardment of London, but with heavier bombs than those now used. And as Sir Winston has said: 'If the bombs of 1943 had been applied to the London of 1940, we should have passed into conditions that might have pulverised all human organisation.'

Certainly, apart from the deep tubes, there were then no shelters available to withstand the heavier bombs that must be expected. In October, therefore, the whole deep-shelter policy was reversed. It was decided to begin work immediately on the construction of eight deep-level shelters, branching like the spokes of eight wheels from existing deep tube stations, to hold 64,000 shelterers. These, together with the deep tubes, would hold rather more shelterers than the present number sleeping in large, public shelters. This work was put in hand, at vast expense, but none of these deep shelters was ready by the time the Blitz was over. Later in the war some of them were used as shelters or as headquarters and billets for troops.

Meanwhile little could be done to make the existing shelters any safer, though wherever possible this was attempted. For the rest, it was an endless job of repairs, repairs to the public utilities first of all, and repairs to houses. Every night saw gas mains cut, water mains destroyed, railway lines blasted, roads cratered. Every morning what repairs were possible were made. In Poplar, by the end of the year, the total of houses damaged exceeded the total number of houses: many had been damaged more than once. Nor was Poplar unique in this distinction. In October the main sewage outfall was destroyed, and raw sewage was pouring into the Thames which stank, in Sir Winston's phrase, 'first of sewage and afterwards of the floods of chemicals we poured into it'. The vast intricacy of cables and pipes posed endless problems to the gas, water and light repair squads. A broken water main in Bruton Street was found to be made of curiously shaped wooden pipes, laid down in ancient times. A carpenter had to make replacements. The cemeteries were hit, and the dead of bygone centuries tossed up into the battered streets:

'In the early evening of October the 10th', says Mr Cotter, 'following a heavy raid on the 9th, a message came through Control that said: some boys had the Countess of Essex against the railings in Priory Street. I suspected a leg-pull by a police-man pal, but decided to see what was going on in Priory Street. I got over the fence and found a little group of police and wardens with what seemed to be a cloth-wrapped package, about four feet long, propped against the wall. It transpired that some kids had inspected a twenty-five foot deep crater in the local graveyard, had spotted the package at the bottom and had promptly picked it out for closer inspection. A stone tomb at the edge of the crater had been tilted over by the explosion and on one of the side slabs the words *Countess of Essex* were faintly legible. The cryptic message became clear, a nice piece of police work, even the deduction appeared obvious. But not so. On that site, six hundred years before, stood a priory. Chaucer was believed to have acted as a secretary there to a relative of Queen Philippa who, after the custom of the age, had hied her to the nunnery. Some of the nuns were no doubt buried there and at a much lower level than the Countess of Essex—about twenty or twenty-five feet down, a realistic depth for a thousand-kilo bomb in soft earth. We shook the almost weightless package, just a dry rustle, but a few marble-like objects fell out into the roadway. We picked them up and then replaced the bundle at the bottom of the crater, covering it with a few feet of earth. Some time later the whole cemetery was levelled off. I washed my marble. It was some kind of stone with minute carving, and then I remembered that the nuns were wrapped in some kind of treated linen for burial, their beads tied around the upper arm. I thought of Chaucer's Prioress, of whom he sang: *Of smal coral, aboute hir arm she bar a peire of bedes, gauded al with grene.* No green on my bead, but it was a bead, and I thought again when Chaucer sings—*And Frensh she spak full fair and fetisly, after the scole of Stratford-atte-Bow.* Well, this was Stratford-atte-Bow all right, Priory Street, Bow, London, E.3, six hundred years later.'

Nicholson's gin factory in Poplar was also hit, and the gin poured into the river Lea, where it flows under Bow Bridge. The Lea became one solid blue flame of burning gin. Was there any chance, one man wondered, of diving in and attacking it from underneath?

The city suddenly seemed to be full of rats and mice. Some said they had come from the burned-out warehouses in dockland: others that so many cats had been killed that the rats and mice now wandered about at will.

On the night of October 10th, in southern London, there was suddenly an enormous uprush of white light, like a gigantic mushroom with a huge black cap. For a moment whole square miles were brilliantly illuminated. This was a direct hit on the largest gas-holder in the gas-works off Purley Way. Five million cubic feet of gas had burned in a couple of seconds.

Miles Mordaunt went out one night after a bomb had fallen nearby:

'The first street I turned into near ours was quite dark, and appeared to be deserted. I walked through to the far end of it, keeping my eye on the rooftops where the flames appeared to be leaping up as if they were very near, though actually they were almost two streets away. One of the burning houses seemed to be a draper's. A lot of debris was sailing up into the air with great stateliness. It was textile material that had taken fire and been reduced to the condition of an old-fashioned gas-mantle. While holding its shape, it was in an incandescent glow as it rose steadily into the air. The frocks kept a ridiculous appearance of primness, moving like ladies, coming down with the same ladylike movement, managing to come down without the skirt billowing in any way. The extremely fragile burned textiles held their shape very tenaciously as they came down. As I reached the end of the street, a policeman stepped out of the shadows. He was doing what looked like a weird dance. He was beating out pieces of this smouldering textile material that kept landing on him. While of course his uniform was not in danger of taking fire, it would have made it look very mothy. More tenacious even than the dresses were the stockings, which wriggled down through the air like snakes. Several of these looped round him in a most persistent way. I helped him beat out some of these things on his shoulders, and said goodnight, and went back. . . .'

Night by night, during that October, London was vanishing. Down below ground, people might be singing: the nightclubs might be full: above ground, there was only the sound of explosions, of aeroplane engines, of guns, the whispering of fires, the rare shout of a warden, running footsteps, the rattle of shell fragments, an occasional ambulance, fire engine, mortuary van, the rumble of falling brick and stone. And there were still cats. I quote Mr Mordaunt again:

'The familiar London of streets rapidly disappeared and one became used to a nightmare new landscape consisting of sand dunes from burst sandbags, and heaps of rubble where houses had been. When one went to these during the actual Blitz, in the small hours of the morning, when the only light was from incendiary bombs or burning houses, one of the noticeable features reminiscent of the more civilised period were the cats whose homes had been destroyed. They were usually present in force, leaping about madly, occasionally pulling themselves together, and trying to get back to what they knew as home, or people they had known. This characteristic made them useful to us as guides. The newly-made rubble was often very treacherous to move on, and even a dog would have disappeared in it, but the cats seemed to be able to leap and light about on it like birds.'

That was London, in October of 1940, when there seemed no reason why the bombing should not go on for years.

CHAPTER SEVEN

IN AN Order of the Day issued to his air crews on October 18th, Goering, the Commander-in-Chief of the Luftwaffe, said: 'Your indefatigable, courageous attacks on the head of the British Empire, the City of London with its eight and a half million inhabitants, have reduced the British plutocracy to fear and terror.' And for the next month his air crews continued dutifully to drop most of their bombs on the plutocrats' capital. The first raid-free night that London had known since September 7th was that of November 3rd-4th, but on the next night the bombers were back, and for a further ten days there were once again heavy raids each night. On November 14th Coventry was the target, but on the 15th, 16th and 17th it was once again London. And then German strategy changed.

Just as the target had been expanded from the East End to London as a whole in late September so, in late November, it was again expanded from London to almost all the major industrial cities of the United Kingdom. From mid-November until late January the Luftwaffe was over Britain in great strength almost every night on which flying was at all possible, but from November 18th to January 19th, out of twenty-eight raids by one hundred or more planes, only six were directed against London, while out of eleven lighter raids London was the target for two, both of which were diversions while the main weight of the Luftwaffe attacked provincial cities.

From January 19th to March 8th there was a lull. This period saw only five comparatively light raids: one on London on January 29th, two on Swansea in February, and two on Cardiff in early March.

Heavy bombing began again on March 8th, when 120 bombers were over London, and continued almost without interruption until mid-May, but now London was once again only one target among many. It suffered two more heavy, and one very heavy, raids in March: two very heavy raids in April, known to Londoners as 'the Wednesday' and 'the Saturday', both of which were specifically ordered by Hitler as reprisals for the bombing of Berlin: and one very heavy raid in May.

The reason for this change of strategy is not hard to see. Though the plutocrats of West Ham, Balham and Battersea had been quite badly knocked about by the bombs of the National Socialists, their top hats dented and their morning coats hideously begrimed, they showed not the slightest sign, visible across the Channel, of any wish to surrender. In fact the attempt to force the British to capitulate by bombing the concentration of civilians living and working within fifteen miles of Charing Cross had apparently failed. The Germans, therefore, decided to try the third of their plans for conquering Britain, the one which, it will be recalled, Jodl had listed first in his memorandum of June 30th: 'Attack on the English air arm and on the country's war economy and its sources as a whole'. This new policy was inaugurated with the very heavy and destructive raid on Coventry, where so many factories vital to the aircraft industry and war production generally were located, on November 14th. Henceforth, with the exception of Hitler's two reprisal raids in April, London was attacked as an industrial centre rather than as a centre of population (though this subtle distinction was scarcely perceptible to the people whose families were killed or houses destroyed in these later raids).

On January 13th Jodl issued a directive, somewhat out of date in so far as the bombing was concerned since it was already being applied, and which was even more out of date by the time that Hitler incorporated its main arguments in his General Directive No. 23, dated February 6th, 1941.

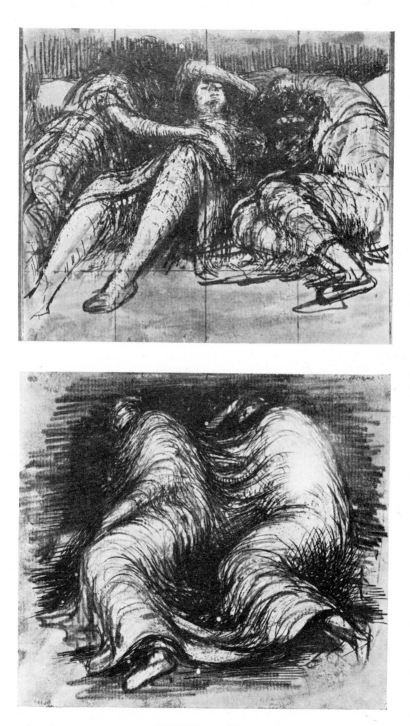

IN THE SHELTERS

Jodl's paper gave priority to air attacks on the British ports, on convoys and on the aircraft and munition industries. He said that so far as the available information went, the morale and the will to resist of the British people had been very little affected by the bombings, although the life of the cities had been somewhat disrupted. And in his final paragraph he stated that deliberate terror attacks against residential areas were unlikely to have any decisive effect on the ultimate outcome of the war. These conclusions, and the consequent change of objective, had presumably all been reached before Coventry was bombed.

To what extent these conclusions were justified, it is not possible even now to say. Certainly the whole of the British propaganda machine was concentrated on one theme: London can take it. Reading the very heavily censored newspapers of the time, the impression one gets is of endless cockney jokes, of grim determination, and of utter self-confidence in the face of dastardly and unfair attack. It is, in fact, almost identical to the picture put out by the German propaganda machine when the German cities were being destroyed from the air three years later. And it is often assumed that had the bombing gone on, and had London been compelled to suffer the very much worse fate of Berlin—amounting almost to total physical annihilation—the Londoners would have proved just as doughty under this ordeal as the Berliners were to do. This assumption may be correct.

On the other hand, it may be incorrect, and for the reason of chronology. When Berlin was destroyed, London had already survived its time of anguish. The people of Berlin saw, from the example of the Londoners, that it is possible to endure almost unlimited hardship. In fact it may be said that London had set a sort of precedent: heavy bombing with high explosives and incendiaries does not cause a nation to rebel against its leaders and insist on surrender. But when London was being bombed there was no such precedent, and indeed expectation had all pointed the other way. In war there is a point beyond which no nation will go: the point at which armies mutiny and civilians revolt. In 1940 nobody knew what that point was in relation to bombing, just as nobody knows today in relation to atomic weapons. But in this same 1940 the Londoners decided that the point had not been reached by the 18th of November. Would it have been reached had the bombing gone on? There is almost no evidence available for such speculation. The newspapers of the time are no sort of guide; the memory of individuals is fragmentary and scarcely subject to generalisation; the so-called official histories are mostly, as becomes the work of Government departments, far more interested in matters of administration and finance than in history as it is generally understood; and the Home Office, where the facts are interred, may not produce them.

As for other sources, they are unreliable. It does seem that the Government were sufficiently worried by the state of London's morale to promote Sir John Anderson, a most talented civil servant, and to reverse their shelter policy in response to the public outcry. Even so the rumblings in the East End appear to have been gathering momentum again in late October. The civil defence services were becoming very tired. Looting was apparently on the increase. The barrels of the anti-aircraft guns were wearing out. And the night fighters were still a failure. Had the bombing of London gone on intensively throughout the second half of November, all December and all January, while the weather worsened and the prospects of ultimate victory remained utterly remote, it is just possible that London's morale might have broken, or at least that the Churchill Government might have been brought down. Possible but, in the opinion of this writer, unlikely. So much for such speculation.

It surely says a great deal for the courage of the Londoners that even after two months of constant bombing there were very few overt and public clamours for an ending of the war, compared to what was heard on Clydeside after only two nights of bombing in March. London, neither a city of humorous Old Bills and cockney chars, nor yet the plutocratic metropolis of Goering's imagination, contained enough brave and sensible men and women to put up with an ordeal the like of which had then not been seen since the sieges of a vanished age.

If there were doubts, even at an early stage, in the German High Command concerning the efficacy of the attacks on London's morale, and if these resulted in a certain vacillation and a perhaps premature change of strategy, tactically the air attacks were carried out with maximum intensity and in maximum strength. A German air force staff officer has stated that even after mid-November, when heavy attacks were being directed against the ports and the industrial cities, London remained the principal target.

Had the active defences been stronger, it would have been necessary for the Germans to attempt to swamp them by concentrating all their bombers over the target at one time. As it was, concentration of attack was not necessary in the early months, and hardly more so later, though the gunners were becoming more successful (the number of shells fired per aircraft shot down, which had been 30,000 in September, dropped to 11,000 in October, to about 7,000 in November and December, and to 4,000 in January, by which time there were a considerable number of radar-directed guns in action). They did not claim many kills at night: 22 in October, 21 in November and only 14 in December. A former German bomber pilot has said that the sight of the A.A. barrage, with shells bursting at all heights, did on occasion worry inexperienced crews, but he adds that since so few planes were shot down they soon became accustomed to these fireworks. The night-fighters did not begin to show successes on any significant scale until March. Thus in 1940 the Germans could bomb London by night almost as and when they chose.

The bomber units came in on separate courses and at different heights, usually between 9,000 feet (which put them above the range of the light and medium anti-aircraft guns), and 12,000 feet. On occasions there were as many as three different 'layers' of bombers over London simultaneously. But normal tactics were to space out the attacks. To increase the strain on civilian morale, the duration of the raids was deliberately prolonged to the maximum, and raids lasting ten, twelve, even fourteen hours were not unusual. In the more massive raids, bomber crews would make two sorties over London in one night, and during the two great reprisal raids of April, 1941, some crews even made three, a veritable shuttle service between their bases beyond the Channel and the target area.

On moonlit nights attempts were made to bomb specific targets in London. In the beginning units—wings or groups—were allotted particular targets. On moonless nights the whole conurbation was bombed, though even so an attempt was usually made to establish some sort of bomb-dropping zone by sending over a pathfinder group ahead of the main bomber force. This force was the celebrated Kampfgeschwader 100, 'the Fireraisers'. Originally only a wing, but later expanded to a group, this unit had various electronic aids to navigation to help it pin-point the target. The two best-known of these were the so-called X-apparatus and the Y-apparatus. The former consisted, roughly, of two radio beams between which the bombers flew. These beams were laid to intersect above the target. On reaching the point of intersection, the bombardier simply released his bombs, while some planes were even equipped with an automatic bomb release mechanism geared to the beam reception. The Y-apparatus was a single beam which sent back an echo from the bomber to the station whence it emanated. It was thus possible for the ground control to calculate how far the bomber had travelled along the beam, and when it was over the target to order the release of the bomb-load.

An intensive, secret struggle took place between the British and the German scientists. The British put out false beams parallel to those of the X-apparatus, to lure the German bombers off course: they also 'bent' the Y-beam. Some British night fighters were equipped with apparatus for picking up the beam and thus, it was hoped, would be in a position to intercept the incoming bombers. This struggle, however, was at a discount so far as London is concerned. The city presented so huge a target, and one so close to the German bases, that navigational aids were a luxury rather than a necessity.

Nevertheless the beams were used in the bombing of London. They were not usually very accurate. For example, on the night that the City burned, December 29th, 1940, the bombers were led in by the HE111s of KG100 flying on X-beams. The map prepared for the night's operation shows that the beams were intended to intersect roughly over Piccadilly Circus. In fact KG 100 unloaded its marker bombs some two miles further to the east, in the neighbourhood of St Paul's Cathedral.

During the early winter, a German air force staff officer has said, the Luftwaffe kept up its attacks almost regardless of the weather, often flying in conditions which, in the past, would have been deemed very dangerous or even impossible. When the JU 88s and the HE 111s could not operate, because they needed a longer runway for take-off and had a higher landing speed, the more antiquated DO 17s flew alone. As a result of these tactics the losses due to bad weather conditions (such as faulty landing, icing up and baling out when badly off course) well outnumbered the losses inflicted by the British defences. The operational strength of the Luftwaffe's bombers in the West began to decline, from approximately 860 on September 1st, to 820 on October 1st and to only a little over 700 on December 1st. And the number of bombers over the target declined accordingly. During the last twelve raids of September the average number was 197: during the last twelve of October 134: and during the first twelve of November 128. Still, the Germans went on for several more weeks putting everything they could into the air. And by making great efforts, involving double sorties, they still managed to mount an occasional 300- or even 400-bomber raid in December.

But this tempo could not be maintained into the new year. A telling factor was the rapid deterioration, in wet weather, of the bomber fields in France and the Low Countries, only a few of which had runways and concrete taxi-ing lanes. During the January raids the number of bombers over the target averaged only 120, and from late January until early March bombing operations against Britain were almost discontinued.

An important contributory cause to this lull in the bombing was dictated by German strategy on the highest level. In December of 1940 the decision was taken to invade Russia early in the following summer. Hitler could not afford to let his bomber force be wasted away in accidents. And the lull gave the German Air Force a chance to rebuild its bomber strength and to bring its operational units up to full establishment. This was done. When the Blitz was renewed in March, the German bomber force in the West—despite transfers to the Italo-African and Balkan theatres of war—was as strong numerically as it had been in September. It had also been partially re-equipped with new types of planes, or improved models of the older ones, and heavier bombs were now available.

As has been explained in the previous chapter, the German attack on London would have been much more cruel in 1940 had they not had to rely chiefly on comparatively light bombs. They were well aware of this, and one expedient that they used was to drop sea-mines by parachute against land targets.

The magnetic mine had been Hitler's first 'secret weapon' of the war, and had caused very heavy losses of shipping during the winter of 1939-40. It had been largely mastered, through the degaussing of ships and other means, by the summer of 1940, though it was still a menace. The original method of delivery had been for surface vessels to sow their mines in British coastal waters, but in November of 1939 seaplanes began to drop them by parachute. Later land-planes were also used for this purpose, the Heinkel 111s of Kampfgeschwader 4 being equipped each to carry two magnetic mines, slung beneath their wings on either side of the fuselage. By the time the Blitz began these magnetic mines, as weapons in the sea war, were becoming obsolescent, and since the Germans lacked a big blast bomb, they immediately began to use them against land targets. On the very first day of the Blitz, KG 4 and other bombers groups were dropping mines on parachutes into the dock area; according to a pilot of that group, he and his comrades were thenceforth usually taken off their normal mine-laying duties whenever there was a major raid on London and were sent out as an ordinary bomber group, sometimes with bombs, sometimes with mines. In the beginning these were dropped complete with sea-fuse, though later the sea-fuses were removed. This expenditure of mines against land targets did not altogether please the German Navy.

On September 20th Raeder told Hitler: 'At present numerous aerial mines are being dropped on London. . . . They have a decided effect, to be sure; however, the time has come for large-scale mine operations, since the new type of fuse is now available in sufficient quantities.' This is a reference to the acoustic fuse. The Luftwaffe, wishing to use the mines as bombs, pulled the other way, and by October 14th Hitler had authorised a compromise whereby the Air Force was allowed to drop the 'old sort of mines' over London on moonlit nights, when, presumably, these expensive objects could, in theory at least, be aimed at targets of commensurate value. And throughout the Blitz these great cylinders, weighing a ton or a ton and a half each, came silently swinging down through the night skies on to the streets and houses of the capital.

It is a curious coincidence that whereas Hitler ordered that they be dropped on moonlit nights in order that some accuracy be obtained, Churchill, four weeks earlier, on September 19th, had written in a memorandum for the Chiefs of Staff Committee: 'The dropping of large mines by parachute proclaims the enemy's entire abandonment of all pretence of aiming at military objectives. At five thousand feet he cannot have the slightest idea what he is going to hit. This, therefore, proves the "act of terror" intention against the civil population.' Certainly these mines, called almost universally and quite incorrectly 'land mines', did inspire great terror. This was due primarily to the violence of the explosion, no part of which was muffled (as with the occasional bombs of similar weight then being dropped) by burial in the ground; but a secondary cause was the usual spooky silence with which those lethal monsters came floating down. For instance one that dropped, silently, on to the Park Hill recreation grounds in Croydon, on September 28th, broke all the windows in the High Street, a good ten minutes' walk away.

And here is a description of another, which fell outside the B.B.C., in Langham Place, and destroyed, among other buildings, the old Langham Hotel. It is a transcript of a recording made for the B.B.C. during the war. The narrator is a man, and few people who were so close to a mine when it exploded can have survived to tell the tale:

'On the night of December 8th, 1940, I left the B.B.C. shortly after ten forty-five and accompanied by a colleague, Mr Sibbick, went to the cycle-shed in Chapel Mews. The customary nightly air-raid was in progress, and as we left the cycle shed we could hear the distant sound of aircraft and A.A. gun-fire. We were just entering Hallam Street from the mews when I heard the shrieking whistling noise like a large bomb falling. This noise continued for about three seconds, and then abruptly ceased as if in mid-air. There was no thud, explosion or vibration. I particularly remember this, as I'd heard this happen once before, and was curious as to what caused it and why it stopped. Then came the sound of something clattering down the roof of a building in the direction of Broadcasting House. I looked up thinking that it might be incendiaries, but this was not so. We slowly walked round to the entrance of Broadcasting House, and I estimate that we took about three and a half minutes in doing so. My colleague went inside, returned the cycle shed keys, cycled off towards Oxford Circus. I remained outside the entrance, talking to two policemen, and enquiring about possible diversions on my route home. Their names were Vaughan and Clarke. A saloon car was parked alongside the curb some distance round from the entrance, and I could see to the left of the car the lamp-post in the middle of the road opposite the Langham Hotel. The policemen had their backs to this, so did not observe what followed. Whilst we were conversing I noticed a large, dark, shiny object approach the lamp-post and then recede. I concluded that it was a taxi parking. It made no noise. The night was clear, with a few small clouds. There was moonlight from a westerly direction, but Portland Place was mainly shadow. All three of us were wearing our steel helmets; my chinstrap was round the back of my head, as I had been advised to wear it so shortly after I was issued with the helmet.

'A few seconds later I saw what seemed to be a very large tarpaulin of a drab or khaki colour fall on the same spot; the highest part of it was about ten or twelve feet above the road when I first saw it, and it seemed to be about twenty-five feet across. It fell at about the speed of a pocket handkerchief when dropped, and made no noise. Repair work was being carried out on Broadcasting House and I, not unnaturally, concluded that it was a tarpaulin which had become detached and had fallen from the building into the roadway. There were no other warnings of any imminent danger. I drew the attention of the policemen to it. They turned round and could see nothing. It had collapsed, and from where we were it was partly screened by the car, and the roadway at that point was in shadow. They told me that they could not see anything. Then followed some banter, but I persisted in saying that I had seen something fall in the road. They then decided to go to investigate. A third policeman, Mortimer, had meanwhile approached us—he was about to conduct a lady across that part of the road. But after hearing that I'd seen something he told me that he was taking her inside the building while they found out what it was. Vaughan drew ahead of Clarke, who stopped at the curb to ask me just exactly where it had dropped. I went over towards him, calling out that I would show him it. It was about a minute since I'd seen the dark object. I went towards the tarpaulin and had reached a spot to the left of Clark about six feet from the curb, and twenty-five to thirty feet from "the thing", when Vaughan came running towards me at high speed. He shouted something which I did not hear. At that moment there was a very loud swishing noise, as if a plane were diving with engine cut off—or like a gigantic fuse burning. It lasted about three or four seconds; it did not come from the lamp-post end of "the thing" but it may have come from the other end.

'Vaughan passed me on my left and Clarke, who apparently had understood the shout, also ran towards the building. Realising that I would have to turn right about before I could start running, I crouched down in what is known as prone-falling position number one. Even at that moment I did not imagine that there was any danger in the road, and thought that it was coming from above, up Portland Place. My head was up watching, and before I could reach position number two and lie down flat the thing in the road exploded. I had a momentary glimpse of a large ball of blinding, wild, white light and two concentric rings of colour, the inner one lavender and the outer one violet, as I ducked my head. The ball seemed to be ten to twenty feet high, and was near the lamp-post. Several things happened simultaneously. My head was jerked back due to a heavy blow on the dome and rim of the back of my steel helmet, but I do not remember this, for, as my head went back, I received a severe blow on my forehead and the bridge of my nose. The blast bent up the front rim of my helmet and knocked it off my head. The explosion made an indescribable noise—something like a colossal growl—and was accompanied by a veritable tornado of air blast. I felt an excruciating pain in my ears, and all sounds were replaced by a very loud singing noise, which I was told later was when I lost my hearing and had my eardrums perforated. I felt that consciousness was slipping from me, and that moment I heard a clear loud voice shouting: "Don't let yourself go, face up to it—hold on." It rallied me, and summoning all my willpower and energy I succeeded in forcing myself down into a crouching position with my knees on the ground and my feet against the curb behind me and my hands covering my face.

'I remember having to move them over my ears because of the pain in them, doubtless due to the blast. This seemed to ease the pain. Then I received another hit on the forehead and felt weaker. The blast seemed to come in successive waves, accompanied by vibrations from the ground. I felt as if it were trying to spin me and clear me away from the curb. Then I received a very heavy blow just in front of the right temple which kocked me down flat on my side, in the gutter. Later, in our first-aid post, they removed what they described as a piece of bomb from that wound. Whilst in the gutter I clung on to the curb with both hands and with my feet against it. I was again hit in the right chest, and later found that my double-breasted overcoat, my coat, leather comb-case and papers had been cut through, and the watch in the top right-hand pocket of my waist-coat had the back dented in and its works broken.

'Just as I felt that I could not hold out much longer, I realised that the blast pressure was decreasing and a shower of dust, dirt and rubble swept past me. Pieces penetrated my face, some skin was blown off, and something pierced my left thumbnail and my knuckles were cut, causing me involuntarily to let go my hold on the curb. Instantly, although the blast was dying down, I felt myself being slowly blown across the pavement towards the wall of the building. I tried to hold on but there was nothing to hold on to. Twice I tried to rise but seemed held down. Eventually I staggered to my feet. I looked around and it seemed like a scene from Dante's *Inferno*. The front of the building was lit by a reddish-yellow light; the saloon car was on fire to the left of me, and the flames

187

from it were stretching out towards the building, and not upwards; pieces of brick, masonry and glass seemed to appear on the pavement, making, to me, no sound; a few dark huddled bodies were round about, and right in front of me were two soldiers; one, some feet from a breach in the wall of the building where a fire seemed to be raging, was propped up against the wall with his arms dangling by him, like a rag doll.

'The other was nearer, about twelve feet from the burning car; he was sitting up with his knees drawn up and supporting himself by his arms—his trousers had been blown off him. I could see that his legs were bare and that he was wearing short grey underpants. He was alive and conscious.

'I told him to hang on to an upright at the entrance and to shout like hell for assistance should he see or hear anyone approaching. I went back to look at the other soldier. He was still in the same posture and I fear that he was dead. I looked around. There was a long, dark body lying prone, face downwards close to the curb in front of the building—it may have been Vaughan. There appeared to be one or two dark, huddled bodies by the wall of the building. I had not the strength to lift any of them. I wondered where the water was coming from which I felt dripping down my face, and soon discovered that it was blood from my head wounds. I could see no movement anywhere, and thought I would look round for my steel helmet and gas mask, which I had slung round me at the time of the explosion. I soon found the gas mask and picked up a steel helmet which was not my own.

'I was then joined by my colleague who had returned, and went with him to the entrance where I shouted for assistance for those outside, and for someone to bring fire-fighting appliances to put out the car fire, as I was afraid the glare would bring down more bombs.

'I walked down to our First Aid Post, where I was treated, and then to Listening Hall 1 where I rested until I was taken away by the stretcher party and sent to the Middlesex Hospital.

Here I received every possible attention and kindness. Later on I was told that "the thing" had been a land mine, and that its explosion or blast had lasted for nine seconds.

'The effect of the blast on my clothes is possibly of interest, I was wearing bicycle clips round the bottoms of my trousers at the time; after the blast was over my double-breasted over-coat was slit up the back and torn in several places, but was being held together by the belt. My trousers and underpants were pitted with small cuts about an inch long, but presumably the bicycle clips had prevented the draught getting up my trousers and tearing them off. A woollen scarf, which was knotted round my neck, undoubtedly saved my neck and chest from small fragments such as were removed from my face, which was not covered.'

A little earlier on the same evening, a bomb had actually hit the B.B.C. while Bruce Belfrage was reading the nine o'clock news. Though the crash was audible all round the world, the broadcasting equipment continued to function and Mr Belfrage, with admirable sang-froid, to read the news. After the crash and a very brief pause, his voice was heard, impassive as ever: 'The story of recent naval successes in the Mediterranean is told in an Admiralty communiqué issued tonight. . . .'

A number of parachute mines did not explode and provided a more obvious and in many ways more terrifying menace than unexploded bombs, since it was known that the proximity of metal, or any sort of vibration, might set them off. St Paul's Cathedral, which had already had the most widely publicised UXB in September, had its UXM, during the 'Wednesday', in April of the following year. It was found by Mr Gerald Henderson, the Sub-Librarian, whose description is quoted by the Dean in his book:

'Shortly after 4 a.m. I discovered a sea-mine enveloped in a green silk parachute at the north-east corner of the Cathedral. It was about 8 feet high and lay close to the site of St Paul's Cross. I was somewhat dazed by the events of the night and did not realise at once what the shrouded object might be. It crossed my mind that the silk might have been blown out of some warehouse. I went up to the place and drew aside the silk covering. It then appeared that the object beneath it was a shining steel sea-mine. It was like an inverted, elongated pear in shape and had rows of "horns" at the top and bottom. It had dropped perpendicularly, and most fortunately had remained in that posture. I was afraid that I might cause the mine to topple over if I dragged the covering silk and remained still and perplexed for some little time, holding the silk in my hands. I then returned to the Crypt and told Canon Alexander what I had found. After that, accompanied by Mr Tanner, the Dean's Verger, I went to the police-station at Snow Hill. After some delay we saw the police-officer in charge, who reported the mine to the Admiralty. He sent a constable back with me to make his report. When we arrived at the Cheapside gate to the Churchyard I unlocked it and was putting the keys back into my pocket when the constable, somewhat agitated, said: "I should leave the keys and your helmet here, if I were you, sir, these things go off, they say, if any steel is brought near them." I told him I had almost touched it when I first saw it. I then took him towards the Cathedral and, having peered at the object through the shrubs, he said he had seen enough and departed.

'Later a naval officer with two ratings arrived. I took them to the mine and they proceeded to deal with the "horns". Ultimately the mine was removed—alas! with the beautiful silk parachute. I heard later that while the last "horn" was being rendered harmless a fire engine was driven, contrary to police instruction, at full speed from Cheapside to Cannon Street. This caused the mechanism to start into action and there was great danger that the mine would explode after all. Shortly, however, the ticking stopped and the last "horn" was removed.'

Dealing with unexploded bombs was dangerous enough in all conscience, and the officers and men of the Royal Engineers who carried out this unpleasant duty were much decorated for their bravery. Dealing with unexploded mines, though there was usually no digging to be done before these could be got at, was in many ways just as dangerous, since there was no telling what new fuses and booby-traps the Germans might not have built into the monsters. This was normally the duty of the Royal Navy, and Professor Peter Danckwerts, at that time a naval officer who won a George Cross for neutralising mines in London, has described his experiences as follows:

'In the Blitz of 1940 I was a Bomb Disposal Officer belonging to the Navy and attached to the Port of London. My job was to dispose of bombs which fell in the Port of London area. This wasn't very rewarding because most of the bombs fell in the water and weren't seen, so I didn't have a great deal to do, and I was feeling a little frustrated. Well, one night I was down in the basement of the Port of London Authority building which was a very safe, comfortable place during the Blitz. There was a lot of noise going on outside. The floor was heaving from time to time. The telephone rang and the call was from the air raid controller in a North London borough who said that an object had dropped in a shopping street there, and the local bomb disposal officer thought it might be a magnetic mine. He didn't know, because he'd never seen one, but he wanted to know whether, if he put it on a lorry and took it away, it was likely to explode. I said I thought it was quite likely to, but it turned out in fact that he'd already done this and taken it away and it hadn't exploded, so he was lucky. Well, the next morning I went out with an officer from the Admiralty—I'll call him "R"—who is an expert in mines, to see this thing, and there were also two other mines dropped that night which we were going to see. The first one, which this bomb disposal officer had taken away, was lying in the middle of a big common and it seemed to me an enormous thing. It was eight feet long and about two feet in diameter, thicker than a pillar-box and longer than a tall man. It was dark green and it had a huge parachute spread out behind it, not a silk one—it looked like Aertex or something of that sort. It weighed a ton, it had fifteen hundred pounds of high explosives in it, and it was full of various gadgets which you could see let into the side. This was an ordinary magnetic mine of the sort the Germans had been laying in the sea and in the estuaries and harbours of England, but during the Blitz, when a lot of them were dropped, it got to be known as a land mine, although in fact it was just a perfectly ordinary magnetic mine, which went off on land if dropped on land. This officer from the Admiralty, "R", demonstrated to us how the thing should have been dealt with. First of all, in the side, there was a little fuse which was called the bomb fuse. This fuse was supposed to set the mine off if it fell on land and not on water, and he took it out. He had some special tools. It was very stiff, but he took it out and he threw it on the ground, and about ten seconds later there was a crack and the fuse went off. He said that this demonstrated how careful one had to be dealing with these things—if you rolled the mine about a bit with the fuse in it, it was liable to go off. If the mine hit water the bomb fuse didn't function because the mine sank into the water and the pressure of the water pushed in a little pin and stopped it; but when these mines fell on land, the fuse started buzzing and it buzzed for fifteen seconds, or rather it was supposed to buzz for fifteen seconds and then go off, but some of them buzzed for a few seconds and then stuck, and so if you rolled the mine about it buzzed for the rest of the fifteen seconds and then blew up.

'As "R" said, the important thing when dealing with these mines, if you had to move them at all before you took the fuse out, was to listen very carefully all the time, and if you heard it buzzing to run like hell, because you might have up to fifteen seconds to get away.

'There were a lot of other gadgets in this mine which he showed us how to take out. There was an electric detonator down at the bottom of a hole in the side of the mine which was very hard to get out, since it needed a special shaped tool.

Opposite it was another little hole in the mine, and he un-screwed the cover of this and there was a tremendous *whoof* and a spring, three feet long, shot out of it across the field. The other two of us were most alarmed as we hadn't known this was going to happen, but he said: "Well, it's all right, you can come back, this always happens, it's part of the show". And then finally there was a great big screwed-up cover which we eventually managed to get undone, and underneath it was a large clock made of perspex so that you could see the works, and connected to a lot of wires of different colours. This was the clock which, if the mine fell into water, started ticking and after it had ticked for about twenty minutes turned the thing into a magnetic mine. So we took that out, and cut the wires, and then the thing was quite safe.

'Then we went off and looked at the other two. One of them had fallen on a little house while the family were having supper. They were sitting in the kitchen, and there was a tremendous uproar from the scullery, great crashings, a lot of slates falling and so on. They had tried to get in the scullery to see what had happened, but couldn't, so they went out of the front door and round at the back door of the scullery, and then they found this mine standing up against the back of the scullery door. It was still there when we got there and the supper was still on the table.

'Well, after this demonstration I went back and I took a fuse from one of these mines with me. I worked on it and took it to bits that evening with a torpedo officer, who was working in the Port of London at that time, and we reckoned we knew pretty well how it worked. This was just as well, because in the course of that night we got another telephone call, this time from South London, to say that three large objects on parachutes had dropped in their particular area. The local Army bomb disposal officer said this was a job for the Navy because he thought they were mines, and the A.R.P. Controller wanted to know what I was going to do about it. I said that actually I wasn't supposed to deal with mines at all, but only with bombs. He said: "Oh, my God, who does deal with mines?" I said: "I'm afraid that the nearest people are down in Portsmouth." He said: "That's all very well, but I've got several thousand people evacuated round these mines, I can't wait for the people to come up from Portsmouth." So I rang up *H.M.S. Vernon* at Portsmouth, which is the torpedo and mining school down there, and asked the duty officer whether I could go and deal with these mines. I said I thought I knew how to do it, and he reluctantly said yes. So I went and woke up the torpedo officer who'd been playing with the fuse with me, and my Chief Petty Officer, who was another torpedo-man, both of them very good with gadgets and getting difficult things unscrewed and so on. Of course we didn't have any of the proper tools for this job. (One was supposed to have non-magnetic tools, quite apart from which most of the things were very hard to unscrew unless you had tools of the right shape.) But we got a lot of screwdrivers and, most important of all, we took a ball of string, that is the essential thing for bomb disposal.

'Well, we set off, in a car we had got from the Admiralty, and we drove through the Blitz. It was a horrible night. We drove round craters and wrecked trams and blazing gas mains, past anti-aircraft batteries which were bang-banging away. We had an imperturbable driver, I was full of admiration for him, but eventually we got down into the wilds of South London and of course we got lost. We didn't know where we were, we didn't know where any of the three mines we were looking for was either. We were wandering around back streets with shrapnel coming down and not getting any closer, and it wasn't till we saw a man in a dressing-gown walking along with a suitcase that we felt we might be getting warm. So we stopped him and asked him, and he said: Oh yes, it had fallen in the garden of a house near his. So we made him come back with us and show us. We went into the back garden of this little house. This was our first mine, and we saw it lying there among the bushes, a parachute spread over the wall next door. We went up and had a look at it with our torch, and we found unfortunately that the all-important fuse was underneath, so we'd have to roll it round before we could get it out. My Chief Petty Officer and I rolled it over very, very cautiously indeed while the third member of the party kept his ear as close to it as he could and listened to see if it buzzed. It didn't. So when we'd got the fuse round to the side, we unscrewed it. But we didn't take it out because the Germans had on occasions put things under fuses in bombs so that when you took the fuse out the bomb blew up, and it was quite possible to do it in these mines as well. Having unscrewed it, when it was loose in its socket, we tied a bit of string to the top and then we retired over the garden wall into the next garden, and then over the next garden wall into the garden beyond that, and then round the corner of the house, paying out the string, and when we got there I gave a yank on the string. It seemed sort of elastic, and when I let go the string sprang back again, so we had to climb all the way back and look. Of course the string was tied up with a rose bush or something. We freed it, and then went back and had another pull, and that was all right—when we got back we found the fuse was lying on the ground. I took off the exploder and it was then quite safe. But I did just try throwing it a few yards and sure enough, it fired, it went off, so the thing was still in a fairly sensitive condition, and we were quite right to have treated it with respect.

'Well, we sat down on the mine and had a cigarette after all this, because this was really the most difficult part of the job. While sitting on the mine I noticed that my hands were covered with soot, and also that the other people's faces had a lot of soot on them, and then I realised that the mine itself was covered with soot. I think this was because it was hung outside the aircraft, underneath, and it was covered with soot as a precaution so that it didn't show up in searchlight beams or something. One always got absolutely filthy dealing with these things.

'Well, we went around South London the rest of the night and well into the following morning, looking for the other two mines. We kept on meeting people who hadn't actually seen them but thought they knew where they were, and they'd take us along somewhere and we would find nothing. Eventually we did find the next one. It was standing upright on its nose in the middle of a recreation ground. It had made a dent in the ground just deep enough to hold it up. We went up to this and laid all our tools out on the grass, which was rather long, and then of course we lost them. We couldn't find any of them again, so we had to go to a bus depot, where we broke open the emergency tool-kit and got their spanners and things out and went back and dealt with that mine. And then the final one was in a field by a gasworks in Kent. The sun was up by then, it was a sunny morning and we had a large, interested crowd which had to be held back by volunteers while we dealt with it. So by this time we'd done three mines and we had a parachute each as a souvenir, which we were very happy about, and a lot of miscellaneous explosives from these mines which we'd taken out, and we went home feeling very pleased with ourselves.

'When we got back we were summoned to the Admiralty, the Torpedoes and Mining department, and we found quite an uproar going on because it turned out that a lot of other mines had been dropped in London that night. They'd been found in roads and back gardens, hanging off trees and railway bridges and the roofs of houses, and some were standing up on their noses on the top of houses, though of course they usually just came through the roof. In fact I think about twenty per cent of the mines that were dropped didn't go off, and each one that was dropped meant the evacuation of perhaps a thousand people in some cases. The importance of these mines to the Navy was that each one of them was likely to be a perfectly good magnetic mine, with inside it a complete magnetic mine unit, which was capable of sinking a ship if the mine had been laid in the sea. So the Navy were extremely keen on getting as many of these as they could, because they had to follow the development of German magnetic mines in order to develop their counter-measures. The Navy naturally took steps to stop anybody except people whom they felt they could trust not to blow themselves up from dealing with these mines, because they wanted the things intact. We found ourselves eventually officially accredited mine disposal officers. We used to go out every day; we were given the proper tools which we hadn't had before; we only worked in the daytime, and we weren't allowed to work at night, as we had been doing; and every morning we were sent out with a list of assignments. Mines were dropped every night and we'd be assigned a few, usually in the most remote and unheard-of parts of London. Sometimes we'd find they were quite easy, lying in playing fields or allotments, and some would be rather edgy, mines standing on their noses on the top floors of houses for instance, so that one didn't have a clear run for getting away in fifteen seconds if the thing started buzzing. However, we had no troubles at all, unlike other people. There were actually cases of people who started taking the fuses out of these mines and heard this buzzing noise and ran; it seems incredible, but they got far enough away in fifteen seconds to avoid being blown up by fifteen hundred pounds of explosive. But we had nothing particularly spectacular to deal with, again unlike other people who had to deal with mines which were welded to live rails, or inside gasometers, or hanging off the roof of the Palladium (with free tickets for life as a result). One mine we found had a rude message addressed to Mr Chamberlain chalked on the side, although Mr Chamberlain had been out of office for some months by that time. We found another one which certainly made us pause, because it had a rhyme in German on the side: something to the effect that when you think you've got it, it springs out on you. We didn't like the sound of this at all, and circled round it for quite a time before we tackled it. However, nothing particular happened.

'As a matter of fact we did do another night job, although we weren't really supposed to. This was in the Seven Sisters Road in Islington and the mine was again lying in the back garden of a house. I tied the string to the fuse and laid it out across the road, and through the house opposite, into the back garden of that, and I was just about to pull the string and get the fuse out when the string was pulled out of my hands altogether. I dashed through the house out into the road, and there I found an air raid warden, unconcernedly walking down the road with the string wrapped round his boot and the fuse of the mine rattling along the road behind him.

'We did about a dozen mines, our little team, and then we were eventually called off, because it was reckoned we'd done our quota. I've been asked whether this was a particularly frightening job, and I think the answer is that it wasn't particularly. Because one thing one has to remember is that it isn't any more dangerous to deal with large quantities of explosives than it is to deal with small quantities. You can be killed just as easily by a hand-grenade, shall we say, which has an ounce of explosive in it, as you can by a mine which has the best part of a ton. And the other thing is that it's really quite impossible to believe, when you're dealing with a great solid object of this sort, that it's suddenly going to blow up and disintegrate under your hand. I think the only way you can be convinced really is by seeing it happen to someone else at close quarters. Indeed, on the whole this kind of job is apt to be rather stimulating, rather dangerously stimulating, in fact almost demoralising, I think. You find you're getting a lot of credit for doing very little work and taking rather a small amount of risk; at least the time spent in taking the risk is very small.

'There is a tailpiece to this story. In 1945, when the German forces surrendered, I met a colonel of the Luftwaffe and had a long technical talk with him. He had been in charge of the design of airborne mines at one time, and I asked him why they dropped magnetic mines in London as bombs, without any attempt to drop them in the river or in the docks. Why had they just scattered them over London as perfectly ordinary bombs? He said: "It was that Luftwaffe staff. I had a frightful time with them. I tried to stop them. I pointed out that these had been designed as mines to sink ships, and not as bombs to blow up houses, but they wouldn't listen. All they wanted was something with the biggest possible bang to try and demoralise England. They were trying to finish the war off quickly and we didn't manage to stop them dropping them on land." So it may be some comfort that at least every one of these mines that was dropped on London probably meant one less hazard to ships in our harbours and estuaries, and thus made some contribution to winning the Battle of the Atlantic.'

The dropping of these mines in large quantities was un-expected. And it is important to realise that during the Blitz there was a constant uncertainty as to what the Germans would drop next. Gas, for instance, was always a possibility: to begin with, even a probability. On the very first night of the Blitz a group of firemen working on a blazing warehouse became suddenly aware of a strong smell of pear-drops. Their training had taught them that this was the first and sure indication of one of the poisonous gases. They therefore put on their gas-masks and, thus encumbered, went on fighting the fire. (These may have been the group of firemen, all in gas-masks, whom Mrs Spender saw that night, while trying to get her ambulance to Oriental Road, in Silvertown.) It was some hours before they discovered that the burning warehouse contained large quantities of amyl-acetate, which, vaporised by the heat, gave off the sickly, dangerous smell, but which was no more harmful than the familiar smell of nail-varnish remover.

Nobody knew what might not next fall from the skies. There were vague rumours, which I remember hearing at the time, of a most monstrous 'radium bomb', a faint echo of pre-war researches into nuclear fission. Other rumours, which seemed more credible then, were equally unfounded, even though these were on occasion given the authenticity of

Government authority. Thus early in November an A.R.P. notice was sent out to wardens which said: 'Tins of toffees are believed to have been dropped by enemy aeroplanes. They are shaped like handbags, and some have a coloured tartan design, with puzzle, on the lid, marked Lyons' Assorted Toffee and "*Skotch*", and bearing the name J. Lyons & Co., Ld, N.14, or Cadby Hall, London. Any found to be handed immediately to police, stating where found with time and date.' Needless to say, none of these diabolical contraptions ever was found, and the origin of the rumour is unfortunately lost in obscurity.

Mr Mallet, who in 1940 was living in Chelsea—'carting X-ray equipment for the hospitals' is his own description of his job—was a fire-watcher. He has said how people at his post were always discussing strange and weird bombs. One new weapon of which he heard tell contained a huge coil spring, like the spring inside a gramophone, '. . . and if you got in the way of this thing, they said that it'd either cut your legs off, or your head off, or cut you in half. You just laugh at things like that at the time, you think they're talking out of the back of their neck, you don't take any more notice of it. But those things flash through your mind later on.' One windy night, during a raid, he was down by the Chelsea Old Church. 'They was dropping different things all over London again. Presently I heard something come down and go with a dull thud. It may have gone in the river, I don't know. Then I heard this noise.' It was a strange, scraping, metallic sound, which seemed to be coming closer in the semi-darkness. 'Well, immediately I heard this noise it reminded me of what they were saying about this coil spring. I didn't stop to look, I just took to my heels and started to go. I went up Church Street as far and as fast as I could. All I could see was the houses on either side of me, and I didn't even bother to look whether any doors were open or not.' Because, as he started up Old Church Street, he had realised that this thing, this noise, was following him, rattling and scraping along the street just about as fast as he could run.

It was, indeed, gaining on him. 'I just belted hell for leather up the road. I thought, this darned thing, whatever it is, it can't turn round a corner surely. So when I got to Paultons Street I turned the corner, and as I did this thing went by me. It stopped up the road about a hundred yards further on.' He saw it, in the half light, a dome-shaped object in the centre of the road. For some minutes he waited at the corner of the street, ready to dodge back should it show any sign of life. After a little while curiosity won, and he made his way cautiously towards it. 'And when I got up to it, what I found was this bloody dustbin lid that had chased me up the road.' And, Mr Mallet added, when he told me this story: 'You can laugh at it now, but by Christ you never did then.'

When the raids started the Germans had two principal incendiary weapons. One was the oil-bomb, a large drum of oil with an explosive fuse which scattered the burning contents for several yards in all directions. This was a clumsy and not very effective fire-raiser, and was later abandoned. The other was the thermite incendiary. This was about a foot and a half in length and weighed only a couple of pounds, so that a bomber plane could carry thousands of them. By the time they reached the ground their momentum was enough to take them through a normal tiled or slate roof, and they would then burn furiously, the magnesium alloy container fusing on impact. Sometimes they were simply poured out through the bomb-bays: sometimes they were held in aluminium containers which exploded near to the ground, thus scattering the incendiaries over a comparatively small area. Sir Aylmer Firebrace, Chief of the Fire Staff with London Region during the Blitz, has written in his book *Fire Service Memories*:

'It was a strange experience to be in the centre of a concentration of I.B.s. One moment the street would be dark, the next it would be illuminated by a hundred sizzling blueish-white flames. They made a curious plop-plopping sound as they fell on roads and pavements, but this was not often heard above the shrill whirring noise made by the pumps. They never gave me the impression that they had been dropped from the skies—they seemed rather to have sprouted.'

When first they landed they were quite easily smothered, with sand, a sandbag, or almost anything else to hand: they could even be picked up with a pair of tongs or heavy gloves, dropped in an empty bucket and carried away to a safe place, while in a roadway or on a stone roof they could usually be safely left to burn themselves out.

But in December the Germans began dropping incendiaries with a small explosive charge in the nose which exploded when the heat reached it. A man or woman who was then dealing with one of the things would be badly hurt, perhaps blinded, perhaps killed. From then on about one in ten of the incendiaries dropped contained this small explosive charge, but of course all of them were potential grenades and had to be treated as such. Dealing with them became far more perilous, and if they were not dealt with at once, they would soon start a blaze.

Every night of the raids there were fires, though until late December none approached the magnitude of the huge docks fire which had started the Blitz. In a blacked-out house, the occupants of which were in a shelter, an incendiary bomb that had come through the roof would often not be seen, nor the fire detected, behind the black-out curtains, until the upper floor was thoroughly ablaze. This happened frequently to warehouses and office buildings, locked up for the night and deserted, and, as will be seen, was partly responsible for the huge City fire of late December. But between the docks and the City, there were many great blazes, which would have been regarded as enormous in peacetime, but which, sandwiched between those two vast holocausts, are now almost forgotten.

Mr Maurice Richardson was a member of the Auxiliary Fire Service at this time, and he has said:

'My first fire was a small electrical works somewhere off the Grays Inn Road. That was very easy because there was a nice thick wire netting which one could jam the branch through and support it, so one could play the hose on the fire in utmost comfort. And it was really rather pleasant because there was nothing frightening at all, it was a small fire, it was just like a sort of night out. Well, that only lasted half an hour. Then we found ourselves in the City, bombs dropping somewhere about and we went under a shelter and hid for a while. We ended up at work on an enormous fire. It was about four in the morning, beginning to get light, and I became absolutely fascinated by the sparks, the clouds of sparks: they were really very pretty. We looked up and saw them, and they felt exactly like snowflakes. When they hit you in the face it was exactly the same reaction, of course, since the nerve centres which register heat and cold are very much the same. They were extraordinarily live and hypnotic. But the actual size of flames themselves, looking back on it now, I don't think the fires were quite as big as I'd expected. Sometimes of course they were very big, but when they were very big you didn't go right into them. I remember one on Tower Hill, which was an enormous fire. There were more than eighty pumps working on it altogether, and the pump I was on that night was coupled up doing series pumping with a whole group of pumps; which means that the only man who's needed is the man who works the motor. So the pump's crew were roaming about Tower Hill in little isolated knots, lying down in shelters and smoking and trying to find a pub which might still be open, or where the landlord, even if it was shut, would give one a drink. The whole effect was curiously disorderly: it reminded me rather of Stendhal's description of the Battle of Waterloo. . . . You didn't know quite what was going on, even though it was your fire.

'But of course it wasn't always like that, because sometimes one had to work tremendously hard. The worst thing that could ever happen to one was to get left at the far end, so to speak, with the branch, with the nozzle of the hose, under one's arm and the water coming through. One man can hold it quite easily, but it kicks very violently, and when the water's coming through you can't put it down. The worst thing that can happen to anybody at a fire is to be out on the branch, sometimes you can be many lengths of hose away from the pump, you see, and nobody comes near you, and you can't put it down because if you put it down, well, it attacks you at once. The water coming through gives it tremendous force, as though the thing is alive, this great heavy brass branch. I remember once getting stuck on the end of a branch for what seemed to be hours.

'The most notable part of the noise, apart from bombs dropping at intervals, was the throb of pumps. At a big fire you have so many of these engines going, that that is almost all you hear. Very occasionally one would hear the noise of bombers but not very often, intermittently, you know. The noise that was a typical big fire noise was the throbbing of the pumps, which kept everything else out. Sometimes there'd be a sort of hiss and a crackle from flames, and sometimes a sort of frou-frou kind of noise, as if the flames were all blowing about like skirts of fire, but the noise that was in one's mind most of the time really was the noise of the pumps—at least, that's how it seemed to me.'

The great fire raid of December 29th was not, from the German point of view, a particularly large-scale operation. Only 136 bombers were over the target, and they dropped 127 tons of high explosive and 613 canisters of incendiaries. In five previous raids on London (and in nine provincial raids) greater weights of incendiaries had been dropped: on November 15th 1,142 canisters of incendiaries had descended on London, and on December 8th, 3,188, or over five times the weight dropped on to the City three weeks later. Nor was the target deliberately chosen: the X-beams which guided the leading bombers of K.G.100 over London intersected a couple of miles further to the west. But it was the City that caught the weight of the attack, and in particularly difficult circumstances.

This was a Sunday evening, the end of Christmas week.

Despite appeals by the Government, many City office blocks and warehouses were securely locked against burglars, and many of these had no fire-watchers to put out the incendiaries as soon as they landed. Almost all the churches were also locked up and unguarded, with the notable exception of St Paul's Cathedral. The City that was still standing on the afternoon of December 29th, 1940, consisted, apart from some of its churches and the halls of the City Companies, entirely of buildings erected after the middle of the nineteenth century. The modern ferro-concrete blocks, of which there were few, were usually immune to the direct action of the incendiaries, which burned out harmlessly upon their flat roofs. The late Victorian and Edwardian buildings, on the other hand, with pitched roofs of slate or glass, caught easily and quickly. And there was a westerly wind blowing at some fifty miles an hour to fan the flames.

So the firemen found themselves confronted, very soon, with a vast number of fires, many of which were quite inaccessible. And then the water failed. The emergency main from the Thames to the Grand Junction Canal, a 24-inch underground pipe constructed just before the war, and running through the City, was broken by high explosive bombs. The sheer number of pumps operating caused the pressure drawn from other sources to drop to nothing, in many individual pumps the jet fading away quite quickly to a mere trickle. The few static water tanks then existing were soon drained dry. And the Thames that evening was at such an abnormally low ebb that its saving waters were out of reach to most of the pumps installed on its embankments and bridges. Little use could be made of fireboats: some were immobilised, downstream of the Tower Bridge, by an unexploded parachute mine, while one of the very few in a position to supply water collided with a submerged wreck and was temporarily out of action. The water, in one fireman's phrase, seemed to creep back into the hoses, and the heavy brass branches were alive no longer.

The raid was a short one. It began a little before seven and lasted only a couple of hours. (The Germans had intended to come back later, to stoke up the fires, but the weather closing in over their bomber bases mercifully made this impossible.) By the time they had gone, there were almost fifteen hundred fires burning, some in Shoreditch, Finsbury and Stepney, but over 1,400 in the City. Many of these quickly joined up to produce two huge conflagrations, one of about a quarter of a square mile, centred around Fore Street, which was simply left to burn itself out, and one twice this size which consumed everything between Moorgate, Aldersgate Street, Cannon Street and Old Street and which produced the biggest area of war devastation in all Britain. On the edge of this greater area stood St Paul's.

A fireman named Sharp made a recording for the B.B.C. a few days later, and this is what he said:.

'My particular corner of the fire was at a narrow crossroads near Fleet Street. One of the corner blocks on the far side from me was well alight, walls fallen away, doors and windows and floors inside alight and dropping. The other was only half gone but the fire was eating it up; as I watched, a glow appeared in its dark windows, then panes cracked, flames gushed out, and soon that was laid open too. There was a boom and a roar as the gas main went—a girder became red-hot and sagged. A piece of crumpled metal a foot square fell on the pavement and slowly uncurled. The fire services, of course, were hard at work.

'Two of the corner blocks hadn't been touched and I started talking to a fire-watcher who was looking after one of them. He'd already put out two incendiaries on the premises, and several in the street, running to them when they fell and dousing them with sand before the flames took hold. He kept on going in to the building to see what was happening, for the flames were pretty close. And on his next visit I followed him, thinking I might be able to help.

'Everything on the ground floor was all right—the air wonderfully cool. Then up stone steps to the second floor, an

office. Its windows were uncurtained; the fire glared at us from
a few feet away across the road, and a red smoky haze hung
over desks and typewriters and files and calendars. The paint
round the windows was bubbling, a lot of glass was broken,
but nothing was on fire. On the third floor, the managerial
floor, linoleum underfoot, mahogany partitions, doors with
frosted glass panes. We tried the doors. They were all locked.
We went upstairs again, another huge office, and here there
was trouble—all the black-out curtains were drawn across the
windows and several of them were smouldering. We drew
them or pulled them down. The window frames were burning
in about a dozen places. Simple to put them out if we had
water, but we hadn't any water. There were plenty of buckets
of sand about, but sand wasn't any use at the moment, so we
emptied the buckets and went up to the roof to search for
the cistern. By now two youths of the fire-watching staff
joined us and we went up several flights of stairs along duck-
boards, round the edge of a precipice, a gulf of fire, and up
some steps without a handrail. You couldn't see far for smoke
and swirling flames—just a few spires and chimneys and
broken rooftops. I was glad when we'd filled the buckets and
come down, but we had to go up again and again, filling
buckets, hopping downstairs with them, throwing the water
upwards at the windows. And then we found a fire on the
managerial floor. You could see a glow and then a flickering
light through the frosted glass; we broke the glass with a
chair. We couldn't very well deal with fires on two floors,
with the hand bucket system, so the fire-watcher went off to
find a stirrup pump while the three of us carried on. The
office inside was full of smoke and a nice little bonfire was
burning on the desk. I bent my head low to get it below the
smoke, stumbled in with a bucket of water, threw it at the
fire, missed, and stumbled out. My eyes were smarting, I
could hardly breathe. The two youths did the same. Then we
went up for water again, and again. More and more little fires
were starting. Far more than we could deal with, using our

primitive method, and we were beginning to despair when—
whoosh . . . all the windows blew out and a column of water
hit the ceiling, and clouds of black smoke swirled up. . . . The
firemen had found time to turn the hose on the building and us.'

Another man broadcast on the day after the raid, in these
words:

'For miles around the sky was a bright, orange-red—the
balloons in the barrage stood out as clearly as on a sunny day.
St Paul's Cathedral was the pivot of the main fire. All around
it the flames were leaping up into the sky. And there the
Cathedral stood, magnificently firm, untouched in the very
centre of all this destruction.

'As I walked along the streets it was almost impossible to
believe that these fires could be subdued. I was walking
between solid walls of fire. Groups of shops and office buildings
came down with a roaring crash. Panes of glass were cracking
everywhere from the heat, and every street was criss-crossed
with innumerable lengths of hose.

'Men were fighting the fires from the top of hundred-foot
ladders shot up from the streets, others were pushing their
way into the burning buildings, taking the jet to the fire.
There was a vast number of men there, and apart from
occasionally helping to lay out a hose, I saw that there was
nothing I could do to help. So I went instead to some of the
public shelters.

'They were underground shelters mostly, and the buildings
on top of them were alight. The people had to be got away
from them and got away quickly, and then taken across to
the underground station. Sparks were driving down the street
like a heavy snowstorm. Obviously small children couldn't
walk across to the station in this, and so some of us went
backwards and forwards carrying them in our arms.

'I took off my mackintosh and covered them up complete
with it. It must have been rather frightening for them to be
carried across by someone they didn't know, and not being
able to see anything. But it was the only way to protect them

women + children with bundles. List of subjects for shelter drawings.

1 View from inside shelter at night time, with moonlight + flare light on bombed buildings.

2 Two half figures in closed-in space, with opening showing burning building outside.

3. Single figure against shell splintered wall.

4. Head in a shelter - head in a box closed in.

5 Figures wrapped in blankets.

6 Figure in a bombed street.

Tilbury shelter

Figures showing faces lit up - rest of bodies in silhouette.

Figures lying against platform with great bales of paper above also making beds.

Perambulators with bundles.

Dramatic dismal lit, masses of reclining figures fading to perspective point — Scribbles + scratches, chaotic foreground. Chains hanging from old crane.

Sick woman in bathchair. Bearded Jews blanketed sleeping in deck chairs.

Lascars Tunnel (bundles of old clothes that are people)

Bunks with women feeding children

Dark wet settings (entrance to Tilbury)

Men with shawls to keep off draughts, women wearing handkerchiefs on heads

Muck + rubbish + chaotic untidiness around

PAGE FROM HENRY MOORE'S SKETCH-BOOK

from these sparks. And by the time we got the last one across we should have had to do it anyway because the building above the station was on fire. Luckily the station escaped, and they were all moved off in trains, to get food and drink. And then some much-needed sleep.

'Even the firemen themselves found it very difficult to save their eyes, and many of them have got burnt lids this morning —tiny sparks get caught up under the eyelids. I got a small dose of it myself and it's rather painful. Many of the firemen were very much more fiercely attacked by the sparks, and they were actually blinded for a few hours.

'We saw innumerable offices and shops alight. And wherever we went there was the roar of engines and water and the sickening thud as floors and roofs fell. As in all fires, at moments it really was a very beautiful sight, but for sheer wanton destruction I haven't yet seen anything to equal it. Nearly all the people I talked to were very angry—much more angry than before, and very tired.'

Mr Eric Lewis is a businessman. He had been to Wales for Christmas, but got back to London on that Sunday afternoon, and since it was his turn to be on duty in the large, modern block off Basinghall Street where are the offices of the mining finance company for which he works, he went straight to the City.

'I think it was somewhere about half past six and the raid had already started. Places were blazing, and when I got to the office, which is quite near the Guildhall, in a small alleyway, places were on fire and the whole alleyway was covered with smoke and what looked to me then like a blizzard of red-hot snow. Anyhow, I went to the office, because I happened to be on duty, and people were gathered there and things were getting worse. The maintenance squad, who generally looked after the building, came to me and said: "Look here, the fires are getting quite near and the Guildhall has nearly gone, I think we ought to try and save some of the things which are in the chairman's room." They had a great regard for the chairman, naturally, and so I said: "Well, if there's any danger I wouldn't bother about it, but if there isn't, you can go up and see what's there, and bring down the more important things". Two of these fellows rushed up. They hadn't been gone very many minutes when down they came, and one of them was carrying the most insignificant load that I've seen, something off the mantelpiece, and the other fellow simply brought a blotter which happened to be on a desk. Anything of real value I know must have been left exactly where it was before.

'Actually the building in which we were did not catch fire itself, but all round everywhere was a mass of flames, and one really felt rather like the sprig of holly on top of a Christmas pudding with the brandy blazing all the way round. That was even emphasised more when one looked at the Guildhall, which was one mass of flame. The firemen on top of their ladders were very tiny, and there was very little water available, and with the hoses playing on the fire at the Guildhall it just looked like little boys peeing on an enormous bonfire. That's what it did actually look like. Going out into the streets, they were naturally very much illuminated, and there was a tremendous contrasting effect between the lighted up part of the streets lit by the flames and those which were in shadow—it was quite fantastic. You saw those dark figures whirling their way with these hoses through the streets and the alleyways, and the other ones which were shown up almost like limelight at a theatre.

'Of course one couldn't do anything about it, so we stayed where we were, in the building, and just mooched round doing nothing. It was rather peculiar what one felt. I myself, if somebody had asked me before, I'd have said I'd have run round in a terrific panic, rather like a little Welsh pony at a fair, but actually one had a peculiar sense of numbness and disregard for almost anything that was happening, an incapability of discriminating. It seemed as though one had had an injection, for the whole of one's limbs and one's brain were really in a stuporific state.

'Of course this may be due to the tremendous scale on which things were happening, and the insignificance of the individual in contrast to that size. One didn't know where to go or what to do. Even when policemen kept coming into the building and saying: "You'll have to clear out, you'll have to clear out", I'd no idea where one could clear out to, and as a matter of fact I didn't mind. One moved slowly, one thought slowly and one waited inevitably for what might happen—fortunately nothing serious did happen—and one was there next morning and one accepted everything that happened the night before with a peculiar, almost inhuman, fatalism, which one would have regarded as completely unreal to oneself, had one been asked about it some weeks before.'

All over London eyes were turned towards the great blaze. The Deputy Chief of the Air Staff was working late at the Air Ministry that night, and he went up on to the roof to see the City burn. It was, he has said, a fantastic sight. He tried to engage the sentry on the roof in conversation, but that elderly aircraftman was more interested in the sexual activity of the cats. It was such an extraordinary spectacle, that the Deputy Chief of the Air Staff went down and fetched up his chief, Air Marshal Portal. For some minutes they listened to the stream of German bombers passing overhead, and to the swish of the incendiaries falling into the gathering flames. As they turned away, the Deputy Chief of the Air Staff remarked to Air Marshal Portal, with an emotion which he has said was akin to anger: 'Well, they are sowing the wind.' Then the two senior officers went downstairs and returned to work. The name of the Deputy Chief of the Air Staff was Arthur Harris.

Perhaps the most famous photograph of the Blitz was taken by Mr Herbert Mason on this night. It shows the dome of St Paul's rising majestically above the swirling pink and black clouds of smoke. Mr Mason has described what he then saw in these words:

'I remember only too well the night of the 29th December, a Sunday night. Shortly after the alert it was obvious that the

City was the target for the night. It wasn't long before incendiaries were coming down like rain. Within an hour or so the whole of the City seemed to be lighting up. In the near foreground buildings were blazing furiously and it wasn't long before the Wren Church of St Bride's was a mass of flames. The famous wedding-cake steeple was being licked. In the distance through the smoke you could see the fires increasing, and as the evening wore on an artificial wind sprang through the heat caused by the fires, parted the clouds, the buildings in the foreground collapsed, and there revealed in all its majesty was St Paul's, a hauntingly beautiful picture which no artist could recapture. Down below in the street I went towards Ludgate Hill, which was carpeted in hose pipes, a scampering rat here and there, a reeling bird in the flames. The heat became intense as I approached St Paul's Churchyard. Firemen were fighting a losing battle. Pathetically little water was coming from their hoses. Suddenly a fresh supply would come and a hose running riot would lash out and knock firemen from their feet. The heat was so intense that embers were falling like rain and clattering on your helmet. Cheapside was a mass of flames, leaping from one side of the road to the other.

'Back at my vantage point on top of the *Daily Mail* building, where I was, I could see that this night I was going to obtain the picture which would for ever record the Battle of Britain. After waiting a few hours the smoke parted like the curtain of a theatre and there before me was this wonderful vista, more like a dream, not frightening—there were very few high explosives. It was obvious that this was going to be the second Great Fire of London. The tragedy of this second great fire of London was the fact that there were so few fire-watchers. Single-handed I could have prevented thousands of pounds' worth of damage being done, but the buildings were locked, there was nobody present to force an entry. There were so few people. It was pathetic.'

Eight Wren churches went that night as well as the Guildhall which, however, had been so thoroughly restored in the eighteen-sixties that this was more of a sentimental than an architectural tragedy. Guy's Hospital was licked by flames and had to be evacuated. The Central Telegraph office, the G.P.O. telecommunications plant and three City telephone exchanges were put out of action. Five railway stations and sixteen underground stations were closed. One hundred and sixty-three people were killed, and over five hundred so seriously injured that they had to be taken to hospital. Sixteen of the dead were firemen.

A young fireman and his team, on their way back from a successful attempt to save Dr Johnson's house behind Fleet Street, lost their way among the narrow, burning streets. They found themselves in an alleyway where a trailer pump crew were fighting a fire in a printing press building. He has said:

'I thought when I saw them that they were too near. Just at that moment a wall, which looked as if it was bulging danger-ously, crashed down on them. As we looked round, all we could see was a heap of debris, with a hose leading towards it.'

But Saint Paul's was saved. A watcher across the river in Lambeth saw this:

'An unforgettable sight. The whole of London seemed involved, one great circle of overwhelming disaster, save in one corner where the night sky was clear. One could not distinguish buildings through the great clouds of smoke, except when there was a sudden spurt of yellow flames which lit up a church tower, and it seemed impossible that the City, that London could be saved. There was only that one bit of calm sky in the distance as a symbol of hope that the circle would not be completed.'

That clear patch of sky was above the Cathedral, which at least one over-anxious American correspondent had already reported destroyed to his newspaper. Indeed, it seemed incredible that it should survive.

Twenty-eight incendiaries landed on Saint Paul's that night, and watchers on the roof of the *Daily Telegraph* building say that a veritable cascade of them was seen to hit the Dome and bounce off. The Dome is, in fact, a double dome, and between the outer dome, visible from the street—or from the air—and the inner, which floats above the nave, there is a hollow space containing dry old beams, and almost inaccessible. Had any incendiaries penetrated the skin of lead that is the outer dome, the Cathedral must have been almost certainly burned down.

Hundreds of feet above the burning City the men of the St Paul's Cathedral Watch, clerics and laymen attached to the chapter as well as many volunteers, often architects, who had chosen to do this duty, fought the incendiaries. Almost at once the water supply failed, but luckily the foresighted leaders of the Watch, Dr Allen and Mr Linge, had insisted on supplies of reserve water, tanks, baths, even pails of water, being scattered throughout the structure. With this water, and with stirrup pumps, the Cathedral was saved. It was not easy. Bombs which had lodged in the roof timbers were particularly dangerous and hard to tackle. Some burned for three quarters of an hour, though simultaneously tackled by two squads, one above and one below.

But the most dangerous incendiary of all was out of reach. It had struck the Dome perpendicular to its surface and was lodged halfway through the outer shell. Though the Dome was not actually burning, the bomb was blazing, the lead about it was melting, no man could reach it, and it seemed only a matter of minutes before it must fall inside the Dome, among the beams and other dry timber. As the Dean has said: 'We knew that once a fire got hold of the Dome timbers it would, at that high altitude, quickly be fanned into a roaring furnace. . . .' And then, suddenly, as the men who loved the Cathedral waited and watched for what seemed the inevitable catastrophe, an extraordinary thing happened. The bomb fell outwards, landing on the Stone Gallery where it was quickly and easily extinguished.

Though the Chapter House, the Dean's Verger's House, the

Organist's House—all very close to the Cathedral—were burned out and one of the Minor Canons' houses was seriously damaged, the Cathedral emerged from this night of inferno almost unscathed.

To many it seemed a sort of miracle. St Paul's, during that winter, had simply and majestically taken its rightful place as London's church. A theatrical producer has told this writer that every morning, after a raid, he would look first from the windows of his Hampstead flat towards the City, to make sure that the great Dome still stood. And a simple woman in Bethnal Green, the one who, when the raids started, 'donned her helmet and out she went', remembers the night of the City blaze as follows:

'I went up on the roof with some of the firemen, to look at the City. And I've always remembered how I was choked, I think I was crying a little. I could see St Paul's standing there, and the fire all around, and I just said: "Please God, don't let it go!" I couldn't help it, I felt that if St Paul's had gone, something would have gone from us. But it stood in defiance, it did. And when the boys were coming back, the firemen said: "It's bad, but, oh, the old church stood it." Lovely, that was.'

CHAPTER EIGHT

THE GREAT City fire had revealed beyond dispute the inadequacy of the fire-prevention and fire-fighting arrangements. The Government was taken aback, and, it would seem, frightened as well. On New Year's Eve the Minister of Home Security, Mr Herbert Morrison, made a school-masterly speech over the B.B.C. in which he accused the people of 'slacking': had they not been slacking, they would apparently never have allowed the City to burn. Since they could not be trusted to protect their homes and offices voluntarily, compulsion would have to be introduced. And in January new regulations were passed which gave the Minister powers to compel persons of both sexes within certain age limits to carry out part-time civil defence duties. Men between the ages of 16 and 60 had to register, and were ordered to do up to 48 hours per month duty as firewatchers: this order was later extended to women. Another regulation laid down that business premises must be guarded and supplied with fire-fighting equipment.

This marked a fundamental change to the nature of civil defence. Hitherto in principle and largely in practice a voluntary matter, it now became more and more an affair of conscripts. This was probably inevitable in the circumstances, and so far as the prevention of fire went the new arrangements were very successful. Though they tried, the Germans never again succeeded in setting fire to any large area of London.

The arrangements for emergency water supplies were also thoroughly overhauled, great quantities of hose and transportable canvas dams being made available and large numbers of static water tanks built into the basements of demolished buildings. Finally the whole Fire Service was nationalised, the local fire brigades—which often had disparate equipment and methods—were merged, with the Auxiliary Fire Service, to form the National Fire Service. This, however, did not take place until after the period with which this book is concerned.

The more active defences also made considerable progress during the comparative lull, from mid-January to early March. A German pilot has said that he realised, with considerable apprehension, that anti-aircraft shells were exploding near his aircraft when he was actually flying in cloud. This, he realised at once, meant that the guns were now being equipped with radar. And early in the New Year it was decided to enlarge Anti-Aircraft Command by drafting women of the A.T.S. into it. Though they did not actually fire the guns, they carried out every other sort of duty and, according to General Sir Frederick Pile, these mixed batteries were most successful. Again, however, no mixed battery was in operation until after the London Blitz was over.

But it was the night fighter that really made the most progress during the first few months of 1941. The story of the night fighters is given by C. F. Rawnsley and Robert Wright in their book *Night Fighter*, and it would be invidious to reproduce it here. Briefly, however, the mounting successes of this arm can be ascribed to the growing skill of the pilots and navigators, and to the much greater efficiency of the radar installations, both airborne and on the ground. The system, in essence, was that the ground radar detected the enemy bomber and ground control guided the night fighter towards him until the fighter's own radar set could pick up the enemy. The fighter would then close to within visual range, perhaps two or three hundred feet, identify the enemy, and shoot him down. This required a very high degree of skill on the part of the pilot and navigator and split-second organisation on the part of ground control. These were achieved, and from mid-March on, according to a German bomber pilot, the night fighters became far more of a menace to the enemy than the guns. Indeed, he has said, when pursued by a night fighter he would deliberately fly into the gun zone, or even in among the barrage balloons, to shake off his pursuer.

Group-Captain Cunningham has said:

'The German raiders that started the night bombing, the earliest ones that came in, were usually the most skilled air crews, and their task was to go and put their incendiaries on to the target, and the follow-up aircraft were then given the rather easier task of just unloading their high explosive on to the incendiary fires beneath. We got our greatest satisfaction in catching the head of the raid, but as time went on, and the enemy bombers realised they were being intercepted by fighters, they adopted much more difficult tactics. There were considerable evasions throughout their flights, and although our skill gradually improved and developed, it still remained a difficult job to close in and shoot down a German bomber.

'The light conditions that we used to have to meet when going in to attack these German aircraft would vary enormously. Some occasions there would be a bright moon and a starlit sky, on others it would be dark. My own preference was the dark night, or the no-moon night, because although we had to go in somewhat closer to readily identify and then shoot at the target, there was less chance of being seen by the gunner or gunners of the bomber, who were there with the sole purpose of looking out both above and below the aircraft with a gun to shoot down the fighter that was coming in on them. From experience, and by making full use of the dark part of the sky to make your approach to the enemy aircraft, there was a jolly good chance on a dark night that the fighter could get really close in and get his guns to bear on the bomber before he'd ever been spotted. There were numbers of occasions of course when this didn't happen and we were shot at before we were able to shoot at the bomber.

'I well remember coming up behind a Heinkel 111 with a bright moon on the port beam. And as I came up very close to the aeroplane, just prior to opening fire, I could see the moon shining on the gun barrels of the rear upper gunner's guns, that were not pointing directly at me (but they should have been), and then I spotted them move, and he opened fire a few seconds before I was on to him, but that was all— I did get that one.

'I think the most vivid memory I have of a combat was of shooting down a Heinkel 111 that was just going out over the South Coast near the Isle of Wight. I imagine it must have had very nearly empty fuel tanks, because the moment I fired at fairly close range, I was between two and three hundred feet behind it, there was a blinding flash and the whole thing disintegrated. In my fright I pulled hard on my control column to avoid flying straight through all the wreckage, but I couldn't avoid much of that. This Heinkel had stopped flying and burst into flames, the wing had come off, and all I was left with was a great glow of flame somewhere beneath me and the whole sky was alight. I began to think that I was as well.'

Squadron-Leader Rawnsley, who was John Cunningham's navigator, has a very vivid memory of this kill. He says:

'I was looking along the fuselage from inside, and instead of darkness I noticed that every sort of chink and cranny seemed to be outlined in red fire, and there were things going bump in the night, and things scraping along the keel, and I rather thought we'd had it and I remember remarking to John: "Are we still in one piece?" And John said, in rather a doubtful voice: "Well, yes, I think so", and we sort of checked up, I heard him checking up on the instruments, I had a look at the radar set and I could still see a contact, that was rushing down on the right. I looked out of the window to see what was happening and there was the Heinkel, spinning down like a great big catherine wheel, into the cloud, and the wing which had blown off was coming down just like a falling leaf, that fluttered down, and we were just left alone up there with the moonlight shining on the clouds, like great ice cliffs towering up for thousands of feet all round us, and every now and again there'd be an enormous flash of lightning coming from this cloud which lit up everything in a sort of steel-blue light just like daylight.'

These dark battles—the detection of the enemy, the stealthy approach in the night sky, the sudden burst of cannon fire from sharp astern, and, with luck, the disintegration of the enemy —took place far out of sight of London's weary millions. The news of the successes of the night fighters was nonetheless extremely heartening to the tired people on the ground. In January and February the night fighters had shot at only nine bombers per month: in March the figure was 25: in April, 34: and in May, 116, a startling increase.

The civilian population needed encouragement, for though the raids on London were few after the lull, some of them were exceptionally vicious and violent.

On March 8th 125 planes bombed the capital: on March 9th, 94: and on the 15th, 101. These raids were comparable in weight to those of the Christmas period. But the four further raids that London was to suffer that spring were the heaviest of all. On March 19th, 479 bombers dropped 467 tons of H.E. and 3,347 incendiary canisters: on April 16th, 'the Wednesday', 685 planes dropped 890 tons of H.E. and 4,200 canisters of incendiaries: three nights later, 'the Saturday', came the heaviest raid of all, with 712 planes dropping 1,026 tons of H.E. and 4,252 incendiary canisters: and on May 10th, London's last, 507 planes dropped 711 tons of H.E. and 2,393 incendiary canisters.

When it is realised that only once during the autumn—on October 15th—had the enemy dropped more than 400 tons of H.E. in a night, the ferocity of these later raids becomes self-evident. The especial savagery of the Wednesday and the Saturday is explicable in that these were specifically ordered by Hitler, as reprisals for the bombing of Berlin, and he had laid down that they were to be as heavy as possible. Many German aircrews flew two, and some flew three, sorties on those nights. And the bombs dropped were now much heavier, the incendiaries more efficient.

Though the civil defence services were highly experienced and most competently trained by now, the sheer weight of these last four massive attacks seems almost to have overwhelmed the ground defence. Had the Germans launched attacks on this scale at the beginning of the Blitz, or had they carried out sustained and repeated attacks on this scale in April and May, there is some doubt as to whether London could have endured them without at least a drastic revision of the whole system of shelters, evacuation and defence. But luckily they were few, they were spaced, and London was given time to recover between these tremendous punches; for this was the time when the Luftwaffe was doing its best to smash the provincial cities as well. (It must not, however, be imagined that the weight of attack on the provincial towns was in any way comparable to that on London. London, which had received some 19,000 tons of bombs before November 14th, had over 5,000 more tons, in fourteen raids, after that date. No other target was bombed more than eight times, or received as much as 2,000 tons of bombs.)

Since by April the move of the German armies to the Eastern Front had already begun, these last, heavy raids were in no wise a preliminary to invasion. It may be asked why the Germans carried out these murderous attacks. One explanation may be that Hitler hoped that his 'reprisal' raids would cause the British Government to reconsider their own bombing policy: a more likely one is that these raids, by concentrating the attention of the world on the British Isles, were intended to mask the move of the armies to the East, that they were in fact part of a vast cover plan: a third, and also probable, explanation is that even at this late stage Hitler and Goering still hoped that it might be possible to knock Britain out of the war by air attack alone, thus giving the Wehrmacht a free hand in the East: and finally, violent air operations of this sort undoubtedly appealed to Hitler's sadistic nature. In any event, brutal as they were, the attacks failed to achieve any of their objectives save possibly that of masking the forthcoming Eastern Campaign from the Russians.

But brutal they certainly were, and the strain on the men and women of the Civil Defence Service, already very tired after the long autumn and winter, was great. In the preceding chapters, the effect of the raids has been usually described mainly from the point of view of civilians, as will be the case in the next chapter which deals with the bombing of the Café de Paris. But it cannot be stressed too strongly that the brunt of the battle of London was borne by the firemen, and perhaps even more so by the wardens. Therefore, to end this chapter, here is a description of a major incident of the Wednesday raid. For this I am indebted to Mr L. W. Matthews, a Post Warden of D Post in Chelsea, who was directly concerned in the event described, the bombing of the Chelsea Old Church.

On the night of 16-17th April, 1941, almost seven hundred German bombers attacked South and Central London for nearly eight hours. Civilian casualties were over one thousand killed and two thousand seriously injured, and among the buildings hit were eighteen hospitals and thirteen churches, one of which was Chelsea Old Church.

Owing perhaps to its position on the river and proximity to the centre of Government, the power stations and similar objectives, Chelsea had already suffered considerable damage. Taking its size into account, it was one of the most heavily bombed boroughs in London, only Holborn and Shoreditch receiving a heavier tonnage of bombs per acre. On the night we are concerned with, five parachute mines, a number of other high-explosive bombs and many hundreds of incendiaries fell within Chelsea's boundaries, in an area of about six hundred and sixty acres.

While the Rescue, Fire and Medical Services could be relied on to do all that could be done when people were actually overwhelmed by disaster, trapped in the debris of their homes, perhaps gravely injured, it was the fire-watchers and the wardens recruited from local residents and shopkeepers who always bore the first shock of attack. The wardens' first duty was the reporting of air raid damage: and for this local knowledge was essential. For example, a big high-explosive bomb on an empty warehouse was unimportant beside a small one on an occupied dwelling, and each warden's post kept up-to-date census records of the population of its area. They had many other duties: first aid, care of those made suddenly homeless, and so on; but it was the information they provided about each 'incident' which brought the specialised services into action and enabled the Controllers to deploy them to the best advantage. The wardens were also responsible for the training and organisation of the firewatchers, or Street Fire Parties, later known as Fire Guards. Armed with stirrup pumps and buckets, sometimes with dustbin lids borne as shields, the firewatchers dealt with the scattered incendiary bombs, each of which could cause a major fire.

Chelsea Old Church was guarded by a party of volunteers from the congregation and nearby business premises formed by the Vicar, the Rev. Ralph Sadleir, who took his turn on the duty rota and arranged for them to use his study on the first floor of Petyt House as the Fire Party Post or headquarters. Arthur Mallett, the only survivor of the six firewatchers on duty the night the church was destroyed, says he told the Vicar the room was too good to use for such a purpose. 'There was a fine polished table to sit at with our tea', he said, 'and it was furnished with his own belongings, books, a grand carpet and so on.' There were tiers of bunks for six persons on the small stage or dais at one end of the room. Mallett himself usually slept curled up on the rug in front of the fire.

There was a leader appointed for each night in the week. Normally Wednesday's leader was Mr Bottley of Gregory Bottley & Co., Mineralogists, 30 Old Church Street, and Mrs Bottley made one of the party, but they had gone away the week before on a three weeks' trip to North Wales to obtain geological specimens, and their places on the rota were taken by their manager, Mr Fred Winter, and by the optical lens maker, Mr Sidney Sims. Both men had been with the firm since leaving school and were highly regarded. Sims was engaged to be married, Winter was married with two children.

With Mallett, Winter and Sims on duty that Wednesday were Mrs Greene, Michael Hodge and a Mr Franklin. The latter was a carpenter employed by the Westminster Carriage Company, 48 Old Church Street, and was not strictly speaking a member of the Fire Party but had attached himself to them for company, and they included his premises in their patrols.

Michael Hodge was aged seventeen and very tall for his age. He was waiting to go up to Cambridge but was talking of enlisting in the Black Watch. He was staying at the Grosvenor Hotel with his parents and used to come down to Chelsea on Wednesday evenings by taxi.

Yvonne Greene of 34 Old Church Street, a Canadian and newly married to a Canadian army officer, was a part-time Auxiliary Fire Service driver. At five minutes past nine on the evening of the 16th, when the sirens began sounding the 'Alert', she was off duty, but rang up the Fire Station at South Parade to find out whether she was needed there before going down to join the others at Petyt House.

All day people had been saying to each other: 'Summer has come early after all.' Mr Kealey, the wine merchant of Justice Walk, was on duty on the Monday of that week, Easter Monday, and remembers it was cold; there was even snow. But on the Wednesday the sun shone all day long, and in the evening a little of its warmth lingered in the narrow streets around the church, though a cooler air was coming off the river with the ebbing tide.

The local wardens' post map of those days shows an area bounded on the North by the King's Road, South by the river, West by Beaufort Street and East by Oakley Street. The Old Church dominated the river frontage. The wardens' post itself was a ground-floor classroom in the Glebe Place side of Cook's Ground School (later Kingsley School).

Try to see this area as it was then, with sparse wartime

traffic accelerating in the main thoroughfares as the sirens' wailing rose and fell, warning and challenging. Doors were opening and shutting in all the darkened streets as people left home for the shelters in Paultons Square, the Rectory Garden or the Embankment Gardens. Street Fire Parties met and looked up at the sky, already throbbing with approaching bombers.

Wardens were converging on the wardens' post, to join those on duty. They came blinking from a dark corridor into the small classroom, reduced in height and space by steel joints supporting heavy baulks of timber overhead, helmeted and dungareed men and women hampered by their respirators, hooded lamps, belts hung with pouches containing report pads, axes, extra torches and first-aid packs. As patrols were paired off and dispatched to report on the numbers of persons occupying shelters and the state of manning of fire party posts, a pattern of routine emerged. Messages were exchanged with the Control Centre under the Town Hall, with other wardens' posts and with the warden posted as look-out on the roof of the school. Those not detailed for a duty settled down in deck chairs to read, write or chat over a cup of tea.

Warden David Thomas was questioned about the mural he had started that morning on the wall beside the telephone switchboard. Working from a sketch made a few days before, he had begun a coloured drawing of the Old Church. Another artist, W. F. Measom, offered to provide Thomas with one of his own sketches of the little shops to the West of the Church and the Old Café Lombard, demolished before the war, to complete the picture. (After the war the Wardens' Post became the School Meals Service Kitchen, but thanks to ex-warden A. R. Maxwell-Hyslop, of the Ministry of Education, the picture was glazed and preserved for the time being.)

The telephone rang: the rooftop lookout reported parachute flares dropping in the south-east and, a few minutes later, over Lots Road Power Station. A patrol came back with the numbers of people sheltering in the Embankment Gardens shelters and the state of the fire parties in that sector. Another patrol had nothing to report but mentioned that bombs were falling across the river in Battersea and fires had been started in the south and south-east.

At half past nine the Post Warden left his deputy in charge and went out on a cycle patrol of the area. In spite of the noise of gunfire and aircraft it was quiet enough, cycling slowly in the middle of the road, for him to hear the swish of the tyres, the occasional tinkle of falling shell casing or a greeting from someone watching in a doorway. In the foggy shelters a few words were exchanged with 'regulars' near the entrance. 'Come to tuck us up?' 'Noisy tonight, isn't it?'—and then, outside, a deep breath of fresh air.

On returning to the school he climbed many stairs, past floor after floor of deserted classrooms to the flat roof. This had been asphalted to make a playground: barred embrasures looked out from the six-foot walls. By one of these a warden and a telephone were protected by a sheet of corrugated iron. Bright sparkles of anti-aircraft shells crackled high overhead and elsewhere bombers droned across, and back, and above it all, without interruption. There was a big fire near Victoria; as they watched, the fire took a fresh hold. It was as if a blast furnace had split open: a corona of flame pulsed upwards: the reflecting arc of sky expanded suddenly, and details of landscape seen only in silhouette suddenly became visible.

Many who have experienced it have remarked on the uneasy exhilaration of such a scene: you had a grandstand view of a glorified bonfire night, you enjoyed the spectacle and felt at the same time a prickle of horror, 'a horror of great darkness'.

Downstairs in the post a fresh brew of tea was waiting.

At half past eleven the roof lookout reported a heavy explosion and clouds of black smoke in the eastern half of Chelsea, near the river. This was not in Post Don's area and no action was called for. They learned through an adjacent post that the Royal Hospital Infirmary had been hit and the

A.F.S. station at 21 Cheyne Place put out of action. There were many casualties and widespread damage, due apparently to a single heavy bomb. There were rumours that part of a 'land-mine' had been found.

By one in the morning about forty trapped casualties had been reported at the Royal Hospital Infirmary. A wardens' post nearby had dealt with more than that number of walking cases and homeless persons. Nothing had fallen in Post Don's area. The Post Warden was conducting his senior officer, the District Warden, on a tour of the area, and they were returning from watching incendiary bombs rattling down on warehouse roofs across the river when they saw the six members of the Old Church Fire Party leave the shadow of the tower and walk away from it along Cheyne Walk towards Danvers Street.

The Post Warden had returned to Cook's Ground School and was just sitting down to make an entry in the Log Book, when two heavy explosions occurred close at hand. The time was twenty past one. Everything in the room jumped, dust was shaken down, the sound of breaking glass and splintering woodwork came from elsewhere in the building. Leaving the telephonist in charge of the Post, the Post Warden despatched all available wardens to investigate and went out himself. The District Warden joined him in the corridor. His windows had been blown in on top of him as he sat in his office, but he had escaped injury.

As they turned the corner from Glebe Place into Upper Cheyne Row lights were visible in some of the houses; windows and window frames complete with blackout had been sucked out into the road or pushed into the room. Tiles, broken slates, lath and plaster, bits of wood and glass littered the roadway, but this was only minor damage.

Justice Walk was blocked half way in from Lawrence Street, and it was evident that the centre of damage was somewhere on the other side of it.

As they ran round the corner into Cheyne Walk they were brought down by a length of garden railing. They saw flames

227

leaping up in a thinning dust haze. Near Danvers Street in a shallow crater in the road a gas main was on fire. And then it came to them both: 'The Old Church has gone!' There was a jagged stump of brickwork and projecting timbers silhouetted where the eye had expected the massive square tower.

Some of the houses beyond it in Cheyne Walk were demolished, others were hanging shells, blasted through from back to front. A woman was calling for help from one of them. Leaving the District Warden to organise what help was available on the spot, the Post Warden ran back to the Post to send the brief message which would bring the necessary casualty services. The telephonist at Control Centre repeated the message back to him: 'Post Don. Express Report. Chelsea Old Church. Trapped Casualties. Fire. Time of reference 0125 hours. Message Ends.' It was now his duty to collect various paraphernalia, blue hat cover, blue lamps, portable desk complete with log and message pads, and to assume the role of Incident Officer at the 'Incident', for that was what the Old Church had now become.

Part-time warden A. R. Maxwell-Hyslop had returned to London from the country about dinner time that evening. He had not previously met Mr Matthews, the new post warden. Here is Mr Maxwell-Hyslop's description of what he saw that night:

'I had come up to London that afternoon. I'd been down in the country at the weekend, and I'd had 'flu and I particularly didn't want to have to get up that night. When the raid started first of all I said I wasn't going to get up, and then it got so heavy that I knew that I must, and I think I was actually dressing to go on duty when I heard these two very loud explosions, almost simultaneously. I didn't know where they were and I actually went out of the flat I was living in and turned the wrong way to start with, so I came down to the Old Church from the King's Road, down Old Church Street. Right at the top of Old Church Street there was glass out, and bits of debris and then on the right I saw a big sheet metal sliding door into a warehouse, it was all buckled in a kind of wavelike pattern, and I realised that it must have been a very big explosion somewhere very close. Then I went down Old Church Street and at the last turn I could suddenly see a great pile, a great mountain of rubble, and behind it the bright flames of a burning gas main, and I realised that the church must have been hit.

'That was the most awful shock because people who live in Chelsea often talk about living in a village, and sometimes it's thought to be an affectation, but that night I don't think any of us felt that. The church always had been in Chelsea very much the heart of the village, and it was like seeing something that one loved killed in front of one's eyes.

'I went on down Old Church Street and came to this rubble and there I met Mr Matthews, the post warden, whom I hadn't met before; I knew it was him because he had a special mark on his white helmet which identified him. And I said to him: "I was going to be married in this church." And he said—"I was married in this church." And then we separated again. I can remember one old lady coming out of the top of that pile of rubble. I can remember thinking then—and I've never been able to understand it since—that she must have been thrown twenty or thirty yards in the middle of this enormous mass of timber and brick and broken glass and goodness knows what, and yet somehow she'd settled in there and more stuff had piled on top of her, and yet she didn't seem, when we got her out, to be hurt at all. I've never been able to understand how that could happen. Well, then the raid went on, and there was this horrible noise and the bright light of the burning gas main, and some time later on I heard somebody shouting what sounded like: "Look, there's another!" And I looked up and there coming overhead, coming down from the King's Road towards the river, was a parachute, and I was quite certain it was another mine. And all I could think of doing was to get down behind the pile of rubble and I lay down and I counted twenty waiting for it to explode and thinking that

I was sure to be killed but not being so frightened of that as of the noise I was going to hear. And after I counted twenty, and nothing had happened, I began to feel rather silly. I heard people shouting on the embankment, and I got up and I saw that they were leaning over the embankment; and a little later, up came this frightened-looking German airman and was taken away by a couple of policemen. There were incendiaries later, two lots of them, and we scattered to help put them out. The only other thing that I remember is a silly little thing. I was talking to the district warden and another man just between the wardens' post and the church, and in the middle of a sentence we heard another stick of bombs coming down, so we all went down on our faces. As we got up again after these bombs had exploded, we went on exactly from the point in the sentence where we'd stopped.'

The population of Chelsea fell during the Blitz from 58,000 to 16,000. Mr Cremonesi, the grocer of 26 Old Church Street, had closed his business and was serving as a War Reserve Policeman attached to Chelsea Police Station. On the 16th he had come off duty at ten in the evening and on returning home had joined the Old Church Fire Party on the embankment to watch the novel display of flares: 'They were the biggest we had ever seen', he said, 'like enormous chandeliers hanging over the river.' They had gone into the post at Petyt House for tea, and were in and out of it for some time, patrolling their sector and watching the raid going on all around them. At about a quarter to one in the morning, as nothing had happened, he went home to bed.

He woke up to find the window-frame on his bed and the room full of dust. He got up and dressed as best as he could among the debris of his bedroom, behind the shop. The shop itself was completely wrecked. Debris littered the roadway outside, and further along the street was blocked. Through a fog of dust he could see a fire burning beyond the wreckage of Petyt House and the church. Above that on his side of the street there had been some small houses. Now they were just a pile of rubble. He found an Inspector Lewis of Chelsea Police already investigating the top of the mound. 'Here's somebody!' Cremonesi couldn't see anything but put his hand down through a space and touched warm flesh.

The last thing Miss Maud Matthews could remember was that she had been heating some milk in a saucepan to help her to sleep, for the raid was so noisy. She had been in the top back room of number six and there had been a Miss Bond in the front room.

While Cremonesi released Miss Matthews, who was pinned by the neck but uninjured though completely naked, Inspector Lewis found and released Miss Bond, who attracted attention by pushing a utensil on a stick up through the debris and rattling it.

On his return to the Incident the Post Warden's first task was to estimate the extent of the damage and numbers and position of trapped casualties. A quick reconnaissance over the rubble gave him his bearings. Church Street was blocked a good way up. He sent a report by runner that all vehicles must approach by Cheyne Walk. The Express Report would automatically bring a Rescue Party, Stretcher Party and Ambulance; reinforcements would probably be needed.

The Church itself was no more than a great heap of rubble and broken timbers. The blast had lifted the old bricks and blown out the powdery mortar like a winnowing fan: not much point in looking for anyone in that. The first house in Petyt Place had been demolished, but the others, though ripped open, still stood, and lights showed in one of them. A man with a minor wound was given first aid. Other wardens were detailed to search all damaged houses in the vicinity.

Behind the ruins of the Church the end wall of the nurses' home of the Cheyne Hospital for Children rose undamaged to about two thirds up the second floor: there the brickwork had been sucked away along a clean line from back to front, leaving the top floor exposed in section from the floor joists to the roof space. There was a made-up bed, a chair, an open wardrobe and a ceiling light still burning. With a gas main alight just round the corner, there was little point in worrying about infringements of the blackout regulations, but from force of habit one of the searching wardens climbed perilously up the exposed staircase, now supported only on one side, and switched it off.

An eerie hallooing in the cavernous darkness of one of the damaged Cheyne Walk houses seemed to promise the whereabouts of casualties, but turned out to be a policeman engaged in a search on his own.

The warden in charge of parking arrangements came up to report that no ambulances had arrived. The women extricated by Maxwell-Hyslop, Cremonesi and Inspector Lewis were despatched to hospital. Thanks to Cremonesi's local knowledge, people who had been sheltering in the basements of the little houses behind Petyt House were quickly found and led out from the back, among them an old man of ninety-one. The Rescue and Stretcher parties arrived, and a search began for other residents of the little houses who, according to the wardens' census records, were missing. A gap in the pavement giving off a heavy odour of town gas suggested a way in, but proved impassable until a very small Rescue man the others called 'Yorkie' wriggled through and searched what was in fact an empty cellar. Some of the men began tunnelling into the wreckage: others began working at 77 Cheyne Walk, the *New Café Lombard*, where it was feared some of the fire party might be trapped with another party of three known to be posted there. The body of a man who might be one of them but had not been identified had been found by the bus stop across the road.

Someone came up with the news that one of the fire party had escaped and was now at his home at 27 Old Church Street. It was important to find out what had happened to the others, and handing over to a deputy, the Post Warden went to find Arthur Mallett.

He was lying on a couch in the darkened, blitzed ground-floor back room with other members of the family huddled round him.

Here is Mallett's account of his almost miraculous escape, for he was the only survivor of the little party of fire-watchers:

'During the blitz of 1940 and '41 I was asked if I'd volunteer to join this A.R.P. Fire Service, wardens' post, so I said all right, being as I was up early in the mornings I thought it'd be a good idea that I could be called any time I liked, so I slept at the post more than I did at home actually—I don't know, can't hardly remember when I went to sleep. Anyhow, this precise evening I was there, there was the crowd of us all around in the fire-watching post down in Petyt House, Old Church Street, just down by the old Chelsea church. Everything was nice and quiet, we used to go in there, sit down and have a game of cards or tell tales and read books, go to sleep if we wanted to. Well, what I usually used to do was to go down there and stop up till about twelve or one, then I used to turn in and ask the firewatchers if they'd call me early in the morning as I'd got to get off to work. I used to leave any time from half past five to six in the morning. So that's how things carried on with me. Anyhow, that night somebody suggested that they'd never been up on top of Chelsea Old Church, so I said: "I've been up there two or three times." I said: "The old warden, or whatever he was of the church, he used to come round and ask us if we'd go up and unfurl the flag because it was always getting tied up and twisted around the flag-post on top of the church, and he was a bit elderly so he couldn't climb up the pole, and it was a fairly high church and it was a bit windy up there—he couldn't hardly take a ladder up the winding staircase, so what I used to do, go up to the top of the church, climb up the flagpole and unfurl the flag for him, whenever there was a flag flying up there." Anyhow, we all get up on top of the church and we can get quite a good view from there. We was looking down into dockland area, towards dockland area, and it was quite bright, and it looked very much as if they'd got a raid on down that way. We didn't take much

233

notice of it, one or two there, there was a girl there, a Canadian as a matter of fact, I think her name was Mrs Greene but we always called her Canada. She seemed a bit on the nervous side, so I said: "Well, you had enough of it, all of you?" They said yes, so we decided we'd go down. It was a creepy old place really, I suppose, to some of 'em, I mean it was a bit on the nervous side coming down that winding staircase. Anyhow, we came down out of the church and we went back into the wardens' post. Well, just as we got back into the wardens' post the alert went, so right, we all don our tin hats and everything, helmets, gas-masks we had with us, some were old ex-Army ones, I know, but anyhow, we had them all strapped on to us and away we go, down on to the embankment. When we get down there there's a hell of a lot of shrapnel and stuff coming down, I think they let everything fly. So I'm standing there, all of a sudden something comes down beside me, a big lump of shrapnel or something, so I went over, picked it up and I looked at it and I said to myself: "Christ", I said, "this is expensive metal to be throwing about." And I was looking, then I see it was where the nose-cap had rubbed over the piece of shrapnel and made it look as if it was phosphorous bronze. So being disillusioned, about not making any money out of it, I just was going to dump it. But that second there was such a thud at the side of me, like a fifty-six pound coal-sack dropping on the soft ground. I didn't take a lot of notice, I was still looking at this piece of metal, I was just going to throw it away again, and then I looked: "Oh Christ", I said like that to myself. I looked, there was this big cylinder laying down beside me. I could have picked it up. Anyhow, I turned round to the other firewatchers, I said: "For Christ's sake, run!" Anyhow they run, they was about twenty feet farther away than where I was. Anyhow, they run towards Chelsea Old Church, even then I didn't run, I stood there, and I thought: "Well, I don't know, it's about time I got cracking". I see them running, I had no more to do, I started to run. Well, as I neared the bottom of Old Church

234

Street I set up such a speed that I couldn't turn the corner. I thought: "Bugger this, so right ho, I'll carry straight on." Anyhow, there was a little iron post and a fire post down beside the old church, it was about the only covering, and I thought: "Well, this post is stuck in the ground well, that won't move in a hurry". So I crouched down beside that. Well, as it happened there must have been another land mine come down behind the church. As it did so it exploded and blew the one off that I'd already left. Well, the next thing I remember was—I looked, and when I looked I couldn't see anything. And I thought: "Well, I don't know, the eyes have gone", and it put the wind up me for the minute. But I just sat there, closed me eyes again, I looked up in the air, I thought: "Well, I'm bound to see stars". There were a few out, so I looked up, I looked up, I see millions of them, but they wasn't stars. It was as if I'd been hit on the head with something and you're sort of dazed. So I sort of crouched down again, sat there for a few minutes more, I suppose, it seemed like hours, but I just sat there, and when I looked up again I see a little bright one in among the lot, so I thought: "Ah, that's all right, I am all right." Anyhow, when I got up I found half me trousers had gone, that was the trousers on me right leg. Then I felt something running down me left leg. I thought: "I'm not looking at that." So I stood up for a few minutes and then I could see why it was I couldn't see. There was so much dust and that flying around that I was completely blacked out. Well, I turned round to look up Old Church Street, naturally, because I live up there. When I looked I couldn't see anything —it looked just like a mountain of rubble. "Blimey", I thought, "that lot's gone." Anyhow, I looked out towards the embankment and as I looked out towards the embankment I see a young fellow there that I knew, a chap named Mascall, and he was crying, walking towards me. So I went up to him and I said: "What's the matter, Jimmy?" So he says: "Cor", he says, "ain't it terrible?" He says: "Nearly our lot, wasn't it?" So I said: "Oh, don't let that worry you", I said. "You're all right",

I said. "Get a cup of tea or something", I said, "you'll be all right." Well, I turned round. I thought: "I'd better get up home now and see what's happening up Church Street." Then I remembered all the other firewatchers that was with me, so I started shouting out all their names, I called them all out, what I knew, the nicknames I called 'em by, I didn't get any answers. Eventually I started to climb over all this rubble, it must have been about twenty—maybe fifteen, twenty feet high. Anyhow, I climbed over it and as I started to climb over it, I met my sister, Alice—she'd come down to find out whether I was all right or not. She said: "You all right?" So I said, "Yes", I said, "I've got my trousers torn, Alice". So she said, "Well", she said, "the roof's gone on the house and the windows are out." So I said: "You got a cup of tea up there? That's the main thing." She said: "Come on, we'll go up home." Well, as I got over the rubble I met Mr Cremonesi. So he shouted out something about: "You all right, Arthur?" I said: "Yes, I'm all right." The next thing I see him diving over the top of some rubble. He was whereabouts where Mr Dakins' people were, that's just the other side of Petyt House. Well, when I looked Petyt House had gone, everything around there, all the houses there on the embankment were gone. I did hear a woman calling from a basement. Well, being as me leg was bleeding and I didn't look at it, I didn't bother about me leg, all I was worried about was the woman calling—it was down the basement. I see two or three people there, I can't remember who they were now, but anyhow I told 'em that this woman was down the basement, and I said to them: "Get down there and get her out." So I see them going towards her, so I thought: "Well, that's about all I can do, I've got to be away at six o'clock to work." So I thought: "I'll get home and get some sleep." And when I came up Old Church Street I went indoors and I went to lay down on the bed, the next thing happens, the Chief Warden comes round, he wanted to know what happened. Well, I was too fed up to answer him, all I wanted to do was to get to sleep and get to work, so I near enough told him where to go, straight away, and I went indoors and lay down for a couple of hours. Well, I felt so rough and dirty and that, that I was on this work at the time, I was carting X-ray equipment for the hospitals, so I thought: "Well, there's only one place I know where they might have some tea, and that's at the Fulham Road workhouse, or institution as they call it now." So I had no more to do, I went up there, and I knew Mr Bentall the baker, I went down to see him, so he said: "Hello, Bill", he said, "what's the matter with you?" So I said: "Well", I said, "they've just blown Chelsea Old Church up," I said, "made a bit of a mess down there," I said. So he said, "What do you want?" I said, "I want a cup of tea first off." Anyhow, he comes back with a big pint mug of tea, and I think that's the best pint of tea that I've ever had in my life.'

Mr Matthews returned to the scene of the disaster. He has written:

The ambulance station at Blanche's Garage was out of commission. Trapped casualties were now estimated at ten. Another stretcher had been sent for.

In the debris of number six Old Church Street the Rescue men had reached Emma Chandler, aged sixteen. Her face had been uncovered and she was talking normally to the man beside her. The Rescue Party Leader explained that she was trapped by joists jammed by heavy masonry. Each piece would have to be sawn through and shored up, with the constant possibility of everything subsiding into the cellar below. There was a powdering of ochreous dust over the torch-lit group. However carefully they worked, there was a continuous rattle of particles among the debris.

Mr Matthews has amplified what he has written about that night, in these words:

'Perhaps I ought to try and paint a more precise picture of the incident. By this time there was a big pile of debris, the rubble at the bottom of Old Church Street, right across the roadway. We had to climb, scramble over it and all sorts of holes and craters in it. I remember my own wrists were grazed from it and we were continually falling into the holes, it wasn't at all the sort of textbook method of conducting an incident. We had to find each other to begin with. We had torches but they quite often got broken. We had a method of keeping a record of the incident, a sort of rough log on a piece of paper on a board which was fastened round our necks on a dog lead, but of course falling into holes, dropping it, you had to carry the thing in your head most of the time. But there was this pile of debris and beside it, just a little way up Church Street on the right-hand side where the rubble of the cottages was, the rescue party were working. I don't think they needed very much light because there was a good deal of general light on the scene, but there were hooded torches and in the middle of the party, the men who were working, there was this girl trapped, and of course they had to work very carefully, because if they'd gone at it too roughly the debris would have collapsed on her. The work could only go on very slowly there. Just a little way across the road, in Petyt Place, the houses were rather badly damaged, and there were some big houses in front of those in Petyt Place and at one point I heard a weird sort of noise going on—somebody calling. I thought at first that it was a casualty trapped there, then I found that a police-man was going around and calling for casualties and making this weird sort of hallooing noise to see if anyone was there. All sorts of little things like that happened during the night. The other site of damage at the bottom of Danvers Street was very bad indeed and it didn't seem likely that anyone could be alive there, but some of the rescue party were working there, tunnelling into the debris to see if they could find anyone. The incident went on and there were certain technical things which one needn't repeat—connected with reinforcement of rescue parties, there was, for example, a lot of gas, town gas, coming out of the broken gas pipes, so that parties standing by were often overcome with that. There were little bits of salvage, rather pathetic little things that belonged to people, a work-man's tools for example, gathered up, belonging to one of the

238

people who was later on to be brought out of the debris dead, handbags, trinkets and so forth—these were all collected up, it was all part of our job to collect these things.

'Then suddenly somebody called out: "There's another one coming!" and I remember looking up and seeing what I thought was another parachute mine coming down. It was absolutely terrifying. You couldn't look away from the thing and there you were, just trying to make yourself as small as possible in the debris, and I suddenly realised it wasn't a mine, it was a man, it was an airman on the end of this parachute, and he dropped down quite fast over the roadway and down on to the foreshore of the river, on the embankment. A number of us rushed across there and then we looked rather cautiously over the wall. We had ideas about paratroop invasions. I remember a couple of firemen training a hose and I was clutching my axe and I expect everybody else was wondering what we could do if the man turned a gun on us, but someone went down the steps which are just a little way along the embankment there, and got hold of him. My recollection is that it was one of our wardens, called David Thomas, but anyway, he brought him up, and he was a youngster I should think in his early twenties. I remember he was wearing a green flying suit and he was pretty well the same colour himself. He was very correct in his behaviour—he didn't say anything, he didn't do anything, he just stood more or less at attention. I remember feeling his arm quite rigid when I got hold of him, and then something rather surprising happened—most of one's ideas were upset I think that night. Somebody rushed up and kicked him in the seat, very hard. I suppose it was somebody who'd had someone killed or was just over-come by the strain of events, but anyway he, the man who kicked him, then rushed round to the front of him and succeeded in getting a pistol out of the pocket on his leg. He had a sort of pocket in front of his flying suit, and anyway, somebody else took the pistol from the little man, I don't know what he'd have done if he hadn't had it wrested away

239

from him. Then a War Reserve policeman came along at that point, and shortly afterwards another one, and I remember seeing them marching this German airman off along the embankment, just as if he'd been drunk and disorderly on a Saturday night.'

And still the raid went on.

The great flares which hung as though fixed in the sky illuminated this little scene, the trees in Battersea Park and the rubble underfoot with equal brilliance. The throbbing of bombers and thudding of guns, the screaming fall and explosion of heavy bombs, the continual *noise*, had its own marked effect.

Incendiary bombs scattered over Post Don's area made spurts of fire all over the map. Fires were started in Paultons Square, Upper Cheyne Row, Danvers Street and Old Church Street. Mr Cremonesi's own premises were on fire, but this was put out by a policeman, while he himself dealt with another fire at number twenty-five.

In every street there was a smell of bonfires and a sense of excitement. Women and elderly and unfit men vied with each other in lugging pails of water from one vantage point to another and pumping breathlessly until the flames were beaten down and they were left with their own small, charred, sodden victories.

Similar scenes were being enacted all over Chelsea (indeed all over London) and pins labelled 'H/E' were being steadily added to the Borough map at Control Centre to denote further major incidents. About four in the morning a parachute mine exploded on one corner of Chelsea Square, killing two firemen and a warden and injuring others. Another mine on Cranmer Court, just behind Chelsea Police Station, gave the German airman, who had baled out over the Old Church and who had been taken there, a considerable shaking.

And then all of a sudden it was quiet and the first sirens were sounding the All Clear in the distance. The sirens at the foot of Albert Bridge took it up and died away again. It was five to five. The raid had lasted seven hours and fifty minutes.

240

BASEMENT SHELTER

With the ordinary cold quiet of early morning came a dull calm, a pause for looking about, realising it was over, and accepting the fact of survival.

Through smoke, and a rain of charred paper, the sun was coming up. Pieces of human remains were being picked up and put into bins.

Round the corner at the *Cross Keys*, with one wall blown into the bar, they were serving spirits as hard as they could go. Daffodil heads nodded round the Hans Sloane monument and in the Embankment gardens.

Emma Chandler was chatting quietly with Dr Castillo and a nurse from the Mobile Unit who had given her morphia; she was to die several hours later, after they had freed her.

Everywhere people walked they crunched over rubble and broken glass. People were coming out of their homes with brooms to sweep it up. The damage always looked less when that was cleared away.

The freshness of the morning could not dispel the acrid smell.

Firewatchers and part-time wardens were going off duty, hoping to get some rest before starting their day's work, but fires were continually breaking out afresh and delaying their departure.

Demolition workers began to shovel away the debris of the tower which was blocking Old Church Street. Timbers like the prow of a ship sticking out of the main pile of rubble were for a time to become a familiar feature of the Chelsea landscape.

That was one incident, in one corner of one of London's ninety-five boroughs, during one of the seventy-one heavy raids endured by the great city throughout the winter of 1940-41. Thousands of wardens, night after night, worked as Mr Matthews had worked that night, among the fear and the stench and the ear-splitting noise, to save the lives of their fellow-citizens. The anguish that Mr Maxwell-Hyslop felt when he saw St Thomas More's lovely little church in ruins was repeated a hundred-fold as other churches and cherished buildings were desecrated and smashed. That was the Blitz.

CHAPTER IX

ON MARCH the 8th London had had its longest respite from bombs since the Blitz began, almost six weeks of raid-free nights. The whole atmosphere of the capital had changed greatly since the hectic autumn days. In the larger aspect, the war was entering the long, exhausting, uncomfortable, almost inhuman phase which, for the British Isles, was to endure until D-day, then over three years ahead. In the previous autumn it had been almost a personal war: English men and women had envisaged themselves directly engaged against the men of the Germany army. Without allies, almost without an army, these men and women had expected to see their own streets and meadows transformed into battlefields and many, perhaps most, had been prepared to fight and to die in defence of their homes with whatever primitive weapons were to hand. Now, in the spring of 1941, the prospect was different. Invasion was still considered—by ordinary people at least, though rather less so by the Government—as a very real possibility. However, should the Germans come, it would be the task of the reformed infantry and armoured divisions to defeat them, while the Home Guard and the civilians would only have a very secondary role to play. It would be, in fact, a battle between 'war machines' and though of course there would, as in all battles, be ample scope for individual heroism, the individual as such would inevitably be at a discount.

Civilian life in London reflected this. Describing the atmosphere in the capital during the previous autumn, Miss Elizabeth Bowen has written in her novel *The Heat of the Day*: 'Faces came and went. There was a diffused gallantry in the atmosphere, an unmarriedness: it came to be rumoured about the country, among the self-banished, the uneasy, the put-upon and the safe, that everybody in London was in love—which was true, if not in the sense the country meant. There was plenty of everything in London—attention, drink, time, taxis, most of all space.' If this had also been a period of horror and chaos, it had been one of extraordinary courage and improvisation too, as novelists-turned-firemen fought fantastic holocausts, as beetroot sellers showed unexpected talents for organisation, as normally unassuming men and women quietly and simply assumed responsibility for the safety and wellbeing of their hitherto ignored neighbours.

By the spring of 1941 all this had been organised, rationalised. The men of the auxiliary fire service were no longer amateurs: the shelters were decent dormitories: civil defence had become, in a way, a drill. Many of those who had fled from London had returned during the long lull, and Londoners no longer looked at one another with that instant sympathy which Miss Bowen has called love. The moment of passionate resistance and endurance was over. A normal life, or at least a normal wartime life, had been re-created; in the world of appearances, the theatres, shops, restaurants, pubs were functioning after a fashion; in the world of sensibilities, the dull and obvious emotions, whether worthy or unworthy, were no longer rendered invisible by the high flashes of courage and skill. Endurance was now the mood, and the honeymoon of bravery, after the terrifying wedding night with death, was over. People did their jobs as best they could, and amused themselves as best they could, and thought of the morrow. The Blitz, in fact, even when it was first resumed in March, was already a thing of the past. The young officers who danced and died at the Café de Paris on March 8th were intended for other battles, in Africa, in Asia and in Europe. In a way that Saturday evening at the Coventry Street restaurant is comparable to the Duke of Brunswick's ball before Quatre Bras.

The Café de Paris is approached by a long flight of stairs,

leading down from an inconspicuous entrance between the Rialto Cinema and the Lyons' Corner House in Coventry Street, Piccadilly. These stairs run down to a sort of foyer, off which are the cloakrooms, and which contains a bar. At the time in question the chief bartender was Harry McElhone, who used to own Harry's New York Bar in the Rue Daunou and who had left Paris when the Germans occupied that city. From the foyer or entrance hall the visitor steps out on to the balcony that circles the restaurant proper. From this balcony a double curved stairway leads down to the dance-floor, and between the stairs, at ground level, is the bandstand. Above the stairs and band, and facing the entrance hall, the balcony is deeper. Standing there, looking down at the dancers and diners below, one might almost imagine oneself upon the bridge of a ship, looking down upon the quarterdeck.

Nor is this comparison fanciful. Once upon a time the site of the Café de Paris was a bearpit, which explains both its shape and the fact of its being, as it were, sunken below the level of the ground. When it was transformed into a restaurant, some time before the First World War—it was called the Elysée Restaurant—it was modelled, with an almost weird prescience, on the first-class dining room and ballroom of the greatest liner in the world, then a-building. This liner was called the *Titanic*. The ballroom of the *Titanic* was immediately aft of, and below, the bridge. An architectural innovation was that the captain, without actually leaving the bridge, could step through a door and be above and among his guests. And the décor, containing much glass, which still existed in the Café de Paris on March 8th, 1941, was the same as that of the great liner's ballroom. In fact the Café de Paris was a replica, in miniature, of that ballroom. Its customers were, in the second generation, the same sort of people for whom that doomed liner had been built.

Since it was underground, it was believed to be safe. It was advertised as London's safest restaurant. This, however, was quite untrue. Above the restaurant are only two roofs, its own, and the roof of the cinema above that, for it is underneath the Rialto. Dr Morton's remark about the shelterers under the arches in Bermondsey applied to the rich as well: where they believed themselves to be safe they felt all right. And a powerful contributory factor to this sensation of safety, in Piccadilly as in Druid Street, was the absence of noise. In the Café de Paris it was not possible to hear the raids banging and roaring away outside. (And outside, of course, it was equally impossible to hear what was going on in that underground restaurant.) The Café de Paris, which had reopened during the height of the Blitz, rapidly became one of London's most popular restaurants. It was expensive, smart and gay. The big hotels, with their steady clientèle of rich, and therefore usually middle-aged, residents, lacked the appeal to youth of this most handsome, excellent and apparently safe restaurant, with its superb jazz—Ken Johnson, 'Snakehips', was there with his Caribbean band, undoubtedly London's best—its lovely décor, and its excellent food. For a young officer on leave, and not caring about the expense, the Café de Paris was the ideal place to take his wife or sweetheart.

Among those present that evening was Lady Betty Baldwin, the daughter of the former Prime Minister. Her war work was with the ambulance unit in Berkeley Square, and she was in charge of one shift, but that night her shift was off duty. She therefore decided to have an evening out, and went to the Café de Paris with three friends. She has told this writer that she remembers remarking on the quality of the people who were there that evening—a thing, she says, which somehow she would not normally do. The men, almost all in uniform, seemed extraordinarily handsome, the young women very beautiful, the whole atmosphere one of great gaiety and of youthful charm. This was so striking that she could not forbear to comment on it, and it compensated for her moment of irritation at being unable to obtain her favourite banquette. The restaurant was crowded, and this banquette was taken. A little later all the people seated at that table were dead.

Though most of the diners had come to the restaurant by taxi, the homes of many were far away. Thus Lady Betty's escort was a Dutch officer. A Canadian convoy had recently docked at Liverpool, and a group of officers and nurses who had come to London that day were spending their first free evening on English soil at the Café de Paris. Mr Ulric Huggins, then an officer of the Royal Navy, had recently arrived from Bermuda and was dining with his newly married wife, a friend named Limbosch who was a Belgian army doctor, and the doctor's girl, an Austrian nurse. As already stated, the bandsmen were West Indians, the bartender an American, the waiters inevitably cosmopolitan. The star entertainer that week was Douglas Byng, but on the night in question he was performing at a big charity ball in Park Lane.

A very pretty English girl, now Mrs Trouncer, has said:

'Well, what I remember of this particular night is that we'd decided we'd dress up to go out. I can't think there was any particular reason for it, but I think that everybody was so worried and so gloomy that, you know, we thought we would. So I did have a long dinner dress on—that I remember. And we went to one or two bars and we were feeling very gay and very happy and we went along, I suppose it was about half past nine, and as you say the place was very full, and everybody was very gay.'

Mrs Wittman, a most beautiful woman, has said:

'I should never have been there, had I taken my mother's warning, because she's very psychic and she had a dream a few days before, seeing me in her dream with my eyes bandaged and so on, and sent me a telegram begging me not to go. Anyhow, I had to go up for a regimental wedding and so we were all in town together, my husband and friends, and the Blitz was so bad we thought we'd like to get further underground. And the Café de Paris, having advertised so much how deep and safe it was, we thought that was the place. So they put a tin hat on my head and we walked and got to the Café de Paris where we felt much safer.'

A lady, Miss Irene Ballyn, has written:

'On the evening of Saturday, March 8th, I gave a small sherry party at our flat in Bayswater. As the evening wore on one of the party suggested going on to the Café de Paris to feed; Douglas Byng was billed to appear in the cabaret, and the friend in question was most anxious to hear him. Opinion was divided, but I was resolutely against the idea: was it premonition or not? I still wonder. Another suggested Quaglino's. Still undecided, we left in taxis.

'My friend who wished to go to the Café de Paris and I were in the same taxi, but the argument as to where we should go continued. The taxi-driver, warning us that it might well be a sticky night, implored us to make up our minds. The alert was on, and when we reached Marble Arch we were confronted by a taxi upside down in the middle of the road and other signs of blast. At the sight of this the driver of our taxi said: "Now you've blooming well got to make up your minds. What's it to be—Café de Paris or Quaglino's?" My friend gained the day and we proceeded to the Café de Paris.'

Ken Johnson, known by the public but not by his friends as 'Snakehips', was exceptionally well-educated for a jazz-band leader, having among other degrees a musical doctorate. He was then sharing a house with Mr Gerald Hamilton, and, since he hurried over his dinner at the *Ecu de France*, was a little earlier than usual in arriving at the Café de Paris. Mr Leslie Hutchinson, the trumpeter of the band and a close personal friend of Ken Johnson's, remembers:

'Mr Ken Johnson came in in a hurry, and said: "Man, it's terrible outside—just terrible." '

Mr Yorke de Souza, the pianist, has added:

'Ken himself was a very charming person to work with, very happy, a happy-go-lucky chap, and everyone in the band liked him very much. Well, the night in particular, the place was very crowded, and Ken himself was rather early—he usually came to work a bit later, but this particular night he was about half an hour early and the place was just warming up, things were just getting going, people very happy, dance-floor very crowded, and it was a bit after nine o'clock, I should think, when we got on the stand.'

Miss Ballyn arrived at this time:

'We were received by Charles, the head waiter, so much liked by all who knew him well. There was nothing servile about Charles, he was gracious, there was nothing patronizing about him, though he was friendly. The tables around the dance-floor were packed, but Charles could arrange for us a table on the balcony. Perhaps, said he, we would have a drink in the bar while waiting? So to the bar we went, and it was while we were there that it happened.'

Mr Simons, a company director, was then a warden in Hampstead. It was his night off duty, and he had come into the West End for a game of bridge at his club. After a rubber or two he became bored with the game, and thought he would go to the Café de Paris on the offchance of running into some-one he knew. He was walking around the balcony, with his overcoat slung across one arm.

Mrs Blair-Hickman, an extremely attractive Canadian girl, was there:

'It was just like a Canadian old home week, there were lots of Canadians, nurses, kilted officers, all sorts and types and sizes, and a lot of blue blood too, I gather. We got there only a few minutes I think before the bomb fell. We hadn't even ordered dinner. The boy I was with and I decided to dance, we went out on the floor, and the tune was *Oh Johnny!* . . .'

Mrs Wittman had just sat down:

'We ordered our meal. We were sitting at the bottom of the stairs, and one of the men who was with us said: "How about dancing?" Paddy is a very good dancer, and I loved dancing, and yet after one round we stopped in front of the band, which was Snakehips Johnson's, and I said: "Look, do you mind if we sit down? We've all night before us. . . ."'

Ulric Huggins and his party were a few tables away:

'We arrived to the best of my memory round about a

quarter past or twenty past nine. We took a table on the left of the dance-floor, underneath the balcony. There was a pillar between us and the main part of the dance-floor. We had a cocktail first and we'd been there some quarter of an hour or twenty minutes. We had ordered dinner, and ordered the wine. The waiter was standing behind me, pouring out the champagne over my shoulder for me to sample. . . .'

Leslie Hutchinson says:

'Well, the band kept on playing, on and on, and Ken said: "Stop the band, and play *Oh Johnny!*" Of course we went to give *Oh Johnny!* and then about the second chorus I just heard like a *ping!*'

Mrs Goschen-Evans was dancing and for a split second she thought that this was some sort of 'novelty dance'.

Mrs Wittman says:

'My first impression was that somebody had, for some reason, thrown a bottle in my face from the balcony, when I saw this blue flash, and everything in the air. . . .'

Mrs Trouncer was on the floor:

'Fortunately on the outside of the dance-floor, quite happily dancing, and the next thing I would say I remembered was that I felt: well, this is the end of the world. It didn't really occur to me that it was a bomb. We'd been blown flat, you see; well, we got to our feet, and I remember turning round and seeing, well, my first sort of impression was that the light upstairs was on and therefore one got this extraordinary macabre sort of atmosphere, with all the dust and the bits of this and that, you know, and it looked rather like one's imagination of hell.'

Mrs Blair-Hickman:

'I always remember, it was like swimming through cotton wool, if you can imagine such a thing. I didn't lose consciousness, I don't think I could have done, I remember everything that happened, and when I sort of came to I was sitting on somebody, quite definitely sitting on somebody. It turned out to be an officer wearing a kilt. And I discovered that my leg was broken—I couldn't stand on it—and my back was very wet—that was blood, I found out later. I didn't feel anything at all except astonishment. We all expected in those days to be possibly bombed, but the actuality was so different, at least to what I'd expected. I looked around, there was a lot of dust, a lot of bodies lying around, and lights burning in the darkness.'

Miss Ballyn, it will be remembered, was near the bar:

'It is not easy to describe the actual moment. One had been in houses when it had happened nearby, as also in streets when houses had been hit, but this messenger of death fell among us. To the best of my recollection there I stood, with a glass in my hand, chatting. Then a sudden and very severe pressure on the top of my head. Then complete darkness. The next thing I knew, on opening my eyes, was that the place was in semi-darkness, the sound of groans, low cries, and whimpering. I was sitting on the floor, my back supported against the wall. A man was leaning over me, he had a glass in his hand. He told me to drink it, it was sal volatile.'

Mr Huggins, it will be recalled, had been sampling his champagne:

'The first impression I got was of darkness and dust, and I noticed the champagne bottle lying on the table horizontally. My first instinct at that moment was to pick up the champagne bottle and put it upright. It must have been a matter of some seconds afterwards that I remember I stood up, with the champagne bottle still in my hand, and poured out drinks for the other three people at the table. And a memory I have very clearly is that, as the champagne rose in the glasses, which incidentally were standing upright on the table unbroken, the foam on the top was grey with dust. And I remember quite clearly wiping the foam off with my finger before I drank. And then I turned round, and there at my feet was the waiter, who had been leaning over me pouring out the champagne—dead, of course.'

There were, in fact, two bombs that had fallen through the cinema and into the restaurant at approximately a quarter to ten. They weighed fifty kilos each. One exploded in front and just to the right of the band, at approximately chest height among the dancers, killing Ken Johnson, another member of his band, and thirty-two other people, and seriously wounding sixty more. The other bomb luckily did not explode, but burst asunder on impact with the dance-floor, scattering its stinking yellow contents over the dead and dying, and making a small hole in the parquet flooring: the pieces were later collected by a Bomb Disposal Unit. One of the two bombs had come down through the balcony, which was holed and sagging. Mr Simons, who had been circling the balcony looking for friends, found himself on the edge of this hole, now minus his overcoat, and lowered himself down through it with the drill movement taught to the men of the civil defence. It was some time before he realised that he had a broken leg.

Most of the lights had gone out, but not all, for there was at least one burning on the balcony, casting a faint light among all the flying dust and debris. Somebody lit a cigarette-lighter and a stentorian voice shouted: 'Don't do that! You'll blow the place up if there's gas about!' There was a pungent, acrid smell, the smell that is customary after a bomb or shell has exploded, and in this case perhaps reinforced by the pounds of high explosive scattered about when the other bomb was shattered. The glass mirrors had of course smashed into thousands of murderous, flying stilettos. Mr Huggins' dead waiter had one small hole in his back, and had most likely been knifed by a glass dagger. Many people there have commented on the extraordinary silence, but this was probably because they were temporarily deafened. For others heard differently.

Mrs Goschen-Evans, for instance, became aware first of a sort of red Christmas-tree light, or a light with a red shade, burning above the bandstand. This must have been near where the head waiter and the manager had been standing, on the 'bridge' above the band, and where they had both been instantly killed. Then she became conscious of terrible screams close beside her. At first she thought that it must be herself

screaming, and tried to stop, and it was only after a few seconds
that she realised the screams were coming from a woman
beside her. A bald-headed colonel was sitting on the stairs,
which were half blocked with rubble shoulder-high, his head
in his hands, groaning pitifully.

Mr Anthony Jacobs, the well-known radio actor, was a
private in the infantry at that time, on leave in London:

'I was in a milk bar in Leicester Square, it was a Saturday,
the moon was shining. Suddenly the milk bar shook, and there
was obviously a bomb somewhere near. Well, a few moments
later I strolled out towards Piccadilly Circus and there in
Coventry Street there was a crowd round the entrance to the
Café de Paris. I think the entrance was brightly lit, in spite of
the blackout, and injured people in evening dress were coming
up the stairs now and again, being helped up, staggering, they
really were staggering, and the crowd began to grow. There
was a good deal of congestion in the narrow street. There was
a curiously incongruous atmosphere, a kind of unawareness of
what had happened—the milk bars, cinemas all around, people
out having a good time, and this little doorway and entrance
where this terrible thing had happened down below, right in
the middle of the West End. I seem to remember that above
there was the sound of aircraft, and moonlight.'

Down below there was horror. A girl had been celebrating
her twenty-first birthday down there. Miss Ballyn says: '. . . .
stripped of all her clothing by the blast, in fact stark naked,
she was carried to me, covered with a tablecloth. She died
while I was holding her.'

An Air Force officer, attempting to assume control, was
shouting instructions and succeeded only in creating a temporary atmosphere of panic. The first ambulances seem to
have been filled with the people who had been on the balcony
or in the foyer, that is to say the less seriously wounded, while
those down below on the dance-floor were left, without help
from the ambulance men, for a long time, perhaps as long as
three quarters of an hour.

Such, at least, is what seems to have happened, but the official facts are not available. Though the civil defence authorities of the City of Westminster have been most helpful, they do not have the facts themselves, and for the following reason: an enquiry was held into the whole incident, and of the failure of the medical and ambulance services, at higher level: Westminster had to send off the file dealing with this incident: it was never returned and has presumably been lost.

What is known is that the Westminster Control Centre was informed that the Café de Paris had been bombed within five minutes of the bombs falling, and the first Rescue Parties, Ambulances and Stretchers were sent off from the depots before ten o'clock, that is to say with admirable promptitude. They did not, however, reach the wounded on the dance-floor for about a further half an hour. It is possible that some were diverted, after departure, to one or more of the many other disasters that had occurred in Westminster that evening. (Garland's Hotel was one building which had received a direct hit only a few minutes before.) Mr William Sansom, in his book *Westminster in War*, explains the delay as follows:

'The staff of the wardens' post nearest to the Café were somewhat depleted. Those remaining were quickly on the spot, but confronted with a vast number of casualties they soon became immersed in First Aid work. This was to be expected —with injured and bleeding figures stumbling from the debris and calling for help. But it was the inevitable consequence that reconnaissance suffered. It led, in fact, to an incorrect message being sent to the Report Centre. The message requested assistance for one hundred *trapped* casualties. Trapping was a usual feature of Westminster incidents, concomitant with the general heaviness of the buildings. The Report Centre therefore took the call without question. They despatched two Heavy Rescue Parties for the extrication of the buried, one Mobile Aid Post to receive them, and two stretcher parties and two ambulances to remove the wounded as they were cleared. In point of fact, there were needed nothing but the Mobile Aid Post, ambulances and stretchers and plenty of them: for the debris was light and casualties were for the most part direct. Meanwhile, with the two ambulances already full, some wounded were removed in taxis—of which there were fortunately many in that district—and others were taken across to the hotel opposite, where a First Aid Post was set up. A little later the A.R.P. Controller arrived personally, assessed the true situation and sent back a call for the badly needed ambulances and stretchers.'

Lady Betty Baldwin, being herself a member of the ambulance unit in Berkeley Square, has described her mounting bewilderment, frustration and finally anger when that unit, her own people, failed to arrive. Meanwhile she and others did what they could amid the chaos down below.

Mrs Blair-Hickman has said:

'A very large officer who I found later was Dutch, a lot of gold braid, peak cap, fully dressed with an overcoat as well (he probably came in off the street), picked me up and carried me through into the kitchens and laid me on the hot-plate, and he set my leg with a wooden stew-spoon, washing it first of all, believe it or not, in champagne, which was the only thing handy. While he was doing that a waiter, a very agitated waiter, was trying to clean off my face, which obviously was very dirty, with a napkin, and the awful thing about that was that my face was full of little bits of glass, it was absolute torture to have him do this. However, he was well meaning, and while he was doing that all round me on the floor there were casualties. There were a lot of Canadian nurses there that night and they were working like Trojans, really trying to help, and there was one boy who was right down beside me, he had an enormous wound in his back, a great big, gaping hole, and this nurse was trying to staunch it with a tablecloth. This boy, probably he was a little cock-eyed, he was saying—Well, it's not everybody who's been cut in on by the Luftwaffe—and then after that they started to improvise stretchers by using the screens, because the stretchers had run out or something, and I was carted up the rickety stairs and laid out in Leicester Square, and I remember lying in Leicester Square and just feeling that nothing mattered particularly, I wasn't in any particular pain, I just felt—dead —most odd.'

Miss Ballyn adds:

'There were by fortunate chance a number of doctors among the guests, and these took charge until the arrival of the first ambulance from Charing Cross Hospital. These doctors, working in the semi-darkness, were doing their utmost. The little first aid available soon ran out, and then underclothing was being torn up to make temporary bandages. Someone had found an electric point in the passage that had not fused. Flex was produced and the grim scene gradually came to light.'

It was very grim. Before the bomb fell, Mrs Trouncer had noticed a young airman, dining with his mother: 'A perfectly enchanting old lady, and I mean he was obviously on leave. He was so sweet to her, and so kind and nice. And the next thing I remember was seeing this old lady completely dead, I mean her head was practically off her body, and the young man came at me and he said: "My mother's all right, she's all right, she's all right, isn't she?" And I said: "Oh yes, yes, yes, she's all right." And I mean she was just as dead as she could possibly be, and I was feeling absolutely really numb in a way.'

Ulric Huggins, it will be recollected, had been dining with his young wife, a Belgian army doctor and a nurse. None of them was hurt at all, and they now set to work. He has described what they did in these words:

'Now Limbosch decided that he was going to act as a doctor in his true capacity here; our job was to bring the casualties, if any, towards this central point, where there was light and where the benches lent themselves obviously to laying out of casualties. So the first thing to do was to clear a space round those, and we started moving the tables back from the benches, and stacking them on top of each other. We went to the next table and as we pulled it away so we found an elderly couple who had been sitting next to us. They were both dead—they'd been exposed apparently to the full direct impact of the blast —there was no visible sign of damage to them, but they were both stone dead. Rather peacefully so, if anything. So we moved them away and took the tablecloth off and just covered them up. I then told my wife, Pat, to go round and collect all the napkins she could, and then I started to go out onto the dance-floor myself. Well, now, the scene there was almost indescribable. I remember coming across a girl lying on her front, I think it was—yes, on her front, and she had a very bad wound in the back. I didn't know whether she was alive or dead, and so there was another man, I forget who he was, some other man in evening dress—I said: "Come and give me a hand with this girl", and we picked her up very gently and we took her across to the bench where Limbosch was wrapping his operations up, and we laid her out there. She thought she was going to die and she had her left, I think, or right thumb blown off. She was in terrible pain.'

The girl in question, Miss Hylton-Simpson, has told this writer that her life was saved at the Café de Paris by the ministrations of Ulric Huggins and his friends. She was under the impression that Huggins had been killed later in the war, and was naturally delighted to discover that this was not so. She has also said that she has a most vivid memory of lying there, in pain, and talking French to somebody who was holding her hand. Why French? she wondered. Presumably it was Mrs Huggins who was holding her hand and they were talking French in that corner because the Belgian doctor was giving instructions to the Austrian nurse in that tongue. Mr Huggins goes on:

'I was carrying people in from the centre of the dance-floor, and the whole of that part is a little confused to me, but I remember one extraordinary case, when I was somewhere out on the dance-floor and I found beside me a tall R.A.F. officer, and he was wandering about rather vaguely, and suddenly I noticed that in his head there was a terrible hole, blood pouring out of it, a great deep hole up in the left side of his head, and so I escorted him over to the bench and sat him down and left him there and what happened to him afterwards I don't know, but by that time people were rallying round the places where the lights were, so that they could do something about it. Napkins were being used to staunch the wounds, and about that period on one of my journeys to and from the bench I noticed something rather extraordinary.'

If the civil defence and ambulance people were unduly slow in arriving on the scene, other, sinister figures were quicker. Mrs Blair-Hickman, it will be recalled, had been lying in a semi-coma across the corpse of a kilted officer. She has said: 'And then I saw somebody creeping around in a vague sort of dreamlike way, and this man came up, and he felt around. He felt my hand, which was lying relaxed—I really was feeling most odd—and I found, I realised later, that what he'd done was take a ring off my finger. He must have done that to quite a lot of other people.'

He had. And this is what Huggins had noticed:

'In amongst the people who were dead, amongst the tables bordering on the dance-floor, I noticed two men, both of whom were obviously not people who would normally come to the Café de Paris, they had caps on their heads and they had sweat rags round their necks, and they looked scruffy and dirty and they were leaning down—I presumed, at that moment, helping, and I just paused for an instant and looked at those chaps—and do you know what they were doing? They were looting. They'd come down the back entrance, and I saw with my own eyes those fellows pick up a lady's handbag, whip through it and take out something I didn't see. They were just a bit further away from me and I couldn't see exactly what it was, and I went up to one of them and said—I think, as far as I remember—Get the hell out of here.'

Those squalid figures cannot have been at large in the Café de Paris for long. Others, including Mr Simons, who were quite conscious, saw no trace of the looters and a considerable number of handbags and gold cigarette-cases, lost in the chaos, were later returned to their owners or to their next-of-kin.

Where had they come from? There were many forms of looting during the Blitz. The most harmless, perhaps, was that of the fireman who pinched a bottle of whisky from a burning pub. Some of the Heavy Rescue men—who, like the firemen, were not local men and therefore did not always preserve the same high standards as the wardens—made a habit of pocketing valuables and breaking open gas meters. When caught they received fairly stiff sentences. And then there were the real criminals who, in the confusion of that winter, found ample opportunity to exercise their talents. Some had official positions: it will be recalled that Christie, the necrophilist and mass-murderer, was a War Reserve policeman, while Mr Miles Mordaunt, who was in charge of a mortuary, had as driver a former smash-and-grab artist from the Edgware Road, of whom he tells the following story:

'Having reason to suspect on one occasion that this fellow was keeping some papers from me he'd found on a body, I shook him roughly, pushed him over, and was horrified to see a cascade crash to the floor, from all his pockets, of what looked like the wealth of King Solomon's mines. Glinting under the lights there appeared to be rubies, emeralds and every conceivable sort of gem. When I peered at them closer I thought I was losing my senses, because they stared right back at me—they were, in fact, glass eyes from some oculist's.'

Such petty crooks tended, then as now, to hang about Piccadilly Circus where in wartime many deserters also congregated. It may have been such as these who slipped down the back stairs into the restaurant with the pretence of helping, but actually to steal.

Or it may have been the work of a more ambitious criminal organisation. Miss Hylton-Simpson, when in hospital as a result of her wounds suffered in the Café de Paris, found herself in the next bed to a girl who had also been wounded that evening by a bomb dropped in Soho. This girl was the proud mistress of a small-time gangster. She told Miss Hylton-Simpson that the gang which her paramour controlled specialised in looting. It had spotters out, who telephoned to the gang's headquarters news of any likely source of loot, such as a blitzed jeweller's. Her lover's men, she boasted, would often be on the spot even before the men of the civil defence. And it is possible that these were the men who stole the ring from Mrs Blair-Hickman's finger.

And in contrast with such baseness, Miss Ballyn tells a story which surely counteracts the squalor and distaste of the other.

An R.A.F. officer had had the fingers of one hand sliced off by flying glass. She led him to the ladies' cloakroom and was washing the stranger's hand under the cold tap. It was suddenly too much for her, and she started to cry. The officer said, simply: 'Don't cry, my dear. It's my hand, not yours.'

With the arrival, at long last, of the ambulances, these brave women and men who had done what they could for the others began, one by one, to depart. Miss Ballyn says:

'I felt terribly alone and rather sick. A friend brushed past me in the semi-darkness and recognising me, led me over the road to the Mapleton Hotel. He gave me a neat whiskey which tasted of nothing. Into the Mapleton Hotel were brought the dead and the more severely wounded to await the ambulances. It was here that I learned that my cousin had been killed. Eventually I found my way to Piccadilly Circus, and in company with two others who wished to go in the direction of Bayswater, we found a taxi and I reached home.'

Lady Betty Baldwin had been badly cut about the head. She worked among the wounded until the Dutch officer who had escorted her out—only an endless hour or so before—feared she was about to faint. He led her up the stairs. She has commented on the hideous sight that met her eyes in the streets: fat men and women rubbernecking, puffing cigar smoke into the faces of the dead and wounded laid out upon the pavement. He hailed her a taxi at last, to take her to her doctor's. Some London taxi-drivers were splendid during the Blitz. Others, particularly in this writer's memory the older ones, were often unpleasant and charged exorbitant prices. She was unfortunate in her choice of cab. The cabby took one look at her bloody head and filthy clothes, and said: 'I don't want no blood in my cab.' Then he drove off.

Mrs Trouncer was also led across to the Mapleton Hotel:

'Now I remember walking up the steps there inside and at some point we came to a mirror, and I'll never forget myself. I had a black dress which was, as I say, torn, white with dust, my hair was white with dust, my face was covered with blood, and you know, I mean one looked quite ghastly and dreadful, but I didn't sort of realise it was me—you know, I looked at this sort of apparition and then a sort of big white light dawned and I felt—Well, of course, it must be. Anyway, there we were and we were given some brandy or something, and then taken to Charing Cross, and they were absolutely marvellous, they couldn't have been sweeter. I mean I had a nasty cut down my face with a scar to my lip, which I've still got, and they patched it up—they said—Well, would you like to stay here, if you want to go home you can. And so we went home, and that's about that.'

Mrs Wittman had been much more badly hurt, and had lost an eye:

'I heard my husband calling me, and by calling back and shouting to each other he found me. He'd only got a cut or two on his head, and he carried me up the stairs to where the bar was and there were lights, and already people coming in off the streets and giving first aid and everything laid on. And a soldier off the street, when he saw me, he handed me a field dressing, yes, a big pad which he told me to hold tightly in my eye and not let go till I could get to a hospital or first aid post as soon as possible. However, when we got up to the top, I was on my feet and my husband wanted to have a look to see what had happened. He took one look at me and he started to faint, so the first aid men, of course, rushed at him,

and started binding up his head and he was trying to tell them
—pointing to me—and they thought he was a bit crazy of
course, I seemed all right. Then they turned to me and said—
Will you give me a hand with your husband and we'll get
him to a first aid post? So I said—Well, I'll do my best. Between
us we helped him up and came out, there was quite a crowd,
waiting, and in a slightly hysterical sort of state, even clapping
survivors and behaving rather strangely; my husband, though
he doesn't remember it, as we came out he was coming to a bit
by then, he said—he turned to me and said—Well, at least we
haven't got to pay for our dinner—at which there was quite a
laugh from the crowd—and we got to a first aid station and
eventually they did look at me and then I was pushed in an
ambulance, which is not a very nice experience but like many
other people that had the same experience, you sit there literally
with blood dripping down, and then I was at Charing Cross
Hospital, wonderful organisation there, and eventually I was
sent on in a private car to the Westminster Ophthalmic
Hospital, and of course all the places I went to, they just took
one look at me and said they couldn't do anything for me
and passed me on to the next, but I was very lucky really.'

Yorke de Souza, the pianist, also had a considerable amount
of glass in his eyes, but was able to get home. Leslie Hutchinson,
the trumpeter, was unhurt, though shocked:

'I grabbed my trumpet and off I went. A fellow showed me
the way out. Everybody seemed to be asking: "Well, well,
what's happened? What's happening, what's happened down
there?" I said: "Oh, I don't know, man, I just come up here."
I was covered with dust, so I brought myself off and went to
play cards as though nothing had happened. Of course all this
time I was very much concerned about Ken Johnson and
Ken Johnson was best man at my wedding and also Yorke de
Souza who lived very near to me. A man came up and said to
me: "Have you heard anything about Mr Johnson?" I said:
"No, I haven't heard anything", and then followed by a lady
who came up and said: "You haven't seen Mr Johnson?"

and I said: "No, I haven't seen him." She said: "Oh, well, you'll hear, you'll hear." And then I was told the news: that is that Ken he wasn't here with us any more. Well, I was shaken as you can imagine, but I decided to cheer up—at least try to cheer up, and I went out of the Café de Paris and when I got outside there was crowds and crowds outside, everybody trying to find out what was going on in there. A man said to me, "Leslie, man, are you all right?" I said: "Yes, I'm all right." Of course I went to a police station to verify the fact that Ken was killed; he was killed, yes. Afterwards I went to a night club, started to get my trumpet out of the case and had a blow, just to sober up things a bit. I know some people may think it wasn't the thing to do, but what else could I do under the circumstances? I thought it was the best thing to do. I had a blow, followed by a long walk home to where I was living, in Camden Road at the time.'

As the time passed Ulric Huggins began to feel that he and his wife had done what they could:

'By this time I was becoming a little concerned about the welfare of my young wife and I reckoned that the two of us, you know, had done what we could, there was still apparently no sign of any official A.R.P. or ambulance people, but the air was clear now, we could see the extent of the disaster and we saw that we probably couldn't do very much more than we had done. The benches round our part of the room were full. So I went over to try and find her, and she was still with this girl, and it was with considerable difficulty that I persuaded her to come away, but eventually when there was another woman somewhere nearby, I think, who said she would take over looking after this girl until the ambulances arrived, I at last persuaded my wife to come on and try and get out of the place.

'Well, now, our actual exit—I'm afraid we saw no more of my doctor friend or his nurse—they were obviously busy, but I was concerned to get my young wife out of this and so we went back to the emergency exit which people were, by that time, using and which there was a fair amount of traffic going up, and I remember quite clearly—it was the dreariest horriblest, horrible little exit you could ever wish for. Stone steps, concrete walls—I don't even think there was a banister on it, I remember we walked up slowly in a rather exhausted state. And we got out to the top and there were crowds of people, not many but quite a small crowd round that exit. They looked at us and sort of attempted to question us, but we weren't in any mood to be questioned that night. I remember we walked then along Coventry Street towards the Piccadilly underground. I was holding on to her, she was fairly exhausted by that time. The Blitz was still going on, in the blackout, and we caught a tube to Baker Street, and only when we got in the tube did we begin to look at each other. And I shall never forget the extraordinary impression I got of her —she'd been in a nice dress and the dress was indescribably filthy, her hands and arms up to about her elbow were blood-stained, her hair was all over the place and she was cheerful but somewhat exhausted, and then she looked at me. My naval uniform was in much the same sort of state—grey—but the sleeves of my reefer, my monkey jacket, were completely soaked in blood and I had to throw that uniform away in the end—it could never be cleaned. I hadn't got a cap, she had left her fur coat in the cloakroom. I remember her complaining rather about that, and I said, We'll go back tomorrow and see if we can find it. And I got her back to Baker Street and eventually back to the flat where she was staying.'

Anthony Jacobs, it will be recalled, had been standing outside the Coventry Street entrance. And his memory of the people's exit seems as suitable an ending as any to this tragic incident, this horrible slaughter in a beautiful restaurant:

'As I said, the crowd was threatening to get in the way, the people were a bit hysterical, wanting to go down and see whether their loved ones were all right—there didn't seem to be anyone in control at that moment, and for some odd reason the only people in uniform in the crowd were a sailor and an airman, I forget his rank, but he was an Other Rank, and myself, an infantryman. So we organised a cordon to keep a gangway clear, for getting the injured people out to the ambulances or somewhere where they could be attended to. Well, I'm afraid quite a lot of them must have been dead, because they were brought up and laid on the steps and on the pavement by the Rialto Cinema, and they lay quite still in their beautiful dresses, beautiful colours, covered in sawdust— sawdust which must have fallen on them when the bomb had exploded down below, and this dust gave them a kind of unreal sheen, they looked like beautiful dolls that had been broken and the sawdust come out. And after a while things got under control and I went home, feeling as though I'd had some kind of a dream. Whenever I go down Coventry Street now I remember that dream, and those bright, dead dolls with dust on them.'

CONCLUSION

WHEN, towards dawn on May 11th, 1941, the All Clear marked the end of yet another very heavy raid on London, few people can have guessed that the London Blitz was over. As it had begun, almost fortuitously and for another purpose, so it ended without any true climax, almost without any real ending, for there was to be one more heavy raid, on Birmingham, before May was out. But it was, in fact, over. On May 22nd Kesselring's Second Air Fleet moved its headquarters to Poznan. By early June its squadrons were also in the East and only Sperrle's Third Air Fleet, its bomber strength much depleted, was left in France and the Low Countries. On June 22nd the German armed forces attacked the Russians from the Arctic to the Black Sea.

Then it was clearly over, at least for the time being. But there was little reason to believe that this was more than a respite. The Red Army sagged and staggered backwards: as the Germans won victory after enormous victory, it began to seem unlikely that Russia would long be left in possession of any effective fighting force: and the Heinkels and Dorniers could, of course, be switched back to the west just as quickly as ever they had been moved eastwards. The civil defence services had to be kept up to strength and full efficiency.

It was to be almost three years before they were called upon again to deal with bombs in any significant quantity, and even so, when the little Blitz of early 1944 took place, the raids were pinpricks compared to what had gone before. But the men and women of the civil defence trained, and watched, and waited. Quite soon the public began to forget what these men and women had done for them. They were to hear, once again, accusations of wasting public money, of being nothing but a bunch of tea-drinkers and darts-players. The public, forgetful at the best of times, is doubly so in wartime, and perhaps many who complained about the wardens and firemen had not, in fact, been in London during the Blitz. The Communists, now that the fatherland of the proletariat was itself involved in the war, even claimed that it was they who had kept up the morale of London's masses during that terrible winter when their principal activity had been muted sabotage.

But all that lay in the future. On May 11th, as the firemen put out the night's fires, as the wardens and rescue parties dug for the buried, as the ambulances rushed the wounded and dying to hospitals and the mortuary vans collected the dead, as the housewives once again swept the glass from their door-steps and the dust and rubble from their floors, no Londoner could know that it was over. Twenty thousand Londoners never did know, for the bombs and the fires had sent them to sleep, for ever, in their London clay.

What had it proved, if anything, this first and fearful on-slaught from the air on a great centre of population? It had proved Churchill correct, when he had said, nearly twenty-five years earlier, that the terrorisation of civilians was unlikely to win a war: a fact that the Allied bombings of Germany were to prove again before this war was over. And for us, living under the threat of infinitely worse aerial attack, this fact is perhaps significant. For those who would protest that no comparison between the Blitz and some future onslaught is possible, it may be replied that in October of 1940 the popula-tion of London expected that that great city would be wiped out just as surely, if more slowly, as we expect in the event of atomic war. But they looked the fear straight in the face and decided that the reality, horrible though it was, was neither so bad as the expectation had been, nor so repulsive as the alternative of surrender to a wicked and cruel enemy must be. Civilian morale did not crack then: there is no reason, despite hysterical publicists and strontium-mongers, to assume that it would crack again, even if conditions were far, far worse.

That is one lesson that may be learned from the Blitz. Another is the extraordinary adaptability, not always rational but nevertheless effective, of the inhabitants of a great city. Some people have talked, in the past, as though the bombing of London were a battle fought between the Londoners, particularly the civil defence services, and the Luftwaffe. This is not quite true. A fight in which one man stands defenceless while another punches him is scarcely a fight at all. But what is true is that the people of London displayed enormous ingenuity in dodging the punches as best they could, and enormous resilience in their ability to recover and to accept more punishment. Thus, though they in no sense 'defeated' the Luftwaffe, they frustrated Hitler's purpose, and that was a very real victory.

It was a tragic victory. London is not a beautiful city; with the notable exception of the Wren churches few of the streets and buildings that went had much architectural value. But the sentimental value of a home, whether it be designed by Nash or by some anonymous building contractor, remains, of course, enormous. And death can be measured against no scale. The death of young men in battle is shocking and tragic enough, though the generations of eternal war through which our ancestors have passed have made this tragedy seem, in the abstract at least and when it happens to others, almost normal. The death by violence of young women and of children is far more shocking, not only because we are even now not fully accustomed to such savage attacks on those who do not themselves kill, but also perhaps because such slaughter strikes at the very essence of our society and at its future. And when we look back across this half-a-generation, at the dead of that terrible winter, it is perhaps the women and the children whom we still mourn most vividly.

'During my time in the Fire Service', Mr Phillips of Poplar has said, 'we had some bad times, we had some good times, some funny experiences and some tragic ones. But a sight that I don't think I'll forget ever was that of a rescue squad releasing a small child that had been buried in the collapse of a house. The child had been buried standing up, and was obviously dead. The rescue party were digging away, and they had just uncovered his head and shoulders. It was a terrible morning —rain was pelting down—and I can see now that child's head and shoulders, standing above the debris, white-faced and clean where the rain had splashed and washed the face of the child.'

ACKNOWLEDGMENTS

WHEN first I contemplated writing this book it was soon apparent that there were four major sources of information on which to draw: the newspapers, Governmental and other archives, other people's books, and personal memories and papers. The newspapers, being heavily censored at the time, were not much use, but I should like to express my gratitude to Mr Maywood, of *The Times* library, for his help and for his permission to use that library: likewise to Mrs Wolfe and the Wiener Library for putting their collection of contemporary German newspapers and periodicals at my disposal.

The Governmental archives are, by fiat, unavailable to any save 'official historians' until some considerable period has elapsed after the events with which they deal. The Service departments, however, have shown their usual courtesy in providing what facts may be divulged, and I should like particularly to thank Mr J. C. Nerney, of the Air Ministry Historical Branch, who, though in no way responsible for the views expressed in this book, has been good enough to correct some of my errors of judgment: for any that remain, I alone am to blame. The Home Office, in whose care the archives of the Ministry of Home Security now repose, has also been helpful, though I have had no access to those archives. On the other hand Mass Observation have been most helpful, and have permitted me to read much of the material then collected for the Ministry of Information: I should like to express my gratitude to Mr L. P. England and Miss Mollie Tarrant. The London Transport Executive have also been so kind as to answer questions, and to allow me to quote from their publication *London Transport Carried On* by Charles Graves.

Other publishers who have permitted me to quote from books, and whose permission I now gratefully acknowledge, are: Messrs Cape (*The Heat of the Day* by Elizabeth Bowen), Messrs Cassell (*The Second World War* by Sir Winston Churchill), Messrs Chatto and Windus (*War Begins at Home* by T. Harrison and C. Madge), Messrs Collins (*Night Fighter* by C. W. Rawnsley and Robert Wright), Corporation of the County Borough of Croydon (*Croydon and the Second World War*), Messrs Peter Davies and Pearn, Pollinger and Higham (*Hell Came to London* by Basil Woon), Messrs Faber and Faber (*The Command of the Air* by Giulio Douhet, *War Over West Ham* by E. Doreen Idle and *Westminster in War* by William Sansom), Messrs Victor Gollancz (*Post D* by John Strachey), Messrs Harrap (*Ack-Ack* by General Sir Frederick Pile), Her Majesty's Stationery Office (*Brassey's Naval Annual for 1948, Civil Defence* by T. H. O'Brien, *The Defence of the United Kingdom* by Basil Collier, *Problems of Social Policy* by R. M. Titmuss, *Front Line*, and *On the State of the Public Health During the War*), Messrs Melrose (*Fire Service Memories* by Sir Aylmer Firebrace), Messrs Secker and Warburg (*The Lesson of London* by Ritchie Calder).

As for direct, personal narratives, I have acknowledged sources in the text, and would once again like to thank all who have given me their time, and particularly those who have arranged for me to meet others with interesting stories to tell: among many to whom I am greatly indebted are Mr S. A. Hamilton, Mr Harold Harbour, Mr Ulric Huggins, Lt.-Col. von Ploetz, Mr Sam Shutt, and Miss Marjorie Watkins. Many of the people interviewed by me talked into a tape recorder, the property of the B.B.C., and a fraction of what they said has been incorporated by me in a broadcast programme: I should like to express my gratitude to the British Broadcasting Corporation for permission to reproduce in these pages part of those recordings that were so used and a great deal more that was not. I should also like to express a warm debt of personal gratitude to Mr Robert Pocock, the producer of the programme in question, who displayed a quite amazing tolerance when my interests took me far beyond the scope of our programme.

Finally, the drawings that illustrate this book are taken from one of Mr Henry Moore's unpublished sketchbooks. Made at the time, they are now the property of Mrs Moore. I should like to express my deep gratitude to both Mr and Mrs Moore for their great generosity in permitting me to reproduce them here.